SKOKHOLM

An Island Remembered

Jean Lawman

HALSGROVE

First published in Great Britain in 2000

British Library Cataloguing-in-Publication Data
A CIP record for this title is available from the British Library

ISBN 1 84114 091 0

HALSGROVE
PUBLISHING, MEDIA AND DISTRIBUTION

Halsgrove House
Lower Moor Way
Tiverton, Devon EX16 6SS
Tel: 01884 243242
Fax: 01884 243325
www.halsgrove.com

Printed and bound in Great Britain by Cromwell Press Ltd, Trowbridge.

Contents

This book is dedicated to the late Ronald Lockley

Foreword

Jean Lawman has become a firm friend ever since I first met her on her beloved island in the spring of 1981. My husband Graham and myself had arrived on Skokholm accompanied by a swarm of media reporters who were intent on publishing a 'real-life romance'. Unfortunately this was based on their own preconceived ideas which bore little resemblance to reality. Sharing the posts of warden and cook, we were to live and work hard under conditions that most people would consider extremely primitive. With the departure of the boat that day, we were left there with the current week's visitors, the previous warden, Carol Warman, and her brother Thomas and also Jean. It was a little while before I realized that Jean had lived on Skokholm in the 1970's for six years and her deep empathy with the island soon became apparent.

She showed us many special and secret places, as well as the subtleties of finding razorbills' nests – "there's usually one under here". We were privileged to live on Skokholm for four years and its magic, beauty and many moods have had a profound effect on my own life. Jean has eloquently expressed many of the feelings and experiences I remember from that same time, some so deep and personal that I strongly admire her courage in sharing them with all who care to read this book. Woven skillfully into her tale are the lives and histories of all the more important inhabitants.

The book gives a unique insight into the life of an island warden and, although the scientific studies of bird populations and migration has now ceased, the life is still essentially the same today. Anyone who has visited Skokholm will be immediately drawn back there in spirit as they read, and perhaps those who have not yet made the journey will do so soon.

Dr. Liz Gynn

Acknowledgements

Special thanks are due to Dr. Liz Gynn and Jane Guthrie for reading the draft and providing valuable criticism. Without their encouragement, I doubt that I would have had the confidence to publish.

Dr. Mike Brooke, Professor Christopher Perrins, David Saunders, Stephen and Anna Sutcliffe, Michael Wiles, Graham Thompson, Theresa Purcell, the Wildlife Trust, West Wales and the Friends of Skokholm and Skomer helped in many different ways. I would also like to thank Mick Brown for providing me with the much sought after photograph of Cambell Reynolds and George Sturley.

Introduction

A magnificent oak tree grew at the bottom of our garden in Hampshire and, perched high up in the tree, secure among its branches, I would daydream to my heart's content. I was about ten years old then and many of my dreams involved remote islands and birds, perhaps spurred on by some child's adventure story and my own inborn love of nature. It was nothing more than fantasy but, as I sat swinging my legs out over our suburban lawn letting my imagination run riot, a seed was sown. It lay dormant while the various procedures of a standard education tightened their grip on me.

Fifteen years later however, I was to realise that dream, and it wasn't just luck, as some would have it. It was grasping an opportunity and obstinately following it up until the chance came. If it hadn't come about the way it did, I would have found another route there.

I never regretted that the island in question happened to be Skokholm. There are other islands with larger bird colonies, higher, more dramatic cliffs or a greater degree of remoteness, but none, so far as I have experienced, with equal charm.

This book sets down the memories that linger, most of them quite vivid, of our life on the island during the years 1973 to 1978. I hope it conveys some of the magic of the experience, as well as giving an insight into the natural history of the island, particularly those aspects which I found myself involved with. The emphasis is clearly on birds, but there are also accounts of the flora, the mammals and certain insects, all of these being an integral part of a dynamic and complex ecosystem.

Those years on Skokholm shaped the rest of my life, for better or for worse, mostly for the better I think. The experience developed a lifelong interest and gave me something which will always be with me – a spiritual appreciation of nature as well as an academic interest. My life is the richer for it.

Should I wax lyrical on occasion, it is not contrived, it is simply the way I remember it. A book such as this cannot be anything but a pleasure to write. Skokholm is an island of many moods and I invite you to share some of them with me.

Jean Lawman
St Buryan, 2000

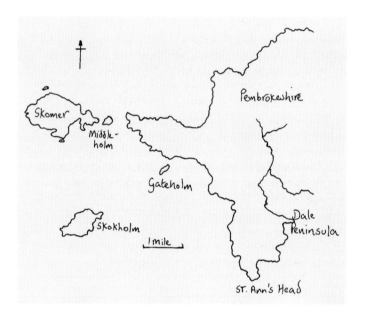

Prologue

It all started in 1971 when I was in London researching the reproduction genetics of Myxomycetes (slime moulds). As if it was going to change the world, my eccentric supervisor would tremble with excitement as our carefully nourished plasmodia met and fused on the agar plate. I never understood the useful applications of the work and I probably never will, but in the middle of it all came something that was to change my world. One day in the lab, even as the nuclei exchanged, I was hopelessly distracted by a letter inviting me to stay for a week on a remote island in Wales. The chance connection was the meeting on Fair Isle of my friend, Ivor McPherson, with Clare Lloyd, a research assistant working on razorbills. The island sounded like paradise to me, so I made the decision promptly and demanded some holiday. So it was that in June 1971 I set off, leaving the plasmodia and my supervisor to fend for themselves

Uninitiated as I was (in spite of the constant day dreaming), it is with much amusement that I look back on that Saturday morning in 1971, waiting in Martinshaven for the 'ferry' to Skokholm to come chugging round the corner at ten thirty on the dot, like any regular boat service. I had overlooked completely the lovely *Sharon* as she lay at anchor in the cove awaiting the arrival of the skipper who was most probably seeing the cows home from milking. Rigid time-keeping had no part here and I had a lot to learn, but I liked what I saw from then on.

That week in June was, I suppose, the main turning point in my life. There were long daylight hours spent out on the cliffs absorbed in watching the activities of what seemed like phenomenal numbers of puffins, hanging over the clifftops looking down on ledges packed with razorbills and guillemots, revelling in the rich array of colourful flowers, catching a lucky glimpse of an oystercatcher chick crouching among the pink thrift, and all that without a ray of sunshine until the Saturday of my departure. Then there were damp, dark nights filled with the weird cries of incoming shearwaters whilst the red beams from the lighthouse swept over the honeycombed ground. All of it new to me, and yet that week I felt more at home and happier than I had ever been before.

Guillemots

The result of that week of discovery was a fond but firm farewell to the Myxomycetes, my hapless supervisor and London immediately. Puffin-struck and disorientated, I returned to my Hampshire home to plan the next trip. It was only a few weeks before I returned to Skokholm, this time with boyfriend, Ray, whom I hoped would become equally obsessed. He did and, after spending a few days on the mainland the following week with me gazing across Broad Sound to Skokholm much of the time, he returned home and back to work. I then took up a vague offer from the warden and crossed to the island for the third time that year in the capacity of voluntary assistant warden/friend of the resident staff. Two gloriously happy weeks on the island followed and then I left on the train for home feeling disconsolate and miserable. Still vivid in my mind is the memory of slumping down on my rucksack outside Portsmouth railway station and bursting into tears as I waited for a lift home. Even Ray's smiling face didn't alleviate my distress. I had a severe form of 'Skokholmitis' and couldn't see what could be done about it.

I soon adapted and found a job but, as no vacancies came up in 1972 for work on the island, we did the next best thing and took off in an old Thames van for a ten month trip round Europe which was a story in itself. Back to work again, this time employed by a pharmaceutical company working with the drug erythromycin. The job had excellent prospects and was very well paid so that when Ray and myself accepted the offer of jobs on Skokholm in 1973 for ten pounds a week between us, my boss and others were convinced that we were well off our heads. How could we turn down the chances of good careers and plenty of money? Wasn't that what life was about? A gut feeling told me it wasn't, at least not for me then. I had an idea there was more to life than that and was prepared to take a few risks to see if I was right. I believed very much, and still do, in following one's own inclinations. What is more, I wanted and needed the island experience.

So it came about that within the space of a couple of weeks, we had shed all responsibilities. We decided to marry because in those days it seemed to be important and, anyway, the Trust was not forward thinking in that respect. Our families were nonplussed and although they shared a little in our enthusiasm, they looked with more than a little trepidation on our future prospects. Perhaps they thought we would disappear forever down a giant puffin burrow or vanish like the lighthouse keepers on the Flannan Isles in *Marie Celeste* style. Perhaps, beneath it all, they were proud of us and, as my mother has since told me, wished they could have done it themselves.

CHAPTER 1

Spring Arrivals

The Sharon was seen by the lighthouse keepers as a white speck cavorting in the boiling waters of the infamous Jack Sound, that channel of water between the mainland and Middleholm. She was an ex-lifeboat of the old type, tapered fore and aft, and was painted in the traditional blue and white. She rode the sea well and had a good and brave skipper, one Terry Davis from Maen Dewi farm near St Davids, a handsome man with a swarthy complexion and the dark skin and hair of a Celt. On board with Terry and his crew, Malcolm, my husband Ray and I were bound for Skokholm Island. Michael de la Brooke, the newly-appointed warden, with whom we were to share our duties on the island, was already in situ, being shown the ropes by the warden from the previous year, John Davis.

Terry on the Sharon

The date was 17 March 1973 and the weather was fair with light winds. We were precisely on schedule, which was little short of a miracle as we were to find out in the ensuing years. It had all gone so smoothly, beginning with our arrival at the office of the West Wales Naturalist Trust, the formalities, shopping for island stores and finally our departure from the little cove at Martinshaven.

We had carried the stores over the rocks and on to a series of ledges and the *Sharon* was able to draw in alongside the rocks on a high tide, enabling us to load her easily. She bounced a little in the slight ocean swell and while the skipper held her in place we passed along rucksacks, cases of canned meat and vegetables, bags of flour etc., more than enough to last us until the next boat in several weeks time. Our eagerness to be off ensured that we worked fast and well. With a last look around the rocks for fear of leaving something vital behind, we accepted a helping hand from the crew and were away to negotiate the choppy waters in the sound.

Any fear of the sea was annihilated by our confidence in Terry's skill and experience. Not for nothing had he received an award for bravery involving a rough sea rescue. I had little knowledge of the sea then and absolutely no fear. My involvement with it had not extended much beyond the waters of the Solent in Hampshire, apart from three very reasonable Skokholm crossings two years before. I was destined to develop a healthy respect for it, something that was not quite fear but more an acknowledgement that it will certainly have the last word if care and caution are not exercised.

I relished the boisterous passage through the Sound where spring tides can flow as rapidly as five or six miles an hour. With an opposing wind it can, and often does, create mayhem. However, it was only when those troubled waters were behind us that I was able to relax properly and enjoy the prospect of impending, physical isolation on a wildly beautiful island. We had gladly left civilisation, as we knew it, behind and looked forward to a more challenging and fulfiling life ahead. Our island would be crowded soon, crowded with thousands of seabirds and rabbits vying for space to breed; courting, fighting and raising young, a general hubbub of nuptial activity, day and night, and we would be there to witness it first hand. We looked out for seabirds on the crossing; a line of auks maybe, a shearwater skimming the bright surface of the sea or the dazzling white speck of a gannet from Grassholm away to the west.

As the mainland receded, and with it Skomer Island and Middleholm, the red sandstone cliffs of Skokholm drew nearer. Those red cliffs were to entrance me over the years as I watched them change colour with different weather and light conditions. I saw them glowing rusty red in the yellow light of a summer's evening, while the next morning they had mellowed to the colour of a ripe damson in a swirling white sea mist. The vibrant colours on the head of a puffin seemed brighter against the red stone and every flower bursting from its crevices was a celebration of nature's palette of colour, never clashing, always pleasing.

Our small island lay near to Milford Haven in South Pembrokeshire. To be more precise, it was roughly four miles from St Ann's Head in a west-north-west direction and about two miles south of Skomer, its larger sister island. It also lay two miles from the nearest point on the mainland, a comfortable distance as far as I was concerned. That point was north-east of Skokholm, and was behind the tidal rock known as Gateholm Island. Gateholm not only stood out physically, it was also distinct because it was composed of red sandstone like Skokholm and glowed pink in the afternoon sun, unlike the pale grey cliffs of the adjacent mainland. I once saw the brightest rainbow I have ever seen envelop, a sun-fired Gateholm in glorious technicolour whilst the sea and the clouds around assumed a deep indigo hue. The red rocks of Skokholm and Gateholm form part of a belt of Old Red Sandstone exposed in South Wales. Within the fine sandstone rock are whitish pellets of a softer material which is largely calcium carbonate and which weathers out quickly to leave a hard and firm pitted surface, good for toughening the tender soles of bare feet and for providing reliable handgrips when climbing.

Skokholm was a rough diamond shape with the long axis in a north-east to south-west direction. It was roughly a mile in length and half a mile across at its widest point. From a height of one hundred and sixty feet at its south-western tip, it sloped down in a gentle gradient to about seventy feet at the north-eastern extremity. Bounded by cliffs, it took the form of a plateau with few undulations, but with scattered, prominent rocky outrops. The largest of these was Spy Rock, everyone's favourite place for philosophical contemplation. Because of the panoramic view, many visitors liked to go there to mark their arrival on the island or to commiserate on their imminent departure. For myself, I went there occasionally to regain lost perspective! The ancient rocks had undergone much complex folding and buckling and there was evidence of this everywhere, particularly in the cliff strata along the South Coast around Theatre Cove and Syncline End, but this was best seen from a boat. To the east, the land masses of Eurasia and Africa gave some protection, but relatively little land lay between Skokholm and the open Atlantic, only Ireland, and that accounted for the very windy conditions and the mild oceanic climate we were to experience. It was to affect us and our lifestyle in many ways, as indeed it determined the whole ecosystem of the island, as I shall describe later.

As we drew closer, the small, north-eastern peninsula called the Neck, which was separated from the rest of the island by a narrow isthmus, slowly revealed its many cracks and fissures, coves and islets. Above the high water mark, a line of white surf nudged the darker rock and then began the lichen zones. First came the black *Verrucaria* and *Lichina* species which tolerate a degree of immersion in salt water, then the orange

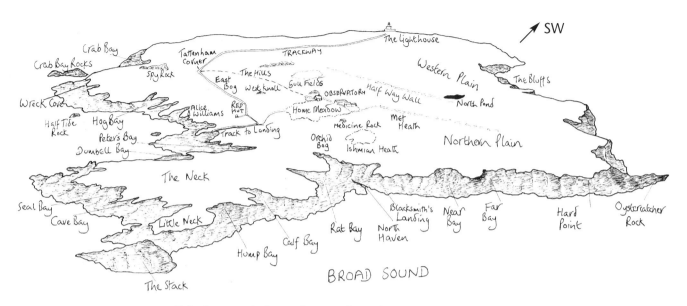

*Caloplaca*s and above that patches of yellow *Xanthoria parietina* with odd tufts of wispy green *Ramalinas*. It looked fascinating and inviting; at least infinitely more so than the rather sterile, pebble beaches I was familiar with in my home county. Surges of childish excitement mingled with adult impatience, as I quietly relished the prospect, of exploring that broken shoreline and discovering its hidden caves, dark pools and penetrating gullies. It seemed for a moment just as if it was that childhood dream come true.

So there we were on our way all those years ago (twenty-five as I write this) to live a life that was still primitive in its day and has even now altered little apart from some modernisation of the island's buildings and utilities (a few miles of sea isn't sufficient to keep the bureaucrats and rule makers at bay these days!). I was twenty-four and Ray was twenty-seven. We were barely older than naturalist Ronald Lockley when he first crossed to Skokholm many years ago at twenty-three; but more of him later. The new warden, Mike Brooke, as yet unknown to us and whom we were to join on the island, was two years younger than I. From the boat we scanned the island through our binoculars for signs of life: a flurry of gulls over the tawny bracken, the small, brown forms of rabbits scampering on the short turf close to the buildings and a pied oyster-catcher flying along the lower shoreline with a shrill 'cleep cleep'. The little cluster of white buildings, by then clearly visible from the boat, were living quarters for the staff and visitors. The site, dating back to around the thirteenth century, was well chosen with a north-easterly aspect and tucked into the lee of a rocky knoll for shelter from the salty south-westerlies blowing in from the Atlantic Ocean. Thus the little homestead with its Snowcemmed walls and roofs sat snugly into the contours and looked delightfully welcoming on that day in early spring.

Just how lucky we were to get out there on the day we planned we came to appreciate later. March is a fickle month anyway and then there is the spring equinox to contend with. The suddenness of a change in the weather around the Pembrokeshire islands is such that no boatman takes a gamble in those waters. The big seas may be negotiable in small boats, but not so the landings on the islands. Our boatmen needed accurate knowledge of how the tides, currents and winds vied with each other to produce wild and powerful tide races and vigorous upwellings offshore. Then there were the huge Atlantic swells which rolled in during rough weather, or even quite unexpectedly from storms hundreds of miles away in the ocean. A large swell made landings difficult if not impossible and sometimes lasted for many days as marooned visitors of the past will know. We learnt that the island boat service could not possibly have operated like a bus service (as I had naively imagined) and the skill and expediency of our boatman was much appreciated once we realized this. We had occasion to wonder at times, when we saw tempers frayed and when the frustration of a wayward timetable made itself felt, but it was not for us to judge, and being marooned was an adventure for those visitors less bound by convention.

Rounding the neck, a small group of purple sandpipers flew off in alarm from the base of the Stack, a large rock some fifty feet high and separated from the island by a channel that could be negotiated by swimming at low spring tides, providing displacement by the swift current was allowed for. In other words you set a bent course. Except for over-zealous lighthouse keepers on fishing expeditions, these wading birds in company with overwintering turnstones, enjoyed a general lack of disturbance in the winter months as they probed in crevices and amongst the weed in search of small molluscs or tiny crustaceans. Their cryptic plumage, especially that of the purple sandpipers, made them very difficult to see on the weathered, purplish brown rock around the shoreline. Many times I stood on the clifftop with visitors, having got my eye in, and tried in vain to point them in the direction of the birds. Meanwhile, they either thought I was bluffing and that the birds weren't there at all or they thought I had a gift of special eyesight, when all it took was a trained eye.

Purple sandpipers evoke special personal memories for me, not least that of being late for my own wedding for want of seeing them! But most of all, I reminisce on the times I spent stalking the elusive sandpipers right down amongst the wave-lashed rocks beneath the lighthouse. I was in their world then; a world of white surf and dark, pitted rock, studded generously with pale barnacles and limpets that were impossibly flattened by constant exposure to the wild seas. There, in this zone of transition between land and sea, I would come across the birds sporting their dusky plumage, even then with a trace of purple in the feathers. In delicate contrast was the ochre yellow colouring the base of the thinly tapering bill and the legs; a little touching up job by Mother Nature. Those birds were so tame that I was often able to get within a few feet of them providing I moved stealthily and made no sudden movement. Sometimes I faltered on the slippery rocks and they would be up and away, sounding off with a burst of nasal 'keet-kitt' calls. They would disappear swiftly round the rocks, a flurry of dark bodies in a haze of white spray, keeping together as they twisted and turned. It wasn't easy to catch them flying in my binoculars, but when I did the white streaks on the wings and outer tail emphasised the quickness of movement and the brilliant co-ordination of the flock. When standing still they appeared rather dumpy, lacking the elegance of many of the long legged waders.

Sometimes I felt guilty for disturbing those trusting birds migrating here from their breeding grounds in the northern tundra. There they seldom encountered human beings and had not learnt to fear them as southern birds have. I often thought of those remote wildernesses in Iceland and Scandinavia and longed to follow them when they returned there in the summer months just to see them on their home territory (it is said that a few pairs breed in Scotland today). No turnstones accompanied them that day in 1973, but it wasn't long before I sought out their high tide roost and found that the two species were very often associated.

Later that year, whilst exploring the channel that divided the Stack from the rest of the island during a low spring tide, I was to find my first anemone of the species *Tealia felina* among the common beadlet anemones. It was in a crevice, waving its lovely pastel green and mauve tentacles around in the lucid water. The great degree of exposure on Skokholm restricted the diversity of the seashore life, but it is still eminently beautiful. It was a harsh environment, even for me, for my bare feet were hardly able to cope with the sharply pitted rock encountered on those low tide forays. There were other times when I donned snorkel and mask and swam for long periods around South Haven and Peter's Bay, numbed by the cold water, but enthralled by the tiny fish darting amongst the forests of *Laminaria* and the crabs scurrying away from my shadow in the open sandy places. The tangled masses of waving fronds moved about slowly and eerily beneath me and were so dense they could have concealed all manner of creatures. Some of our guests were encumbered by vivid imaginations and were too unnerved by it to stay in (or was it just too cold!). The largest and brightest creature I ever saw was a brilliantly coloured ballan wrasse caught in a sunbeam and reflecting all the colours of the rainbow. Those minutes of pure leisure were usually snatched on odd afternoons in August when we were still busy with visitors, but when daytime bird-ringing activities had slowed down with the fledging of gull and auk chicks.

SPRING ARRIVALS

A considerable tide race rushed past the Stack; we felt the boat responding to the surge of water but our skipper held the wheel in check. We passed Cave Bay where a great dark recess in the cliff caught my attention. Inside was a deep pool which I was to creep away to on hot, sticky days, there to lounge in the icy cold water. I loved to throw pebbles in the pool from the blackness at the back of the cave and watch the ripples spreading over the gleaming silver surface. The black outline of the cleft was brilliantly reflected in the water. I tried to photograph it once but it lacked something, probably the smell of the cool salty air and the lulling sound of the surf outside. It was during one of these trips to the cave that I first heard the magical sound of seals singing, a fantasia of pure, unadulterated music and a revelation to my ears. Nor was it so commonly heard that one became accustomed to it and stopped listening. This is surely the siren of folklore.

We were soon round the Devil's Teeth, a striking composition of rock best seen in the smoky light of dawn, and from the top of this we were regarded somewhat imperiously by the resident great black-backed gull. Quickly then we approached the point at which we would turn into the landing place in South Haven. It was in this bay on that first visit in June of 1971 that I saw my first puffins, scores of them floating on the water as if waiting to greet us, just as they were for Ronald Lockley on his first visit in 1926. During his residence in the late 1920s and 1930s, there were many more, perhaps twenty thousand in all compared to the 2500 pairs which was the quoted figure in my time. They apparently inhabited burrows in the cottage garden wall in the good old days. Like everyone else I have met, I remember being surprised at how small they were, but that didn't detract from the pleasure of that first encounter. They never failed to elicit an affectionate response from our visitors when seeing them for the first time. How could they not with their friendly comical look, clownish antics and gaily coloured facial garb? In the latter part of our six-year sojourn on Skokholm, we were startled by the appearance of a white puffin on the water. Not surprisingly it stood out in the puffin crowd and we were very proud of it. Was it really larger than its normally coloured companions or was it an optical illusion? I still don't know but I suspect the latter. There have been further sightings of white puffins since then too.

The landing on a calm day

It being March when we arrived, there was no such reception committee, only a disgruntled shag which we disturbed as it dried its waterlogged wings on a rocky point before we turned in to land. Evil looking and reptilian so people say, but that is because they have never watched the beautiful, sinuous movement of its lithe body beneath the water as it glides, weaves and turns swiftly to snatch a fish. It is a different bird altogether from the primeval looking creature drying out its ragged wings on the rock; something else I was to learn on Skokholm in the ensuing years.

In one sweep we drew alongside the landing steps and the crew (Malcolm) jumped off. While the ropes were being thrown ashore to secure the boat, we were acutely aware of our landlubber image and general lack of experience with boats. To his credit, Terry never made us feel uncomfortable, he knew his job and we (we hoped!) knew ours. However, our uselessness didn't last long and we soon began offloading the mountain of stores. The steps were lime-washed every year by conscientious lighthouse keepers to keep the slippery growth of algae at bay, otherwise they were lethal. It was originally their landing and they considered it their duty to lime it, although we did it occasionally to show willing as it certainly made our lives easier. When clean, they made the landing of bulky stores a relatively easy task both for ourselves and the keepers who would receive their coal, oil and other heavy items from Trinity House boats. The winch was their property and we never used it except once when I had to drive the dumper up on to the rocky bank in order to stop! Only the winch would budge it! Even so the transfer of heavy Calor gas cylinders from boat to shore was tricky, especially when there was a considerable rise and fall in water levels, and apart from dragging them along the ground once they were landed I left them to the men. Precious, and often heavy, photographic equipment brought over by island visitors was anxiously guarded until the moment came for the handover. I don't believe many first-time guests knew what they were in for as regards landings and many times I watched their faces tighten as the time came for the off-loading of valuable gear. The word Hasselblad was shouted in my ear on such an occasion and, at the time, I didn't have a clue what it was. It sounded like a weapon of some type to me and I passed it on with due respect and caution in case it was.

I remember no occasion when luggage (or people) were lost overboard. The sea claimed the odd bag of flour, certainly the odd cabbage and once, when Mike was landed on his own, a load of Snowcem (was he trying to get out of something?). Some of the landings which involved more than a simple step ashore must have caused the occasional heart to flutter as the boat rose and fell three or four feet with the swell. No doubt many ladies' hearts missed a beat too as they leapt into the arms of an island warden (not me!), or a handsome crew member.

Most South Haven landings, were achieved without too much difficulty. Even visitor Albert, a wonderful character well into his eighties, was literally manhandled from the landing steps into the dinghy, which apart from a flimsy bit of rope was totally at the mercy of a lively and unpredictable swell. I can see him now lying in the bottom of it, ever calm and serene with hand raised in a gesture of farewell. At that age you can afford to be philosophical!

There was another occasion when an ex-warden, Mike Harris, revisiting the island with a BBC film unit, became so frustrated at the abortive attempts of the boat to effect a landing in the prevailing south-easterly winds that during a final circuit of the bay he leapt with a war cry on to Half Tide Rock. It was an admirable and a successful feat.

Such is the stuff of island wardens! He was saved the inevitable landing on Blacksmiths (a poor substitute for South Haven on the north side of the island) which followed. Knowing that their arrival would be around dinner time and possibly later, I had put baked potatoes in the oven since they needed no attention. The lengthy delay caused by the alternative landing and all the humping of gear up the cliffs meant that burnt offerings were all that was left. Good spirits prevailed, but it was generally agreed that a lump of sandstone would have been kinder to the fillings! However, hunger was always on our side.

Huge ocean swells rolled in from the west, crashing on to the cliffs in the Mad Bay area, but they also ran along the north and south coast and joined up a little eastwards of the island. St Ann's Head, which we rounded many times on our way out to Skokholm, bore the brunt of that lot. Once such day we were confined to the hold (something to do with regulations!) and if I was ever going to be seasick that would have been the day. I wasn't.

The day could be quite windless, but somewhere out to sea there was turmoil. Then the endless pounding of the surf could be heard from anywhere on the island, a mighty ominous roar that seemed to issue from the bowels of the earth. 'An energy bomb that should be tappable' were how my thoughts ran as I beheld yet another oil-filled super-tanker bound for Milford Haven. They dwarfed St Ann's Head and made it look like a sandspit. All that oil scared me because of the birds. I thought it would happen one day and it did, in 1996, when the *Sea Empress* ran aground.

Facing south-east and therefore protected from a direct pounding, South Haven usually gave considerable shelter and landings were fairly straightfoward unless the swell was heavy or there were strong south to south-east winds, in which case it had to be Blacksmiths. With a tidal range of twenty-five feet, conditions at the landing varied considerably throughout the day. At very low tide it was a dinghy job which meant many trips backwards and forwards with people and gear; wet feet, wet legs, wet tempers sometimes, but usually taken in good heart and with a spirit of adventure.

Blacksmiths was situated just west of North Haven and it was apparently where the Marloes blacksmith was landed to shoe the horses and donkeys on Skokholm. In our years there it was not a proper landing at all, just a few convenient rocky ledges that were mostly used for fishing by those keen enough to face almost inevitable disappointment. Not always though. One morning my cousin and a few friends caught enough mackerel to feed fifteen of us by breakfast time. Few hotels can boast of fish that fresh!

Blacksmiths landings could be quite exciting, often involving a good and timely jump. I once leapt off those rocks to board a dinghy which disappeared to a level about ten feet below me, much to the consternation of the boatman. He insisted that I nearly went through the bottom of it! I can't think why I was so eager to get off! On another occasion, Terry had to anchor the boat fifty yards offshore, as efforts to bring her in had proved much too dangerous. He threw us one end of a rope which was fixed between the *Sharon* and the rocks so that he could work the dinghy in by the hand-over-hand technique. It worked well until somehow contact was lost between himself and the rope (or else it was the rope and the *Sharon*) while he was returning in the dinghy. Off she went with the him standing aboard, yellow oilskin cape acting like a sail as he raised his arms to indicate that he wasn't too pleased with the situation, and his shouting, although we couldn't make out the actual words, confirmed it. He was becoming smaller and smaller as he receded across Broad Sound towards Skomer; a tiny yellow dot in fact by the time his son had started the engines and set off to the rescue.

At very low tides, when Blacksmiths and South Haven were both impossible, there were beach landings in North Haven. They were tricky (and very wet) involving lots of work because there was a steep slope to be negotiated (i.e. the cliff) with all the gear. Hemmed in either side by dripping moss-covered walls, visitors would look about them, once they were safely landed on the beach, for the way out! Those with vertigo looked faint before they even began the ascent. Those without vertigo formed a chain with us to heave up the gear which often included heavy sacks of flour, potatoes etc. Gravity sometimes got the upper hand and items of luggage went hurtling down with no protest at all from the owner, they were just thankful it was the luggage and not themselves! There were some interesting moments for the vertigo sufferers going up or down, perhaps more so down because they often needed to go backwards to avoid seeing where they were going and how far they might fall. I saw this feat performed several times, but most of all I remember a very portly lady, with a 'now or never' attitude, who took the plunge very suddenly forwards and bull-dozed her way down the slope with tremendous speed and determination. Woebetide anything in her way, but she made it in the end and was still the right way up. She burst into tears of relief and we all pretended to weep with her so that she didn't feel too silly. Such were the lengths we would go to to make our visitors feel comfortable! I'm sure she must remember that part of her relaxing week on Skokholm! At that time there were no nesting buzzards or peregrines to be considered in North Haven.

Of course there could be problems at Martinshaven too for folks going off if a strong northerly wind whipped up, and there were indeed a couple of occasions when people were landed at Renny's Slip on the south side of the Deer Park. Another cliff climb, but I doubt that that would happen today.

For one who loved the island as I did, stepping off the boat on to her welcoming shores after a long absence was something akin to the feeling I had as a child waking up on Christmas morning. Days and days of knowing it's going to happen and then at long, long last it does! Our landing in 1973 was more exciting because it was our first year of working there, but spring arrivals in the ensuing years were more heartfelt; I felt I was coming home. Whatever it is, that special charm that touches you on the first encounter with Skokholm, I have never found the likes of it elsewhere.

We were to make our spring return to Skokholm with Terry most years. At first his crew was Malcolm Gray and then, later on when he left school, Terry's son Glynn. Sometimes we stayed on the Davis's farm for a night or two before we were due to sail in the hospitable care of Terry and his wife Ann. This was before we found a winter base in Pembrokeshire in December 1975. Theirs was a small farm with cattle, pigs and chickens. We were always made welcome there and enjoyed Terry's numerous stories, especially one about removing a troublesome tooth from the mouth of his boar pig.

The *Sharon* was eventually replaced by a new boat called the *Arklow* after she sank at her moorings in Martinshaven on the 11 September 1976. It was an horrendous night with a north-easterly gale blowing that registered force thirteen on the Beaufort scale. We understood that several attempts were made to salvage her but all to no avail. By chance, Ray was staying in Lockley Lodge above the cove, waiting to return to Skokholm after a visit ashore and witnessed the event. He was the one who had to inform Terry that she was taking in water; there was nothing anyone could do and she soon went down. News came the next morning via the lighthouse radio/telephone; '*Sharon* sunk' were the words I heard from Mike, leaving me wondering whether that meant Ray too, until he fed me the details. I have to admit that my heart missed a beat or two before I learnt the facts.

I remember the *Sharon* as a boat of great character in which we had made many good and safe crossings to the island, but there were not so good times, one in partic-ular when the seas were what I would call mountainous and Terry looked alarmingly anxious. A swell of such proportions rolled through Broad Sound that it was hard to turn the boat to head back. The tiny figure of Jack the lighthouse keeper waved us away from the clifftop indicating there was no chance of a landing anywhere. Back we went, but only to sit for hours off Skomer waiting for the tide to drop and try again. Later that day we did effect a landing to the relief of us all. There were also a few fish-ing trips when Terry called in unexpectedly and off we went pretending that nothing else was pressing. Ray caught a superb bass on one of those trips. One day we were caught in a heavy thunderstorm off the south coast and I remember it vividly out there in an open boat, the sky hanging over us like a great purple blanket rent apart every now and again by magnificent bursts of green sheet lightning. The boat rocked to the tremendous peals of thunder as we tried to hide from the rain. I don't think I've ever felt so humbled by a storm and it cured my queasy stomach for a while.

In the *Sharon* too, we had cruised through the summer shearwater rafts, Terry cutting the engine as we closed in on them. No noise then save the swish of water against the boat and all around us literally thousands of birds floating placidly on the calm reflective surface. What a spectacle it was in the soft light of evening, so much so that we scarcely spoke. Eventually a few birds would rise and pretty soon they were all up, sweeping around us in an everchanging collage of black, white and blue.

Some years we boarded the *Sharon* at Sandy Haven, her wintering place. It was a pretty creek some distance up the Milford estuary. We had to ferry our gear out to the big boat in a dinghy, and since we had no engine Terry would use the old technique of sculling at which he was an expert. The oar was worked with a twisting motion just beneath the surface and thus the dinghy was propelled. It sounds easy, but anyone who has tried it will know that it's not.

The Sharon in Sandy Haven

Once after a long delay on the mainland due to the inclement weather, our final departure was to be reported in the local paper. It was a low tide in Sandy Haven and it was to be touch and go whether we had enough water to float off with our huge amount of stores. The reporters did their bit with great efficiency, interviewing and photographing us with our pile of stores and livestock (chickens). After much well wishing and hearty farewells, they made it clear that they couldn't waste any more time than necessary on us, so they left. We didn't though; we remained inextricably stuck in the mud and then began to tip as the tide receded, much to the chagrin of all of us (most of all Terry and the chickens for whom feeding time was well overdue). So followed more days of waiting for tide and wind to be right, but this time with the added embarrassment of meeting friends and neighbours who greeted us with 'short season?', or 'tide bring you in, did it?'

In March 1977 Terry's new boat, the *Arklow*, was not ready for service and we attempted to cross in a small craft owned by Robbie, the son in law of Dillwyn Miles (Director of the Trust at that time). We started way upriver of Milford and the journey began well until we were foiled by some awful sea conditions outside the estuary. We trusted in Robbie's judgement and preferred a shorter season on Skokholm than none at all! In 1979, I crossed with the new wardens, Stephen and Carol Warman in a fibreglass dinghy from Martinshaven. The Jack Sound is interesting enough anyway but in a very small boat it is awesomely interesting. Terry was an unknown quantity to the newcomers and they must have found the experience even more daunting than I did. We arrived safe and physically intact if a little wet. Once I had a lift with a group of divers to Skomer via Little Sound, that very small channel between Skomer and Middleholm, and rubbed my knuckles raw in the effort to stay in the boat. Unlike them, I had no wetsuit and was a bit scared going through that torrent of rushing white water.

The *Arklow* was a sturdy ex-fishing boat. Terry modified her and built on a small wheelhouse. For the few times we went on her she seemed good and seaworthy. Her hull was painted dark red and she looked fine but she did not have the character of the *Sharon*, the loss of which must have been very traumatic for Terry. Martinshaven was considered a relatively safe harbour and north-easterly gales of such ferocity were very rare indeed. He was unlucky to be so caught out.

Cambell Reynolds, the owner of the Dale Sailing Company, filled in as boatman when Terry was unavailable or working on the new boat. Some while after we left he took over the Skokholm run completely and also the very lucrative day trips to Skomer. He also was our boatman on the many trips out to Grassholm as well as holding the Trinity House contract for ferrying mechanics and certain items of equipment out to Skokholm, the Smalls and the South Bishop. He was an excellent and experienced boatman. Sadly Cambell, who became a good friend, died of cancer in 1994 aged only sixty-eight, leaving his sons to run the business. I remember him, not only for his good looks and charm, but also for his cool and pleasant temperament which never failed to put you at ease. Everyone had complete confidence in him even in some quite nasty situations (engine failures etc.). I only saw him agitated once and that was when he had to ask some people in the dinghy three times over not to attempt to grab the boat as they approached it. To be fair, it seems the natural and proper thing to do to people not used to the procedure. Calmly he asked 'please don't try to grab the boat', then louder 'don't grab the boat', followed by a much louder 'leave the — boat alone!' It was the only time we ever heard him swear, but he had to get his point across. Frantically reaching out for the security of the bigger boat can result in an upturned dinghy. Cambell was responsible a couple of times for removing us at the end of the season and he did us the special favour of leaving us on the island for as long as possible. I was reluctant to go and would have liked to have overwintered there. He would take our last visitors off with a wink and a nod for us and we knew we wouldn't see him for a long while.

Some years before his death, his faithful crewman George Sturley, another well known and much loved character was killed together with his wife in a fire at their home in Marloes. Photographs of both George and Cambell are on display in the Griffin Inn at Dale. George looked a real 'old salt' always with a wicked smile about his weathered and ruddy complexion. He must have been related to Harold Sturley, an island boatman in the late 1950s who was tragically killed by a stray bullet from the firing range at Castle Martin whilst he was at the wheel of the *Cubango*, owned by Dale Fort. George drove a purple three-wheeler and wore a sailor's smock and a loose woollen hat. I remember being ferried out to the *Dale Queen* (Cambell's boat) in Dale harbour by George in a dinghy piled precariously high with stores. We began to sink as we got further out and just made it with some energetic baling out. It hadn't just

Cambell Reynolds (left) *and George Sturley on the Dale Princess*

sprung the leak, it was like it each trip! It was called a pram dinghy and I think maybe it really was an old pram!

We often gave George a gift of fresh gulls' eggs, of which he was especially fond, having eaten them since he was a boy. We liked them too and must have eaten hundreds, sometimes wickedly hiding the shells from visitors in case they objected, but most people were very keen to try them. They had to be scrambled or used for cakes and puddings because the white wouldn't set properly. They were rich and gave the cakes a deep colour. In our second year we ordered some tins of waterglass (a solution of silicate of soda) to preserve a quantity for cooking.

Cambell and George were a wonderful team and it was a joy to be in their company. One of the memories I have of them is of their brewing tea in the wheelhouse with a kettle hung on a string over a small stove. During the crossing the movement of the boat occasionally brought the kettle into contact with the stove and the water was encouraged to rise a degree or two. Tea would be 'ready in an hour or two' and somehow it was! The first boat of Cambell's, and the boat we knew, was the *Dale Queen*, eventually to be replaced by the *Dale Princess*. The *Queen* was very different from the *Sharon* or the *Arklow*; she was broader and equipped with a large wheelhouse. She was painted dark and light blue with red trimmings. All the island boats were around thirty-five to forty footers. I think the limit then was twelve people plus crew for the Skokholm and Grassholm run and thirty for Skomer.

CHAPTER 2

Settling in

S oon after landing on the island in1973 we were joined by our new companion, Mike, and one of the lighthouse keepers. Handshakes and pleasantries were exchanged, as we continued unloading the boat. A red dumper truck, that I recognized from my previous visits, stood by to ferry our ample supplies up to the Observatory. Thus the three of us staff became rather nervously acquainted. We little knew then of the lessons that we would learn from our close working relationship on the island with Mike, who was a different being altogether from ourselves – but more of that later.

Waving farewell to boatman and crew, we savoured the moment of arrival. For us it had been a natural and unhampered journey. Some of the future wardens were unfortunate enough to be accompanied by a television crew sent to record the event; a boatload of people greedy for material to sensationalise an experience which their very presence devalued. For me it was a very special occasion and I would have resented that kind of intrusion.

It was only a short distance uphill from the landing steps to the Observatory, and what a joy it was to see once again the little lime kiln beside the track. It was in remarkably good condition and was built in the 1800s, but lime was rarely if ever burnt in it according to a Marloes woman who told this to Lockley. The practice was said to be too much trouble. In his book *Dream Island Days*, Lockley wrote that the last fire had been drawn roughly fifty years before, that is around 1880. From cavities deep within its structured walls we were to hear storm petrels churring at night, and to our delight in later years a blackbird raised her brood in the bramble bush growing in the stone basin. I missed very little of the mainland in those island years, but the song of the blackbird was dear to my heart and it was a great event when they first bred for us on the island. Those sweet, melancholy notes carried on the breeze to my appreciative ears as I undertook the evening chores around the buildings. We had gulls mewing, skylarks singing, curlew calling and many more evocative sounds, but there were no rich songsters and that created a gap which the blackbird was to fill. As well as providing them with a nest site, that bramble bush fuelled our annual blackberry and apple pie, a rare treat! As we passed the kiln we noted what we took to be piles of goat droppings in the cavity below the basin where the fire would have been lit. The musty, goaty smell which assailed our nostrils confirmed their identity and it

The lime kiln

was obvious that the feral herd had taken shelter in that convenient little den during the winter storms.

Beside the stream trickling down a rocky gully into South Haven were some early primroses, a tantalizing reminder that spring was not far away. In this sheltered sun trap they flourished along with other plants that thrived in the damp conditions, for example brooklime (*Samolus valerandi*) and common reed (*Phragmites communis*). A mass of fresh green, succulent foliage bordering the stream was the precursor of a mass of white flowers ready to bloom in April. This was common scurvygrass (*Cochlearia officinalis*). It was my first encounter with this sweetly perfumed flower which is so common in damp gullies around the coast of Cornwall where I now live.

The stream was then enclosed by one of four Heligoland traps which we used for trapping and ringing birds. This one we called the Winch Trap, as close by were the remains of the old winch system used to haul up small island boats above the tiny pebble beach, like Ronald Lockley's *Storm Petrel*. Incidentally, he used to collect and use the island's red pebbles as sinkers in his lobster pots. In those years bird ringing was a major part of our daily routine and many interesting migrants were caught in the small wooden box at the end of the trap. One that I have good reason to remember was a nightingale which I caught easily but let go again because it could not be attended to quickly enough for my liking, Mike being occupied at the other end of the island. Stupidly, I felt guilty about it and didn't admit to catching it, but reported seeing it instead which meant that nobody believed me! Rightly enough, Mike was very strict about accepting records but it was a shame because it was the only one we ever had.

For the most part the vegetation in March still bore its winter colours and the general picture was an attractive mosaic of faded pinkish brown bracken, very dead from the previous year, mixed with varying shades of green. The overall scene was truly invigorated by the intensely blue March sky. Such days often came with dry and cold northerly air streams which were not uncommon in the months of March and April. The dried stems and frizzled fronds of the old bracken lay torn and criss-crossed over the ground forming a battered canopy that gave shelter to some of the smaller plants like ground ivy (*Glechoma hederacea*), soon to yield tiny, blue flowers, and dog violets (*Viola riviniana*) whose sprightly, purple heads peeped out from dark recesses. Those were some of our earliest flowers. Impossible to imagine then the deliciously aromatic swathes of bluebells that would paint the island slopes in May a cool and soothing blue, even though already some of the leaf tips were poking through the soil. Later on, the bracken would regenerate and its living canopy act as nurse to the dying bluebells, keeping the soil cool and moist while the bulbs stored up reserves for the following year. That was a relatively simple relationship between two plants, but I had no notion

Dog Violet

then of the much more complex relationships involving the plant communities, the animals and the weather on the island.

Little did I know also of the beautiful orange and map-winged swift moths whose caterpillars fed on the roots and stems of the bracken. Those larvae would have been overwintering in the soft soil beneath the plants and would emerge during the summer, flaunting exquisitely patterned wings of orange, black and gold, to surprise me in my moth trap.

There is a well made trackway from the landing to the lighthouse which was once laid with rails along which a tram carrying stores was drawn by horse (Lockley's horse Sugarback was one of them) and later on by a small motor tractor. All this before the arrival of the 'war veteran' dumper truck from the Channel Islands. Some rusty rails were still evident in places on the island. However, our track to the Observatory left the main track just above South Haven and crossed a large area of well nibbled turf – Home Meadow. On our left just after the fork was a grey corrugated hut, called the 'red hut' because it had once been painted red. I have seen a photograph of it in its more colourful days and I am glad it is a red hut no longer! It was used then as a storeroom for coal and some of the sacks were always left lying around for the resident slow-worms.

Home Meadow was a rabbits' version of McDonalds, but as we had arrived in the middle of the day it was pretty much deserted. Not for long though, never for long! I remember sitting one evening on the bench outside the cottage which overlooks the meadow and counting up to ninety rabbits. Some of our young male visitors once entertained themselves by trying to race them back to the bracken from this bench. My money was on the rabbits and I won! Visitors were usually surprised and often pleased to see so many of them, and with a peak summer population estimate of ten thousand this was understandable.

In those days, situated in the lower, north-eastern corner of the meadow was the largest of our Heligoland traps which we imaginatively called 'the Heligoland'. It was built around a marshy area beside the main spring where some small elder bushes had been planted, and these along with a good summer's growth of yellow flag iris (*Iris peudacorus*), common figwort (*Scrophularia nodosa*), marsh willowherb (*Epilobium palustre*), water mint (*Mentha aquatica*) and some other tall wetland plants provided the migrant birds with a little cover. The trap was enclosed with fine wire netting and gave a degree of protection from the constant, salt-laden winds. On our arrival that March it still looked brown and bare. Between the trap and the track was an uninteresting looking brown hollow, but it was there that I was later to relish the appearance of some red campion flowers mingling with the bluebells; so beautiful the deep pink against violet blue, like hot against cold. On Skokholm, those campions were scarce and only grew in that one locality, but now they are so very familiar around my home in Cornwall, where they can be found in flower in virtually every month of the year.

The track went on up to the buildings and arrived first at the white cottage of stone with its steep roof of cement-washed asbestos slate and its low walls and tiny windows. It was the perfect weather-proof structure for a dwelling on a windswept island. It had withstood the winter storms well and from the outside looked ready enough to welcome another set of visitors, save for the extensive grey smudging on the Snowcemmed walls and roof, soon to be be remedied. Our first destination however was the Wheelhouse, the centre of domestic activity on the island. That building and its adjoining rooms was to the north and was reached by crossing a walled yard that separated it on the south side from a middle block of renovated barns and outhouses.

That first day, a musty, somewhat mouse-tainted smell greeted our nostrils as we pushed open the door of the Wheelhouse, complete with its 'Master' plate, a relic from the wrecked schooner, *Alice Williams*, about which more is written later. Perhaps this hint of male superiority didn't go down well with everyone in these days of sexual

The cottage

equality, but it didn't bother me then and it wouldn't now. Our immediate needs after the hour-long boat journey and hours of loading and off loading was to indulge in a cup of tea, as all the necessary items for brewing had already been sought out by Mike since his arrival a few days before. In following years it was much easier as we were all familiar with storage arrangements. At least that first year we had brought no livestock to be tended to. We hadn't then realized the homeliness and fascination that domestic chickens would bring to the isolated farmstead, so there was no half framed gate made of driftwood and old wire netting which we were later to fix in front of the main door to deter the hens from entering our kitchen and dining room.

The Skokholm mice (house mice) had their fun in the winter, ravaging, chewing and eating anything they could get hold of to fend off starvation, so mouse smells, mouse debris and mouse dung was all pervading in the Wheelhouse at first, and mouse trapping, mouse proofing and mouse deterring was well underway from that initial cup of tea onwards. There were reckoned to be between four and five thousand animals present by the time the population had built up in the autumn, by which time they ranged over the whole island. Cold winter weather, particularly in the month of February, killed many of them, and come the spring the remainder were to be found mainly on the cliffs or around the buildings. Vulnerable food was easily stored in mouse-proof dustbins and cleaning up operations were simple because the mice were then in low numbers and beginning to take to the outdoor life with the advancement of spring. They did however gradually remove virtually all of the insulation inside our cooking stoves and we could do nothing about that. The mice themselves had a fine time of it as one of our visitors commented in the 'chatty log'. After listening to their all-night revelries in the attic of the cottage, he or she concluded that they were holding the annual mice Olympics and there is a charming illustration depicting this in one of the chatty logs! For myself they never bothered me, in fact they could be and were used as scapegoats at times when bars of chocolate mysteriously went missing!

Lockley thought that they were introduced around 1903 when a boat packed with straw, which was taking a horse over to the island from Martinshaven, landed at South Haven. While the animal was embarking, the straw was disturbed and several mice were supposed to have scrambled ashore. However in a paper describing his studies of the Skokholm mice Dr R. J. Berry from the Royal Free Hospital came to another conclusion. The island race, which are larger and heavier than mainland mice, showed more skeletal similarities to mice caught at West Hook Farm, near Dale, compared to those caught in Martinshaven. He suspected that the mice were introduced ten or twenty years earlier when the island was not lived on but was farmed by a tenant of West Hook Farm (now stifled by Dale aerodrome) who made frequent trips to the island in his boat moored below Hook Vale. There was yet another story told that mice were introduced via sacks brought over by rabbiters some time in the 1890s, and it is also possible that there was more then one introduction. The mice were the only resident small mammals on the island apart from the rabbit. The only others were recorded very rarely and comprised two vagrant bat species, notably a noctule and a few pipistrelles.

With the aid of the dumper truck, the off-duty lighthouse keeper had lent us a hand transporting our gear in several loads up to the buildings. We were reminded that in the 1950s there was no dumper truck and stretchers were used to carry up the gear which often included bulky and heavy building materials. So we evidently had reason to be thankful. The old truck was a godsend, not only then but on every boat day in the busy summer seasons ahead. When the lighthouse finally went automatic in 1983, it was handed over to the Observatory but it has now been replaced by a new one, and in the late 1980s our dear old dumper truck was taken by helicopter to Thwaites Museum still working! Prince Charles, it seems, had a hand in that. Saturday mornings, no matter what we were doing, we would have one ear cocked for the soft throbbing of the engine and if the wind was in the right direction we could hear it coming soon after it had left the lighthouse. It was a good sound to us then, undisturbed as we were by general traffic noise. The keepers themselves soon became our friends, but more of them later.

Front aspect of the Wheelhouse

The Wheelhouse was just one of a complex of outbuildings which grew up around the oldest dwelling, i.e. the 'Cottage'. It was once a threshing room and was a place of great character with a solid flagstone floor composed of large slabs of red island sandstone. Those stones were there when Lockley arrived. They would colour up beautifully after a hard scrubbing and a good sluice down. Even with a daily sweep they gradually turned dull during the week and it was good to bring up that lovely earthy red colour that brightened the room and complimented the white walls and wooden tables. That duty was performed every friday night by one of us and we made it a floor to be proud of. I doubt if I was ever proud of a floor before or since, or enjoyed cleaning one! I am certain that a floor could not be more clean or hygenic than that one was.

Ronald Lockley renovated this 'barn' with timbers from the wrecked *Alice Williams* and tiled it with sandstone from the island quarry. It was under that roof that we gathered to eat our meals. Although it probably once had a loft, the timbers were then open to the roomspace below. This posed problems for us sometimes, in the form of avian visitors, namely racing pigeons that stopped off and joined the chickens at feeding time. They would make themselves at home around the buildings and, being attractive and tame, easily engaged our sympathy and protection. They were always individually coloured and marked, with soft, pretty eyes, and they soon seduced us into giving them names. There were inevitably many Percys, and I remember Griselda and George

View north from the Knoll. Shows middle block of buildings with wheelhouse behind. Beyond (left to right) are Skomer, Middleholm and the mainland.

who paired up for a while, as did Toby and Bertram! These birds would treat us to charming sessions of cooing and amorous display. As this was going on all around us among the island birds, it added to the enjoyment of our more formal studies of bird behaviour. Sometimes they overstayed their welcome and became part of the kitchen scene, perching inside on the rafters above the eating tables. It was no use pretending to visitors that they weren't there because, sooner or later, one of them would deposit a pigeon visiting card where it wasn't well received. Many times we deported the offending pigeon(s) in a box, and this way we learnt just how incredible the homing instinct can be for they often came back from the mainland unless taken a good distance away. Try catching a pigeon in a large barn with rafters, cluttered to the last square foot with kitchenware and furniture and you will have some idea of the trouble we had (pigeon racers note!). Butterfly nets, wire razorbill hooks, box traps, bored lighthouse keepers and many more devices were employed. We even tried feeding them grain soaked in our home brew, a concoction guaranteed to induce abnormal behaviour in humans! They didn't even fall of their perches! Sometimes, pigeons in poor condition didn't survive in spite of our care and coaxing (and beer); whether through exhaustion, dehydration or what we never knew.

Swallows too, came in regularly and that was rather nice as they simply flew agilely back and forth until they finally swooped low and went out through the door. The building was re-roofed in 1984 by a work party led by John Lewis and *Alice's* old timbers were burnt for firewood.

Further adornments from the wrecked schooner charmed our eating room. Built into the wall at the western end of the barn was a series of shelves, and set in the wall above them was a superb piece of carved timber from the bow of the boat; it was chequered and painted in black and white. From a row of nails in the wood below, we would hang all the different coloured mugs for daily use. I hope that piece of wood is still there, although I know that the rest has changed, for below a hatch has been cut through to the new kitchen that was once our storeroom. New rules of hygiene etc. have dictated that the kitchen be separate from the eating room. No more does cook chat freely with guests in between passing plates of bacon and eggs rather precariously over their heads. I doubt also that the latter are able to leap up and rescue bits of toast set aflame beneath the grill while cook struggles with twelve eggs frying and rows of bacon and tomatos sizzling in the oven.

Cook had the advantage of the best view as he or she stood at the work surface above which was a little window, and strange birds or unexpected boats had priority over burning toast and ravenous visitors. Only a little window, but through it you could see part of the north side of the island, a small area of sea and the mainland beyond. Some of my best views of peregrine falcons were seen through this window particularly when they pitched on the stone wall outside. Hoopoes, black redstarts and many more migrants were clocked up by the cook and so were many rounds of burnt toast.

Sweating in front of a stove with a huge frying pan of eggs and two grills blazing for an hour or so called for an open window, and this was when the cook often fell out with the visitors who sat shivering while a chill northerly wind swept through the room. The idea, I argued, was to harden them up and to make sure they ate their breakfasts quickly! One advantage of the new arrangement that comes to mind is that the cook must be out of earshot of complicated requests, like grades of softness in boiled eggs or amount of charcoal on toast. Complaints cannot be heard from that distance either, but then neither are compliments!

Inside the Wheelhouse. Shows wheel from the Alice Williams

At the eastern end of the barn over the old fireplace, was fixed the wheel from the wreck, made of wood and brass. It is one of the finest ship's wheels that I have seen, and when polished up and shining made a splendid focal point. Indeed it was this wheel that really gave the room its character. Lockley once took it away with him to his farm on the mainland and it had to be prised away from him. A wheelbarrow wheel had been put up in its place which earned the warden of the day (Peter Condor) some nasty looks! I wonder how they got it back? During his residence, Lockley had a chain attached to it which would raise and lower a kettle over the fire and he also built in settles beside the fire. For us the wheel had no function but was a vital part of the history of the island as well as a unique ornament. It is probably the most photographed ship's wheel in the country! A lifebelt stood in the little window high on the west wall, but this one was not from the *Alice*. I remember it particularly as it was connected with my one and only experience of a poltergeist. One afternoon as I stood by the stoves about fifteen foot along the north wall of the room, this lifebelt suddenly took off from its shelf and landed just a foot or two away from me on the floor with a tremendous thud. Needless to say I was a bit shocked and dumbfounded. I have never been able to explain this as there was no wind at all, and indeed that window didn't even open and the door was closed too. If the phenomenon was connected with someone reaching puberty, as some say it is, I couldn't help wondering which one of us it was! Being a true sceptic, it greatly puzzled me and it still does.

Occasionally a herring gull stood outside that window and pecked viciously at it. Some people said that was a sign of bad luck and it meant a death in the family, but I never went along with that as my entire family would have been dead within a year! No doubt the gull was simply pecking at its own reflection.

Two long wooden dining tables with benches and chairs ran down the centre of the room. We had a third table to be placed in the middle when visitor numbers were high. The warden was seated at the head with the wheel above him as a sort of crowning glory. The other staff members sat adjacent to him. Some tried to get as close to Mike as possible as if the peck order ran up the table. Those less privileged sat right at the far end like starlings on the thin end of a branch! Many tried to sit in the same place every meal time although we tried to encourage more general mixing. They usually persisted and those with less of the great British tenacity gave up. My ability for parrot-fashion learning at least made it easier for me to remember names because names became associated with sitting places. I would repeat to myself the list of names going round the table during the introduction ceremony, but it did sometimes lead to embarassing mistakes. Mealtimes were big social occasions especially for lone visitors; it was their chance to mix, talk, make friends and ask questions. Our chance too to find out about them and, alas, to learn of the happenings in the world outside

Thus we mused on the busy summer ahead as we prepared our tea that day in March 1973. We did not know at that stage how we would cope with increasing numbers of visitors with all the cooking and other work, and we didn't know either how the three of us would get on. For myself, I was quaking with fear at the idea of having to produce all those meals after living in a bedsit on beans on toast for several years. Fortunately, I wasn't on my own; not only did I have Ray who was willing to share the cooking, but I was armed with recipe books as well. It was only the island and the birds that had drawn me there after all.

A certain amount of mildew had accumulated on the tables over winter, but nothing that couldn't be remedied with a hard scrub and an airing outside. Mike had already connected the stove to the Calor gas cylinder and boiling a kettle of rainwater was straightfoward. Matches, tea, condensed milk and sugar were soon located and once we were supping that brew, as far as we were concerned, we were at home. In the ensuing years that feeling of being back home was even better. We even got to like the diluted condensed milk!

Cleaning the cookers was a priority job, but first there were stores to unpack, lots of them. There was food mainly, cases and cases of tins – meat, fruit, beans, milk and vegetables, along with butter, jam, cheese, flour, sugar, fresh meat, loaves of bread etc. We had no boat until the first visitors arrived, and then it was once a week only so that we had to be vigilant in our ordering of stores. When Mike asked for mint sauce to go with the lamb, I realized it had to be a little more than plain fare.

We owe our gratitude to the Trust in that they placed great emphasis on looking after the visitors and ourselves in terms of supplying us with ample, good quality food. We certainly ate better than we would have done ordinarily, with two roast dinners a week, joints of ham, bacon, fresh mince etc. and a good supply of fresh vegetables and salad too. Fresh fruit was only supposed to be for staff (to stop us getting scurvy!) but it often got incorporated into orange and banana cakes, apple pies, plum puddings etc. Accustomed to a western diet, our stomachs preferred it that way. Most certainly Mike's did! Our storeroom was situated where the kitchen is now, a little room on the west side of the Wheelhouse and entered through a tiny black-painted door. There was an awkward protruding step into it and you rather squirmed in than walked in. It was nothing for the cook to be found sprawled on the floor clutching head in hands after a hefty bang on the lintel, salad cream or marmalade sprayed over everything in sight. The low beam above the Wheelhouse door also claimed many victims among the taller of our visitors whose entrance would be announced by a resounding thud and a corresponding whinge. Some of them were never the same afterwards!

In the storeroom were a number of metal and rubber mouse-proof dustbins in which such vulnerable commodities as bread, flour, sugar and dried fruit were stored. These were perfect so long as you could remember what was where, and you put the lids back on afterwards! There was plenty of shelf room for cereal packets, coffee and loose tins and jars. Outside, a corrugated shed was used for storing the bulk of the tinned food of which we had several weeks' supplies. This also housed a row of nesting boxes for laying hens, but they were on ground level.

Calor gas cylinders were stored in there too, and we always had several spares. Our cooking facilities were modern compared to the fifties when they had to manage with primus stoves, but then I think the guests cooked for themselves. As well as two cookers, the Calor gas fuelled a small boiler and a fridge. Not all the rings on the two stoves worked all the time and so it was quite a challenge to cook for large numbers of people. By some misadventure, we once had a complement of twenty-four when our official intake should have been fifteen. That time we had to turn our laboratory into a dormitory. Cooking for the masses as we did could best be described as bucket chemistry, but we did our best to quench the voracious appetite of most of our visitors not used to long hours of imbibing fresh air and taking lots of excercise. Large scale cake or bread making developed my biceps, although eating such fare didn't make us fat; we had too much to do!

We had gone to the island in the capacity of voluntary warden and cook, so Ray and myself shared most of the duties. We cooked on alternate days and that suited us as it didn't become too much of a drudge. It gave each of us a complete day away from it and even meant that we actually enjoyed it a little. As neither of us had had any experience of cooking for other people, we knew we were taking a bit of a risk and that meant the Trust who were employing us were as well. We were determined not to let them down. Fortunately, as the weeks went on, we were eased in gently with the numbers of visitors increasing only slowly over the weeks until we had a full complement of fifteen. I never came to terms with the fact that Ray made the first cake for I had not the nerve. It was a success too and Ray's self esteem rose greatly, whilst I, as a mere woman, felt humbled and embarassed. Things changed though and in a few weeks I was a confident cake maker.

In the corner by the head-banging door stood a small, galvanized gas boiler. It was lit from beneath, and apart from using the kettle for tea and coffee, it provided all the hot water we needed for washing up, washing clothes and tea towels as well as the very rare and privileged occasions when a member of staff took a bath. This luxury was only allowed when there was no problem with water supply and that really meant if the rainwater tanks were reasonably full, and if they weren't it was back to a bowl of hot water! Our warden took to bathing in the Wheelhouse so that he could run the water straight from the boiler into the old fashioned tin bath. More convenience than laziness I'm sure! He used to hang a little note on the door to warn intruders of the event. I am observant in many ways but not in the fine details of a door, and so it was that once I nearly ended up in the bath with him as he sat there in steaming indulgence. It was obviously not safe to rely on written instruction as he did, and in any case it was my kitchen!

We had many rainwater tanks, about seven in all, placed around the buildings to catch water off the roof. The other unofficial use was for 'dunking', which was usually carried out by some of the more boisterous components of a certain schoolparty, especially on birthdays. That didn't exclude staff either, but Ray had (and still has) a certain intimidating air about him when these things threatened and nobody dared to even try him, but I had my turn all right.

In the early part of the season, rain was usually frequent enough for the tanks to be well topped up, but they each had to be emptied sometime at the start of the season to be cleaned. That was another priority job. Our water-carrying vessels were tall, cylindrical, plastic containers with stout handles and little round lids attached by tiny chains. They stood by the boiler and were used to fill it and also to take the cold water to the bowls in the sink as there were no running taps then. The first job in the morning was always to fill and light the boiler so that there was ample hot water for washing up. Many of the male visitors would come and beg a cupful for shaving before breakfast, and very early risers would never be refused an early cup of tea.

Our drinking water came from the main spring below the 'Heligoland' and was stored in a five-hundred-gallon tank that stood on a wooden frame outside the Wheelhouse. There was a kind of bench affair built below the tap on which the 'drinking water only' vessel was placed, and whoever was getting the water was likely to jump up on the bench while it was filling and peep over the wall to take in the view down the meadow and eastwards across the four miles of sea to St Ann's Lighthouse on the tip of the Dale peninsula. It was not uncommon to spot a migrant or two this way, or perhaps an even finer sight such as the one that is mentioned later on in the book.

It was a major crime to use our precious drinking water for washing anything. We also had a strict rule that on no account could anyone wash their hair or themselves down at the spring for fear of contaminating the water. It was of excellent quality and tasted as pure as water possibly can so that a plain drink of water was a treat. That could hardly be said for the adulterated tap water on the mainland that most people were used to. The spring was said to have its origins in the Preseli Mountains to the north-east of us, which on days of good visibility appeared as a range of dusky blue hills in the far distance. I used to find that theory quite mind boggling and I still don't know if it's true. They are twenty-seven miles away after all! The spring never ran dry, even in the drought of 1976, but it did turn brown and take a long time to fill. If it had dried up we would have had to evacuate the island that year leaving the scorched brown turf to the birds and the starving rabbits.

We drew water at least once weekly to fill the tank, and for that we would borrow the dumper truck and ask for volunteers. Those pumping sessions were enjoyed by staff and visitors alike and they were sometimes accompanied by a chorus of Skokholm spirituals. First we would peep under the flat stones surrounding the well for a look at our prize specimen eel, known to some of us Ellie. She, or it could have been a he, was some fifteen inches long and was our proof of the purity of the water. It was a simple pleasure just to gaze into the clear, deep water of the well and dangle your hand in its coolness. To draw the water we would first prime the pump by filling the attached pipe with water and then, with a side-to-side stroke of the handle, pump it into a fifty gallon container perched on the dumper truck. Visitors loved this job and joined in willingly, particularly the men because it was a great time to show of their muscular prowess, if they had any! Each person was supposed to do a certain number of strokes (usually a hundred) and they always did. We had no heart attacks, just a lot of fun and we were never short of helpers while we had visitors on the island. In the past it had been possible to pump water directly up the meadow, through a pipe to the Wheelhouse tank, but that pipe was broken and we didn't mind at all. You could say that these sessions brought out something like the community spirit that still prevails in some villages.

Water pumping sessions nearly always broke the metaphorical ice if there was any. If that didn't work, the bucketing sessions did. This was the transfer of water from the dumper to the tank outside the wheelhouse high up on its stand. Someone had to stand on the wall, and then it required a few people to hand the full buckets up and to refill the empty ones. If anyone was dry after that something was amiss! There was something inately satisfying about these basic tasks. Long after we left, in 1986, a water ram was installed.

The water for our first cup of tea of the season was therefore close at hand, even if the drinking water tank was low and a bit suspect, thanks to a typical, wet British winter. Sometimes on our spring arrival the mugs would be still hanging in place, because

Ray pumping water

departure the year before had been a rushed and unexpected affair so that last minute things were left much as normal.

Over our heads as we sat at the table, apart from some magnificent cobwebs, two lengths of wire hung down from the beams, each ending in a hook on which we hung our only means of lighting, the Tilley lamps. Imagine then a social gathering in this lovely old barn, bathed in the soft white light of their glowing mantles. Shadows flicker on the white emulsioned walls and the brass on the ship's wheel gleams with reflected light. On the wall near the door hangs a long, black plait of coarse hair, not from a recent Chinese cook, but the tail of Sugarback, Lockley's pony, who died on the island. We never had the heart to throw it away. The company's chatter and general frivolity is accompanied by the friendly hissing of the lamps. The floor and the walls are thick and solid and no-one pays any heed to the raging gales and rain outside. That comes later in the dash to the cottage or outbuildings when furious gusts of wind might extinguish the lamps, but it is never far to go. More often the night is fine, and then the star-studded, black dome enveloping our world captures our attention and we stop to stare at the beauty and mystery of it all. There are sounds unfamiliar to the city dweller; the surf, the stranger-than-fiction cry of the shearwater, or the pure whistle of a curlew. All part of the magic of a Skokholm night.

Thus the three of us were brought together over tea within the bounds of an island that was to be our temporary home, Mike, a solitary figure, and ourselves well acquainted. We all wanted to be there without a doubt and we knew our respective positions: Mike as warden and the two of us to share the assistant warden and cook's jobs. That was clear enough we hoped, but in fact our duties were not clear cut, as we shall see later.

What were our reasons for being there as individuals? Ray had detached himself from a business-orientated career and, like me, was looking for something more rewarding, more exciting and less conventional. Although he had less of my obsessive passion for islands and birds, he had a genuine appreciation of wildlife and a tremendous spirit of adventure and had been very happy to go along with the venture. I, from an academic background, had followed my inclination towards living somewhere remote with an abundance of wildlife, a far cry from laboratory work in London. I had an inborn feel for nature, not just for statistics, facts and explanations but for the spiritual side too, and Skokholm offered a perfect blend. Mike was freshly graduated from Cambridge University and, with his brilliantly logical mind, was intent on furthering his career. By arrangement with the Edward Grey Institute and the Trust, he was offered the warden's post for four years while at the same time studying for his PhD. on Manx shearwaters. His motives were, and had to be, research orientated, but that is not to say that he didn't relish the idea of living on Skokholm too. Indeed he assures me that he was as keen as we were.

If I had to present an island image of the three of us, it would be as follows. Ray and I were ex-hippy types. I see Ray with medium length, curly, brown hair kept under control by a white, woollen hat. Once, that hat concealed a sick robin that he was nursing and there was much wonderment as he 'cheeped' his way round the table whilst serving up the lunch. With a generous, unkempt beard, a rugged complexion and faded, rust-coloured smock over his jeans and wellingtons, he had the look of a genuine islander. His stern countenance was touched with humour and concealed a warm, sensitive personality. He was more responsible than I and I tended to leave the serious side of life to him – money matters, bureaucratic demands etc.

I see myself, technically the other half, with shoulder length, sun-bleached hair, which was straight and usually fortified with salt from excessive swimming. I wear a faded blue smock, jeans and soggy plimsolls (or I have bare feet). I have no idea of the impression I gave of my character; I will have to leave my readers to judge. Ray and I were both of average build and physically fit.

Mike, I see, as an ex-college type with a pleasant, boyish face and shortish hair, although he assures me that old photographs show a considerable mane of hair, so it must be his early season image that I have conjured up. What is so striking is the darkness of his hair and skin, so that one could be forgiven for thinking that he had foreign blood in him. He wears more conventional clothes and I see him in a well worn, maroon sweater, brown cotton trousers and black wellingtons. He was solidly built and strong which was a great advantage during our football matches, when he would charge up the centre of the pitch kicking the ball and send it straight into the goal with no nonsense. Most opponents were either too slow or too fearful to go in for the tackle! We found Mike generally friendly, but difficult to communicate with due to his shyness and natural reticence, which meant that it took us a long time to find out anything about him. Such people, I was to learn are usually the most interesting. For example, it was a long time before we heard about his cycle ride down the west coast of the United States, or his exploits with the nearly extinct Mauritius kestrel and, even now, it is not easy to extract information out of him in spite of his extensive travels and unusual experiences. He was hard working, dedicated and genuine in his concern for wild creatures.

We little knew each other that day in March 1973 and had no idea how things would work out between us. It wasn't smooth running, as these situations seldom are, but we managed, and some of the problems we encountered are outlined briefly in a later chapter.

CHAPTER 3

Lockley's Legacy

It is not easy to quantify the inherent charm of Skokholm. I had my first glimpse from the Deer Park on the nearby mainland in 1971 and saw nothing grandiose or dramatic, just a relatively small island with few features save some rocky bumps and the little white dots that were the buildings. But it was that simplicity and the humble proportions which appealed so much, along with the setting. In no way was it an extension of the mainland, as Skomer appeared to me. It was a respectable distance offshore, giving it its own dignity and independence, and the red rock undoubtedly helped to single it out from its sister islands. How could I not yearn to be there?

Getting to know the island in 1971 had been a joy, partly because it was such a comfortable size (two hundred and forty acres) – small enough to become familiar with every nook and cranny and yet large enough for much variety and interest. There were those quaint features whose significance I did not understand at first, like the figurehead of a woman looking down from the cliffs near South Haven, and the well-preserved lime kiln. It was even more of a revelation because, at the time of my first visit, I had not read any of Ronald Lockley's books extolling the beauty of the island and its wildlife and therefore was not influenced by them. Little did I know then how his presence had shaped the island's future or how his work and ingenuity had infused the buildings with such character, particularly the Wheelhouse. I knew nothing of the story behind the strange figurehead on the cliffs which I had noted when I first drew in to land there. Of his studies on the Manx shearwater and bird ringing activities, I had no prior knowledge. Nor was I aware of his struggles with domestic and wild rabbits, trying to breed them on the one hand and trying to exterminate the wild population in the interest of farming on the other. It was some time too before I realized that the herd of feral goats that I loved to watch were most likely ancestors of his stock, mixed with others owned by lighthouse keepers. I knew them as free-living and totally undomesticated animals. His faithful tram-pulling horse, Sugarback, outstayed him and continued to live on the island long after the departure of his master. He is buried near North Pond, but lived on for us as the plaited tail on the wall and in the names of his favourite rocky outcrops – Sugar's Delight and Sugar Loaf.

Perhaps Ronald Lockley's feelings were akin to mine when he first saw the island from the mainland cliffs for he claimed to have lost his heart to it before he even set foot there. His situation and his intentions were rather different though. He first crossed to

Ronald Lockley

the island in May 1926 in a sailing boat rowed by local fishermen in a dead calm sea. He was twenty-two years old, a young and spirited man. Dozens of puffins were gathered on the sea and on the nearby cliffs when their boat approached South Haven – a delightful introduction to the rich variety of birds and plants he was to discover whilst exploring the island. He had a dream of living a Crusoe-like existence at the same time as being able to study the wildlife he so loved. Skokholm provided the perfect setting and, after some lengthy negotiations, he finally took possession on 31 October 1927 at the age of twenty-four. Along with one W. H. Shellard, the father of his future wife, he took on a twenty-one year lease for a nominal rent of twenty-six pounds a year.

His future was extremely uncertain. It was a time of economic depression and there was little return from the resources available to him, like rabbits, shellfish and wool or sheep meat. Life on the isolated island had always been a challenge to the hardy souls who had farmed there in the past, particularly as the rabbits made the cultivation of crops a daunting task. Then after only a few months of possession came an extraordinary turn of events which changed his fortune. On 28 February 1928, during a return journey to the island with his companion Jack, Ronald Lockley 'beheld a strange and tragic, yet beautiful scene'. As unreal as if part of a dream, a wooden schooner in full sail lay upright and wedged in a broad cleft on the east side of the island. She was broadside on to the shore with her broken bowsprit firmly lodged in the red rocks at the base of the gully. It transpired that her captain and crew had abandoned her at the entrance to Milford Haven after she became out of control in an easterly gale. The schooner named *Alice Williams* then sailed her own course for some five miles until the cliffs of Skokholm claimed her forever. Easterly winds and high spring tides had combined to bring about salvation for our needy islander. No lives were lost and one can sympathise with Lockley's honest admission – 'I believe that some of my first thoughts when I first saw the schooner were as disreputable as any beachcomber's'.

Mainsail, foresail and topsail were intact, but the jibsails were torn to shreds. The men eventually managed to board the stricken vessel via the stump of the bowsprit and found the deck cluttered with a useful assemblage of ropes and chains. It was then that Ronald Lockley noticed a lady floating with some wreckage in the sea below: 'a strong, bright face with piercing blue eyes that gazed far-seeing into the blue sky. The woman still wore her hair neatly coiled, with a black ribbon and red roses entwined in it. She also wore a white frock with an old fashioned tight bodice, and around her neck was a rosary of jet and a black cross that matched her raven hair. She floated serenely in the water despite the fact that one of her arms was missing.' She was, of course, the ship's figurehead, and they eventually set her on the cliffs where, until a few years ago, she continued to embrace the salt winds and survey the turbulent seas around the islands. That was the story of the figurehead I had first seen from the boat in South Haven in June 1971.

Alice Williams was purchased by Ronald Lockley for the sum of five pounds, including her cargo of fifty tons of coal, a veritable hoard when driftwood and island turf were the only available fuel. She also provided the much needed wood (fine quality oak) for lintels and beams to be used in the renovation of the island buildings, and indeed some of her timbers became essential parts of the main structure of the buildings. This went a long way to solving one of Ronald Lockley's main problems which was the aquisition and transportation of timbers for major construction work. They also retrieved the ship's bell, which for many years summoned hungry visitors for refreshments but, alas, it had to be replaced long ago.

The figurehead came under our care in 1973. She had been kept painted and in good repair and, at the beginning of each season, we replaced her on the cliffs just along from South Haven where she looked across the sea towards the Dale Peninsula. She appeared serene and proud just as when she rode the bow of her ship, and seemed to care not a whit that she was incarcerated on a small island after seventy-four years at sea, for she had been built in 1854. Her spirit lived on. When I visited 'Alice' she always had company, usually puffins, gulls or rabbits and all around her grew a wealth of wild flowers. I felt that, if she had a personality, she would have loved her summer station out there on the cliffs. She was taken in only at the end of the season, but once she had to come in for running repairs, having keeled over and broken her once mended arm. It was said that the owner of Skokholm, residing at Dale Castle, could see the island from his window and demanded the reason for her absence during this spell of renovation. It was strange for us to think that someone had their eye (or rather their telescope) on us! Today she stays indoors all year as she is considered too valuable and too old to risk a hardy, outdoor life. 'Alice' was a true legacy from Lockley's days; she told a romantic story which will never be forgotten, and her presence on the cliffs in our years seemed to me to be a celebration of Lockley's ultimately successsful venture.

According to Lockley, two ships, one of them being the *Alice Williams*, have been wrecked in Wreck Cove, and anchors, chains and several obscure pieces of metal were often visible on a low spring tide. We never witnessed any shipwrecks apart from a small sailing dinghy that was abandoned and sailed itself into North Haven. I remember thinking dreadful thoughts before we knew her story, like bumping into bodies whilst swimming or finding them washed up on the beach, but all was well in the end. She had been written off by the owner and was eventually sold for a tiny amount by the finder (not me).

The story of Ronald Lockley's life on Skokholm is beautifully narrated in several books. His passion and curiosity for nature are highlighted by his romantic approach to the venture, which is understandable because the magical quality of Skokholm brings it out in you! His books undoubtedly helped to popularize natural history as a pleasurable pas-

Alice Williams figurehead

time as well as encouraging serious long term studies. Many of them are now collector's items. Today, when the survival of many animal and plant populations are under threat, such books are of great value in that they help to generate public concern. In spite of an academic training, my feeling was, and still is, that you cannot get through to the general public with a multiplicity of facts and figures. There has to be something more, and there is, as I was to discover for myself, and hopefully will impart to my readers.

Although Ronald Lockley has been criticised by the academic world for anthropomorphizing his bird subjects, particularly in his monographs on the Manx shearwater and the puffin, his pioneer work on seabird biology and bird migration was of great significance. He was a prolific writer and, along with his books about Skokholm and seabirds in general, he has also written about seals, rabbits, whales and dolphins, including a novel *Seal Woman*. His travel books take the reader to many remote places across the world and even in those, Skokholm never fails to get a mention. Perhaps, like me, he could not get it out of his system. Known world wide as a naturalist and writer, Ronald Lockley died at the age of ninety-six in April 2000 in New Zealand where he had emigrated in 1970.

Of great significance to us was his initiation of bird ringing on Skokholm, a practice which was then still very much in the experimental phase in Britain. As well as tracking migration by ringing and recapture, specialised studies of the seabirds became possible. This work had the greatest influence on the way in which the island was run when we arrived and, for our first four years of working there, we became very involved in all aspects of it.

Ronald Lockley's ringing studies began in the 1930s. The first aluminium rings that he used were obtained from his good friend Harry Witherby, then editor of *British Birds* magazine, and were placed on the legs of some of the larger seabirds. Shortly afterwards, he began to catch small migrant birds for ringing, by driving them into purpose-built traps of wire and wood, and then, in 1933, he set up Skokholm as the first official Bird Observatory in Britain, running the establishment himself until the outbreak of war when he had to evacuate the island. The following is a summary of events after the war.

Skokholm Bird Observatory sign

The West Wales Field Society, later the West Wales Naturalist Trust and now the Wildlife Trust, West Wales, agreed to take over the lease from Lockley in 1946 and a twenty-one year lease was granted to them by the owners of the Dale Castle Estate. Ronald Lockley had started the forerunner to the WWFS in 1938 when it was called the Pembrokeshire Bird Protection Society. Having secured the lease, the Trust issued a licence to the Council for the Promotion of Field Studies, now the Field Studies Council, to manage and carry out research projects on the island. The Observatory was run by a string of wardens including, in the 1950s, the late Peter Condor, ex-director of the RSPB, who was responsible for building the big Heligoland trap by the spring. In 1962, the Field Studies Council agreed to undertake specific ringing studies on the island's seabirds in conjunction with the Edward Grey Institute of Oxford University. Some of these studies were still going on in 1973, particularly those involving oystercatchers, shearwaters and razorbills. In some years during the 1960s, more birds were ringed on Skokholm than at any other bird observatory in Britain. The leasehold was renewed in September 1969 for a period of seven years but, in January 1970, the Field Studies Council decided to give up managing the Observatory. There had been problems when the Estate disapproved of some research into the Skokholm mice and then, in 1967, a chalet was erected on the island without their permission, causing further problems. It was pulled down, but its concrete base remained in the Wheelhouse yard and over it we strung our washing line. At short notice, the Trust resumed responsibility and continue to manage the island to this day.

This meant that when we arrived in 1973, Skokholm was still officially a bird observatory, but it only remained so until the autumn of 1976. That was when the current seven-year lease terminated and, although it was decided by the Dale Estate to continue the lease for a further seven years, they added the condition that all ringing on the island was to cease. From the year 1936 to November 1976, a total of 284,355 birds were ringed using observatory rings, including gannets on Grassholm. This involved 164 species with sixty per cent of them being Manx shearwaters. The figures are taken from Michael Betts' *Birds of Skokholm* published in 1992.

For four years, under the observatory's block licence issued by the British Trust for Ornithology, Ray and myself were able to ring birds as trainees under Mike's supervision, since he already possessed an 'A' ringing certificate. Thus we experienced four seasons of intensive bird ringing. It was new and exciting to us, as it was to Ronald Lockley all those years ago. It was a great privilege to see the birds close to, and even more so to actually handle them. To be able to study in such detail the exquisitely patterned plumage of the wryneck that so reminded me of the scales on a moth, to marvel at the fragility and weightlessness of the tiny, ocean-going storm petrel lying quietly in your hand, or to look closely into the fierce, yellow eyes of a sparrowhawk are just a few examples. We learnt how to handle the seabirds confidently, particularly shearwaters and also, in my case, razorbills. Gulls, puffins and gannets required firm and careful managing once they had been caught and there were special ways to hold all birds, whether large or small, so that they suffered no damage, even to their feathers, and, at the same time, didn't inflict any on us with their sharp bills or needle-clawed feet.

Sparrowhawk

In our six years on the island the three of us ringed thousands of birds, the majority being seabirds. but we also processed many passage migrants and vagrants as well as our resident landbirds. I admonish that, during those four years of ringing, the activity became so intense that I began to be concerned for the welfare of the birds and their environment and wished in the end for them to be left in peace. It disturbed me too when I learnt that migrants are stressed by the procedure of trapping and ringing and are often in poor condition, weighing much less than average after a long migration. On the other hand, since Ronald Lockley began ringing, much valuable information has been forthcoming which has been useful to bird conservation in general and, one hopes, may help to maintain bird populations at a healthy level. Now twenty years after Skokholm, I remain firmly of the opinion that birds should be ringed for special studies only, and then only if there is vital knowledge to be sought which is essential for the conservation of that particular species. Trapping for the chance of a rarity or purely for pleasure is highly questionable as there is no justification for it. Today, most of the basic information has been gathered and one should consider carefully whether the work merits causing disturbance at the breeding colony and inflicting stress on the bird.

On our arrival in early spring, there were often a few early migrants to greet us. Black redstarts, ring ouzels and wheatears were among the earliest, and, since we had a dozen or so pairs of the latter breeding on the island, some of them were our Skokholm males returning home from their wintering grounds in Africa. Males always arrived before the females and it was a treat to watch their energetic displaying. They would fly up from a rock or a wall with a sweet chikking song, tail spread to emphasize the broad, white flashes warning other males of their dominance over a territory. Holes and crevices in walls or rocky crags and even rabbit burrows provided them with a good choice of nest sites. Soon each of our wheatears was wearing a trouserleg of several darvic (plastic) rings arranged in a certain colour combination so that it could be recognized as an individual for Mike's special study of wheatear biology. Eventually he knew who was where, who was paired with whom, who had the largest territory and, over several years, he knew the detailed domestic history of them all. It was his personal soap opera and I shall always remember his surprise (and apparent delight!) when he discovered a polygamist among his flock! Polygamy is now known to be a common trait among many birds species. At least he didn't find any prostitutes among them, as scientists working on penguins have done recently.

One of our main jobs at the beginning of the season was to repair the Heligoland traps, of which we had four. These large, funnel-shaped traps, made of wire netting fixed to a framework of wood, were introduced to the island in 1933 by Ronald Lockley, after he had visited the island of Heligoland, where they were first used. I have already described the whereabouts of two of them, notably the Heligoland situated above the well and the Winch Trap in the gully above the landing. Another was built in the garden of the Cottage where a few small shrubs, mostly elder and a wind-pruned sycamore provided a reasonable amount of protective cover for the birds. This one was called the Garden Trap. Naturally, in what was a very open and exposed landscape, the few bushes we had, together with the island's two sycamore trees, were very attractive to small migrant birds and they also served to remind us that the British climate was capable, in less remote places, of supporting large, beautifully shaped trees and even lush woodland! The fourth trap was the Wall Trap as, not surprisingly, it incorporated a length of earth and stone wall. It was the last to be built and it caught the least birds. Built halfway along the wall that ran east-west from the buildings to our largest pond, North Pond, it caught birds such as wheatears, black redstarts, cuckoos, ring ouzels and pipits. Not only that, it was orientated towards the western horizon so that it would catch the setting sun and, with its black, rickety framework and a flaming red sky, it appealed to my artistic bent, but that was before I moved to Cornwall's West Penwith where they have other ideas.

In some years, winter gales did considerable damage to the traps, ripping away the netting from the framework, which over the years would crack and begin to rot. It is possible that the island's herd of feral goats caused damage too when they attempted to gain access to the lush vegetation remaining inside the Heligoland in winter. They also enjoyed head scratching sessions on the frames from time to time.

A great variety of plants grew well within the trap as it was to some extent rabbit proof and also because it was inclined to be marshy in places, being beside the spring. Some of the plants have been mentioned in Chapter Two, including the water mint that I harvested for use in rabbit stews. Today, although the trap has gone, the area is still enclosed by a fence and is known as the Well Exclosure. Ronald Lockley used to import tree and bush cuttings from the mainland because of the difficulty of growing 'live bushes', and describes how he used to 'push them in the ground and hope'.

Armed with hammer, nails and scaps of wood, Mike and Ray would set to work repairing the traps for another season's use. As soon as they were completed, the thrice daily rounds of driving them began. Essentially, the birds were driven from the wide mouth of the trap, which in the larger trap was some fifty feet across, into the narrow end and finally up a laddered ramp into a small, wooden box. This could be closed by releasing a string attatched to a hinged lid. The person then exited through a small side door and the captive birds were extracted from the outside through a cotton sleeve that covered a hole in the side of the box. They were then placed in a cloth bag with a drawstring and taken to be processed in the ringing room. One day our bantam hen, a great adventurer called Mary Cluckins, decided to seek fresh pastures down there in the Heligoland. She may be the only chicken caught in such a trap. She was not ringed, as may have been her want, but was confined to the hen house for a few days instead! By some misadventure, shearwaters occasionally found themselves inside the trap, and, being unable to take off or find an exit, crouched miserably until found by one of us and placed out of harm's way in a nearby burrow. They were usually, but not always, newly fledged chicks.

On no occasion was a bird to be left longer than twenty minutes in a bag whilst we waited for Mike to arrive and supervise the procedure. The birds usually lay quiet in the cloth bags hung on specially placed hooks in the ringing room. As well as being ringed, the birds were weighed and various measurements taken, along with details of moult condition. Very rarely, a migrant bird would already bear a ring, the details of which were sent off to the British Trust for Ornithology, who informed us of the original date and place of ringing. Such information made it all seem worthwhile.

Bird catching was not restricted to daylight hours. Ronald Lockley's work way back in the 1930s had brought to light much information on the biology of the Manx shearwater, but there were still many questions to answer. Some of these Mike hoped to investigate, so, as soon as we arrived on the island, we were 'invited' to join him on nocturnal shearwatering forays. Already, in March, the early arrivals had begun to occupy burrows by night. We soon learnt the art of catching shearwaters, but that is described

One of the Heligoland traps – the Winch Trap

in detail later on in the chapter on nightbirds. During the day too, usually after lunch, one of us would traipse around behind Mike with a notebook and pencil as he weighed and measured each adult and, later on, the single white egg or chick. Laying began in late April and extended into June, peaking about mid May and keeping us all very busy, so that I began to think that the shearwater was having the easier life!

Little did we know then that, in the latter years of his study, Mike was setting his alarm clock twice in the night for secret trips out to his study burrows, where he was monitoring the frequency of visits made by established pairs during the pre-laying period. This period extended for several weeks. At the time we didn't know anything of his extra nightly excursions and, only now, I wonder whether his regular absence in the late afternoon was to do with catching up on sleep. This information I gleaned while reading his monograph on the Manx shearwater, where I also learnt that some of his experiments researching burrow competition involved blocking a small sample of study burrows with stones. As well I didn't know at the time, because I know I would surely have disapproved. He too was unhappy with it and was rather pleased when the birds dug round the obstructions and continued breeding. Even the small number of birds which didn't succeed in getting past the stones all bred successfully when the stones were removed.

His study birds were located in very shallow burrows or in deeper ones with a section of turf cut out above the nest chamber and replaced either with the original sod or with a tight fitting stone. The latter was obviously the most desirable for long term use. Many of them were in Gull Fields or on Ishmian Heath, where they were marked with numbered posts. It said much for the birds' homing skills when they could find their own burrows with no trouble on the blackest of nights and we couldn't even recognize them individually by daylight without special markers. Lockley's study burrows were located on the Knoll.

Shearwater eggs are chicken-egg size and plain white, as they are in most burrow nesting birds, and I remember sampling the odd one for tea. These were found lying above ground away from any burrow entrance, perhaps because a female returned and found her burrow occupied by another, leaving her nowhere to lay her egg. They were rich, bright yellow and tasty, and I'm sure Mike had many more than me! We were lucky to find them before the crows did!

With Sugarback long dead, and the rabbit population consisting almost entirely of the genuine wild stock (there were occasional throwbacks to some of Lockley's introduced varieties as described in the final chapter), the only living legacy left behind on the island was the goat herd and the one remaining Soay sheep. During my 1971 visit, I had seen this last individual as a lone straggler that kept with the goats for company. Ronald Lockley claimed that the goats and the sheep never mingled, but this one evidently preferred company to complete isolation. The Soays, a rare breed, originating from the island of Soay in the St Kilda group, had been given to him by the Duchess of Bedford who was also a keen naturalist. That aged sheep was not a pretty sight when I saw it; its tawny coat of coarse wool was thin and ragged and its general woebegone look roused much sympathy among visitors. Exactly when it died I have no record, but I do know that there was a Soay skull hung on a nail in the Wheelhouse when we arrived in 1973. They are normally hardy animals which are able to survive well in a rugged environment and look attractive when they are in their prime, with their wool a rich chocolate brown. The rams sport a fine pair of horns.

The lighthouse keepers kept goats for milking at the same time as Ronald Lockley, so our feral herd were most likely of mixed origin. The two herds apparently joined up each day for an hour or so in the centre of the island. Ronald Lockley's goats were of the Swiss Toggenburg strain, while the lighthouse herd were a Welsh breed. There had been introductions at other times in an attempt to improve the strain, including a Toggenburg in 1956. The goats we inherited were an unfathomable mixture and varied in colour from uniform black to dark brown, buff or even a creamy white, whilst others were mixed colours and often had white streaks running down over their eyes and white muzzles. Many had white socks and those markings made them very attractive, especially the kids, and also enabled us to recognize them as individuals.

The billy goats had longer, shaggier coats than the nannys and the mature ones boasted a pair of enormous handlebar horns. The older nannys also had quite large horns which were thinner and more upright. The billy which we thought was the dominant animal when we first arrived was perhaps the most magnificent of them all, being entirely black. We thought he was the leader, but since then I have learnt that a recent study in Snowdonia found that goats live in a matriarchal society, so perhaps our oldest nanny had been in charge after all. Apart from the kids we raised ourselves, the closest we ever got to a goat was when a nanny left the herd to kid and then, if we approached her, she would usually stand her ground.

The herd were a splendid sight when gathered around one of the rocky outcrops like the Sugar Loaf or the Tabernacle, both at the western end of the island which they seemed to prefer. They looked well in the rugged landscape and were to me a symbol of a wild type of freedom seldom attained by previously domesticated animals. They seemed like old, but elusive, friends once we got used to their company. They did very well to survive the winters, considering the intense competition for grazing from the rabbits, and they often resorted to chewing lichens off the rock. In one of his books, Ronald Lockley wrote that lichens always formed part of their diet and he even claimed that they induced an abundant flow of milk! During one exceptional winter, when snow lay on the ground for a period of weeks', several of the oldest goats died while we were absent and we found their remains in the quarry the following spring.

CHAPTER 4

A Walk on the Wild Side

The blue, wind-ruffled seas of March and April brought back numbers of auks to the island, the razorbills and puffins in sprightly black-and-white breeding plumage and the guillemots in dark brown and white. It was a great thrill to see crowds of them for the first time and the event made headline news in our small world. They came and went in roughly four-to-five-day cycles in the early part of the season, forming rafts mostly close to the cliffs, but some over a kilometre offshore. A few arrived, numbers built up over the next few days to a peak, and then all of a sudden they disappeared again. The reasoning behind this was vague, but it did appear to be affected by the weather. Strong winds and rough seas seemed to keep them away, not surprisingly as it was probably detrimental to raft formation. Good counts were more likely to be in calm, sunny weather. We counted the total numbers of all three species during this pre-breeding period, which began immediately after our arrival, and that was in addition to the more accurate census of the breeding birds carried out later in the season and described in another chapter.

The following is an account from my diary of one memorable walk undertaken primarily to count the auks, but which also served as much needed spiritual refreshment during the busy days of early spring when domestic preparations demanded much of our time. The detail of that particular walk remains vivid in my memory, and I have included also much information gleaned over the years about the auks and the other wildlife encountered.

It was one of those brighter than bright days of early April with a chill northerly wind whipping up icy white curls on a steely blue sea, a colour so unlike the vibrant greenish blue of warm summer days. The light had that wintry quality that gave the white feathers on the seabirds a snow-like purity and, on such days, the rock seemed to glow an even warmer red. It was good to be out in the bracing air and I anticipated an exhilarating walk with the added bonus of seeing the auks en masse for the first time. My allotted section of the island was from North Haven to the lighthouse, along the rugged west coast, It was a cool and windy section, so I was clad in a woolly hat to keep the heat in and a smock to keep the wind out. Fishermen's smocks had the added advantage of huge pockets in which you could stuff notebooks, pencils, strings of rings, pliers, snacks and sundry other things. The auks would be gathered offshore beneath their own breeding ledges, engaged in pre-breeding social activity. It was just after

The west coast

nine o'clock in the morning, peak time for counting razorbills and guillemots, but not for puffins, they tarried until the afternoon before they congregated offshore and required a separate count later, usually after four o'clock tea. Peak numbers of all three species seemed to correspond within the cycle, and their numbers increased generally as the month progressed.

I walked down Home Meadow and past the Heligoland, glancing through the wire to see if an early migrant chanced to be lurking in the still bare elder bush, but it was deserted. Then across the heather belt known as Ishmian Heath where little sticks with white painted tops bearing numbers marked some of Mike's shearwater study burrows. 'Is this how individual birds recognize their own burrows,' a visitor once asked him! Then onwards to North Haven where I started my part of the anti-clockwise circuit of the coast. There, above the narrow gut that widened gradually into North Bay, I contemplated the possibility that one day the Neck might become an island in its own right, so narrow was the isthmus that separated it from the rest of the island. Perhaps future wardens will organize expeditions there as we did to the Stack, or perhaps would live there in splendid isolation. Thus my thoughts ran away with me. I lingered there awhile because it was worth spending a few minutes looking over the North Haven cliffs for anything unusual, such as a migrant ring ouzel or a wryneck, not to mention an elusive warbler lurking in the precious patch of scrub on the west side, but there was too much wind that day. So, no birds, but there right below me and not easy to see on account of the choppy water, was the rounded head of a cow seal just emerged. Her nostrils were inflated and she was taking a breath before sinking down slowly to continue sleeping. Seals can submerge for long periods, sometimes up to twenty minutes. I concentrated first on the faintly grey spotted, white throat and the head profile to confirm her sex and then scanned around for others, the large bull perhaps which usually patrolled that area, but there was no sign of him. Our seal counts were never large, only four or five at the most, and they were usually seen around this part of the island which was generally more sheltered. Skomer had a large breeding colony, but on Skokholm there were few beaches or coves suitable for pupping and few hauling out places too. Still I loved to see those alluring animals with their doleful, dark eyes and cute, dog-like faces. On very calm days, if the water was clear, you could follow their smooth, graceful movements beneath the water with binoculars, something of a contrast to the clumsy hauling-out operation required to pull their heavy, blubbery bodies out on to the rocks. Incidentally, the species was the grey or Atlantic seal (*Halichoerus grypus*) and they were the only species recorded regularly there, but it is interesting to note that in September 1963, Mike Harris saw two common seals (*Phoca vitulina*) with some grey seals. These are not normally seen on the Welsh coast.

Seal pup

Crispy dead bracken sticks crunched and snapped beneath my feet as I followed the path along the cliff edge. With a warning thump, a rabbit bolted into cover, flashing a white scut. There my count began with a few razorbills off Smith's Bay and then a larger gathering off Near and Far Bay, where the accessibility of the nesting sites had made them into one of the special study areas monitored by our friend and research student, Clare Lloyd, who had joined us in 1973 for her final year of the study. A decline in razorbill numbers generally over the previous twenty years had prompted the Edward Grey Institute to undertake a special razorbill study on Skokholm, where they had been ringed since 1934. For two years I continued her research by monitoring the study areas.

Those first razorbill groups were small compared with those I expected to encounter further round the coast, and they were the first sizeable gatherings of the year. When all the breeding birds were back, the number of individuals in each raft would correspond with the numbers of breeding pairs in that colony but, later on, non breeders would be joining them. Those groups signified the onset of the breeding season, months of bustling activity that enriched our island experience. For a few days the sea and the cliffs would be alive with them, buzzing about like hundreds of black and white flies. They would soon make tentative flights from rafts to breeding ledges, but it was too early for them to spend much time on land. They were very nervous with 'ledge fright'. As time went on and numbers increased, they would gain confidence and there would be much activity on the cliffs. I watched a razorbill circle the cliff on an exploratory flight. It made a circuit and quickly returned to the sea, landing on the outside of a group. It wasn't an elegant landing. Its feet were extended to act as a brake and, wings flapping, it did an ungracious belly flop, accompanied by a splash. Neither was the flight graceful like that of shearwaters or fulmars, their short stubby wings never stopped whirring, but then I had watched them underwater and that was a different story. Looking down on the crystal clear water from a clifftop, I had seen them zipping along with such beautiful, fluid movement, wings and feet propelling them as they turned this way and that. They went deeper than I could see, chasing small, agile fish zig-zagging through the water trying to evade the cruel beak in pursuit. My thoughts turned to the great auk, whose totally flightless condition predatory man took advantage of and wiped out the entire population by the 1850s. All auks are flightless for a period of about six weeks during the moult which takes place at sea after breeding. Heaven help them then if they enter an oil slick!

Even in those small groups, I detected an air of excitement and purpose in their interactions with each other. That was to become more evident in the larger groups I saw later on. Small colonies were less successful because they were not so safe and they lacked the intense social stimuli generated by large numbers of birds which plays a vital role in synchronizing breeding. Large colonies have all kinds of advantages, including reduced predation, an increased knowledge of local food supplies and minimal disturbance caused by birds doing different things at different times i.e. incubating and feeding chicks. It is considered to be food availability that determines the onset of breeding, in this case the spawning of several species of small fish like sprats, whitebait and sand eels in March and April. Large seabird colonies, such as those on the Pembrokeshire islands, are always located close to areas of oceanic turbulence where the upwelling of nutrients causes planktonic flushes which provide food for fish higher up the food chain. This is correlated with temperature and, accordingly, Clare found that low sea temperatures in 1972 resulted in a late breeding season (about two weeks).

Many of the auks were meeting up with their mates from the previous year, perhaps for the first time since they parted the summer before. After spending seven or eight months at sea, despite storms, monofilament fishing nets and oil spills, many pairs had survived to meet again at their old colony in order to breed again. Indeed, Clare's study demonstrated that nearly three-quarters of them retained the same mate and, as in many other species, pairs which failed to breed successfully were the ones most likely to change mates. I was soon to be handling some of the birds, reading their rings and seeing who was with whom, and in which site they bred.

Much of the pair formation and bonding took place in those gatherings on the sea. Were the faithful old timers feeling the joy I liked to think they were during those reunions? Certainly, there appeared to be much aggression among some of the birds, but I was convinced there was great joy too, as I stood watching the frenzied bill rubbing and mutual preening going on amongst some of them. The potentially vicious beak of the razorbill nibbled so tenderly the neck of its ecstatic mate. And what of the chick they had raised the year before? Had it survived? First year mortality among razorbills, as in many long lived seabirds, is high, and anyway the youngster would not return to the island until two or three years old and then not to breed until it was four or five. If it had survived, then it was probably wandering at that moment somewhere in more southern seas, away from the adult wintering grounds in the Irish Sea or the English Channel. Later, I was to become especially interested in the fledging activity of razorbill chicks and it took up much of my time on summer evenings, as described later on in the book.

My attention was drawn to a dense cloud of gulls over the Neck on Skomer. Our larger sister island was at least two miles away and so I was being more than optimistic as I searched among them for something that might have been one of their nesting peregrines. Peregrines were much less common in those days and even a distant glimpse of one was very exciting. It was not to be, my binoculars picked out a human figure striding over the ground, was it John Davies, our counterpart on Skomer? Impossible to tell, but fun trying to.

Inland of me, pairs of lesser black-backed gulls were already taking up territory in a colony north of Bread Rock and my passing created the usual uproar. Perhaps the Skomer person was looking across at me now! I liked the screaming gulls and looked forward to some delicious omlettes made with their eggs! The census map showed a few razorbills nesting on Hard Point which were noted for future reference, but the next group I encountered were off the Northern Rocks and probably included birds from Little Bay and the Dents. The groups were becoming larger as I approached the main breeding areas on the west coast.

Just offshore and living up to its name, Oystercatcher Rock was occupied by a party of roosting oystercatchers. They had gathered on the southern side of the rock and faced into the brisk wind so that it caught and ruffled the black neck feathers of the sleeping birds making odd pale patches. Many stood on one leg to conserve heat. I studied the composition of birds and rock, a medley of black, white and red on the weathered sandstone. I noticed that while most had bright pink legs, one bird had faded, almost grey legs, most likely a feature of age. Was it my imagination or did the reflection of the sun on the rock wash their white breasts with purple? It looked so. The white neck line, a part of the winter plumage, was still prominent on some of them, most likely the sub adults. Several birds preened vigorously with long, scarlet bills, discoloured at the tip from energetic feeding. The tide was dropping and the more active among them were becoming agitated, moving around and calling to hasten an exodus to feeding places further round the shore or on the island plateau. There were only eleven birds in all, but possibly some had already left, whilst early breeders had already taken up territory on the island.

Oystercatcher

At Northern Rocks, I approached the cliff edge where there was a point overlooking three guillemot ledges situated not far below. Guillemots were always the first auks back on the ledges, possibly because they didn't go far afield in the winter, as Tim Birkhead's work on Skomer has shown. A piece of wood was fixed across a gap in the rock to remind me (and others) not to lean too far! Gingerly I peered over and I was lucky. There were half a dozen birds standing around looking decidedly uneasy, but still they stayed, one of them cocking its head and looking up at me with a soft brown eye and a quizzical expression. With their long necks tilted back and their foreheads tapering smoothly down to the slim bill, they displayed a certain elegance not found in the thicker necked, stubby billed razorbill. Head and back were a lovely dusky brown, smooth and sleek, blending well with the rocks and making them less visible later on as they faced into the cliffs whilst incubating eggs. Would I be lucky and see among them a bridled bird showing a delicate, white line traced round the eye and extending a little way behind. Always I looked out for these spectacled beauties, but that day I was out of luck and not surprisingly so for there were only two or three on the island in all. The bridled character increases with latitude and is uncommon on our southern cliffs. As I searched among them, I was careful not to move quickly in case I caused them to fly. We generally discouraged people from trying to get near to the auks as it was so easy to startle them. Indeed, later in the season a sudden departure meant possibly taking egg or chick with them! Over zealous photographers caused problems and some of the main colonies were designated 'out of bounds'. This may seem over protective considering the disturbance we caused when ringing them, but at that time many aspects of their life history and survival capacity were unknown and the advantages far outweighed the disadvantages.

A fulmar cast a sidelong glance at me as it cruised by on pearly grey wings. It was only feet away and at eye level. I noted the fanned tail, tipped white, and the splayed feet trailing behind. Aerodynamics were beyond my understanding, and so I marvelled at the way it glided along effortlessly on the wind eddying round the cliff tops. It often slowed down and hung motionless for a few seconds in a steady updraft, giving me excellent views through my binoculars. I focused on the snowy white head and noticed a ring of tiny, dark feathers round the coal black eye. They softened the face and thus the fulmar had a gentle look. There was maybe just a few feet between us, but it was the difference between life and death to me, standing as I was right by the cliff edge. It was not a good place to use binoculars! I looked around in vain for pairs sitting on the ledges for I loved to watch them sitting side by side crooning amorously. They always seemed so contented and peace loving, often tolerating a third bird landing on the ledge beside them. Not always though, sometimes the arrival of an intruder provoked much raucous cackling and bill stabbing. I knew also of their insidious habit of spitting oil in defence, an action which can lead to the death of another bird. Even a peregrine facon has been known to die as a result of the fatal oiling of its feathers by a fulmar (notably a peregrine at Bury Head in Devon). I had also heard of fulmars taking over guillemot colonies further north in Britain, but was it not a natural event as their populations expanded, who was I to judge? I was later to get well oiled myself whilst ringing a fulmar chick and the stench clung to my smock for ever. That morning however, I just wanted to enjoy watching the fulmar negotiating the windy cliffs, banking and turning, wheeling and stalling. What freedom, I used to think, but then – are birds free from the chains of the skyways, as the Bob Dylan song goes?

Lockley himself had watched fulmars cruising along the cliffs and even around the buildings, but he never saw them land. Those were early days in the expansion of its range. By the time we arrived, they were well and truly established, albeit in small numbers. They weren't on land that morning any more than they were thirty-three years ago, but I knew they soon would be. It occured to me then (and it was a sobering thought!) that, as fulmars were long lived birds, it was actually possible (although highly improbable) that one of them, even the one I was watching, could have caught the eye of Lockley himself in this very same place!

I came then to North Gully, where the stream from North Pond ran down in a series of little rocky enclaves. It was a favourite haunt of mine and it was my habit to linger there for a while, but only early and late in the season. For the rest of the time it was a dangerous business because of the 'bomber'. This last was a highly strung individual with a formidable weapon in the shape of a dagger-like bill. It was an oystercatcher who had a reputation for drawing human blood when she, or he, had young 'bombers' to defend. The trouble was that you had no warning, coming as it did from behind at great speed. A sudden rush of air, accompanied by a piercing whistle, and the bird all but impaled itself on your earlobe. You couldn't relax in the gully in such company.

North Gully was a place of contrasts. On quiet days you could hear the trickle of the stream above the subdued swish of the surf on the rocks below. Then, it was a pretty place, even when no flowers were out because of the warm colour of the rock, which complemented beautifully the green of the herb-rich turf. Other days, like that particular day, it was quite desolate, with the chilly north wind flicking back droplets of water as the stream spilt over the edge, tossing them into the air. A pipit flew up from the stream bed and my ears detected a plaintive 'pseet, pseet'. It was ever a wonder to me that the raw beauty of the place was perfectly expressed in that simple, wistful call.

It was there at North Gully beside the stream, that I had first found sea milkwort (*Glaux maritima*). It was the only site on the island for this attractive, little plant with its dark centred, pink flowers growing out from the leaf axils. I remember well my pleasure on finding it; it was new to me and that made North Gully even more of a special place.

On the sea below were larger gatherings of auks, guillemots and razorbills together this time. The paler, longer bodied guillemots were easy to distinguish from the latter as they sat lower on the water and their thinner, slightly uptilted bills were very obvious. Whilst preening, they tipped over sideways on the water exposing their white underparts. Many auks, particularly the guillemots, formed lines of a dozen or more strung out on the water like broken necklaces, and all facing the same way. I watched them dive in synchrony, a magic little performance, but I kept losing count because of it! They broke up and formed clusters again. What did that particular display mean? Was it part of the overall plan designed to stimulate the urge to breed and hence promote synchrony among the birds, or did it have a more specific function? I still don't know. Puffins didn't indulge in line displays, but they were certainly social. More so the guillemots though, who would soon be cheek by jowl on their ledges. To counteract this they have had to evolve a whole range of signals and attitudes to check antisocial and aggressive behaviour that would otherwise disrupt breeding success. In a few weeks, their ledges would be packed solid, each bird tenaciously guarding its own space, having to threaten and drive off competitors while at the same time recognizing and greeting its own mate, hence the many different postures and sounds designed to keep the peace and to promote successful breeding. Most obvious of these is the constant bowing and turning away of the head, often followed by preening. That appears to mean 'I respect your space and have no wish to fight', at least that was how it seemed to me. As for the razorbills on the water that day, my notes tell of much bill rubbing, head shaking, spinning on the water, and clumsy chases over the surface using wings and feet, all of which are highly significant in razorbill language I'm sure.

I counted the auks below the Jags where the ledges were invisible from the land, except by way of adventurous climbing. My next vantage point demanded that I stopped to take in the view. Not for nothing was Mad Bay so named. When storms raged in the Atlantic, that bay was in angry turmoil; huge breakers crashed on to the purple cliffs and erupted in a mighty surge of white surf, spitting and foaming its way up the cliffs. Mists of spray were whipped up and hurled over the tops, along with balls of spume that spun along and were tossed over the heads of intrepid onlookers. No storm raged that day however, but it was most exhilarating standing in the teeth of the chilly wind looking along this dramatic coast; for a study in colour it was most inspiring. The red cliffs, plum dark in the shade and rich sienna in the sunlight, were softened at their base by zones of yellow and grey lichen and then delineated by a fuzzy line of white surf nudging the blackened foreshore. Then there was the intense blue of the sky, the sea's lively reflection and, above all, the interplay of light as small clouds moved briskly over, precipitating tiny, dark shadows which the eye chased as if mesmerized by them. Inland of the cliffs was a soft patchwork of green and brown, dulled by encrusted salt. Beyond, I could see the remains of an ancient herring-bone wall, the stones well defined in an intricate but broken pattern. Contemplating the colours brought to mind a disagreement I had had with a visitor over the attractiveness of different rocks. Even on grey days, I argued, our sandstone cliffs glow warmly, unlike the drab coloured granites and basalts found on Skomer and Bardsey, but I was surely biased.

I clocked up many more auks sitting on the sea off Twinlet and Guillemot Point which, besides being dramatic cliffs, were home to our most easily observed auk colonies on the island. There one could sit right opposite the ledges, with no fear of disturbing them and watch the progress of the different pairs as the season progressed. I sat on the remains of Clare's hide and glanced at the diagrams she left me of the razorbill sites on Twinlet, each one with a number. I could run my eye over the rock with its well defined vertical and horizontal cracks and pinpoint each one quite easily; there were roughly twenty-five of them. It was an easy site to monitor. There were a few guillemots there too, but the majority were on the far cliff at Guillemot Point. A row of razorbills nested at the extreme western end of Twinlet and right on the end one year was just one guillemot pair. Perhaps they had an identity crisis! Skomer however, was home to many more guillemots and a study of their breeding biology was being undertaken by Tim Birkhead.

Beyond Twinlet, I approached Steep Bay where the ravens were nesting, and didn't I know it! There, crouching on a rock ahead of me, was the great bird itself, highly agitated at my approach. With its throat feathers puffed out, it rocked too and fro barking warnings at me. I noted the bright point of light in its dark, intelligent eye, the massive beak with glowing tip and the silver sheen of reflected sunlight on the black wings. I doubted not the wisdom and peculiar powers it had been credited with in the past. It was trying to intimidate me and was doing it quite well. I felt I had no business to be there for the bird was on guard, protecting its mate sitting on the nest below and, I hoped, brooding young chicks. Ravens are early nesters and, when we arrived on the island in early March each year, we were eager to check their progress. I had crept once already to the edge of the precipitous cliff and craned my neck to look down on the massive nest, built primarily of heather sticks, containing four perfect, turquoise blue eggs. It was a typical nesting site and a traditional one, cleverly concealed beneath an overhang. Ravens often use more than one site over the years and there was another in Twinlet that I knew of. Although well hidden, the young raven chicks (quaintly named ravelet's by Abel Chapman in 1924) were still vulnerable to attack from crows or gulls if left unattended.

I had (and still have) great admiration for those noble birds and loved to watch their skillful aerial acrobatics. No one could tell me that they weren't just enjoying themselves sometimes. Whilst patrolling the cliffs, a sudden impulse seemed to grip them and they would fold their wings very suddenly and flip completely upside down in a half somersault, momentarily losing height, and then flip back again. Sometimes the pair of them would rise to a good height and then stoop and turn over in unison. They would repeat this several times before soaring away into the distance. Doubtless there is some dull scientific explanation for this behaviour, but why can't it just be high spirits?

I knew that the collective name for ravens was an 'unkindness' and generally thought it unfair, but was it? I wondered that day as I gazed down at my feet where the torn, orange legs of a puffin lay on the turf above the nest; a poignant reminder of a much-loved bird fallen victim to the one which had so roused my admiration. I certainly think the name unfair now because I have learnt to accept nature's way. Her ways seem cruel, but they are essential for the good of the species, ensuring that only the fittest survive. Only man strays from this law.

I became accustomed to finding remains like those above the nest but, more often, they were the ragged wings and feet of shearwaters. Shearwaters form a high percentage of raven prey items on Skokholm in the spring and summer compared to rabbits and puffins, as was reported in a paper published in the 1971 Skokholm report by Dr Z. Bogucki and Barry Chambers. They suggested that most were caught in the very early hours of the morning when they are preparing to leave their burrows. Chicks near to fledging excercise near their burrow entrance and those that linger too long as dawn approaches are highly vulnerable. It is reported that large numbers of ravens gather on Skomer to prey on dead and dying shearwater fledglings in the late summer and autumn, although many of them are suffering from the disease known as puffinosis, discussed later in the book. At other times of the year, rabbits form a substantial portion of the raven's diet.

Often when I saw a raven, I would think of that quote in *Macbeth*, my favourite Shakespearian play.

'The raven himself is hoarse
That croaks the fatal entrance of Duncan.'

Poor Duncan indeed. The previous year it had been poor crows. After the four raven chicks fledged, the family made their way slowly and venomously along the west coast to the lighthouse, wreaking havoc in the Fossil Bay crows' nest on their way. It was completely destroyed and the chicks killed and eaten. I had been monitoring its progress and was shocked at the appalling site that met my eyes, although generally the crows (between six and twelve pairs) did very well. Besides, they weren't exactly innocent themselves.

I thought too of the fate of our British ravens. They were once common in more gentle countryside in Britain, but were so persecuted by gamekeepers and shepherds that by then only remnant populations held their own in wild and inaccessible parts of our country, such as there on the islands and the adjacent mainland of Pembrokeshire. On sea cliffs they were always safer and had probably been on Skokholm since the Vikings gave names to the islands, if not before. On mainland cliffs they were not usually found close to land that held game.

It was a wonder to me that the nest remained intact during the gales and rain that were so often a feature of the weather early in the season when their breeding period began. Indeed, it was incredible that there was any shelter at all to be found on the exposed west coast, but that nest not only survived the storms, it usually accommodated a good size family which invariably fledged successfully. At least they didn't have to face snow, ice and frost, as did their fellows further north. The fact that they breed well north of the Artic Circle says much for their hardiness.

We only had one pair of ravens and they wore no rings, so we couldn't be sure that we were seeing the same birds each year. There was a good chance that they were because ravens are long-lived birds and faithful to their mates. Our pair may have had ancestors that had bred on the island right back through the centuries, so a part of the island was rightfully theirs. Only one year (1966) had there been two pairs. Raven Gully on the south coast must have once been occupied by ravens and they had also used sites in Rat Bay, Calf Bay and Wildgoose Bay. Perhaps the only threat to them was the peregrine, which in recent years has recolonized the island. These large falcons choose similar nesting sites and are known to be capable of forcing them out and taking over the nest.

A lapwing rose from the moorgrass as I detoured round Steep Bay. It threw itself around in the sky, rising steeply, tipping and tumbling, whipping the air with broad, fingered wings, tracing loops and sweeping the ground in seductive curves. Arcs of dark and light plumage exaggerated the brilliantly executed manoeuvres and I stood entranced by the aerial ballet. Shrill mewing cries cut the chilly air, recalling wilder, emptier places, even farther away from humanity. The bird had a nest on a low, grassy bank near to North Pond and, judging by its frantic behaviour, nothing was amiss. I raised my binoculars searching for the thin, white-tipped cane placed a few feet away from the nest. I found the cane, but where was the sitting bird? Then I caught sight of her, just her head with a short, erect crest moving stealthily away in the long grass. That way she would not betray the whereabouts of the nest. She had been alerted by her mate. Her four beautiful, olive blotched eggs would be exposed in the shallow scrape inside a tuft of grass, depending entirely on their cryptic colouration for protection. It was hardly a nest likely to be stumbled upon by accident, although that did happen occasionally. More often I found them by concealing myself beneath a bank or an outcrop several hundred yards away from where I suspected the nest to be. Having already caused the sitting bird to leave the nest by my appearance on the skyline, I would then watch with the aid of the Observatory's Nikel telescope (a 15x60 zoom) for the bird to return and sit. This she inevitably did when all was quiet again, although very slowly and with great caution. Then, having eyed the spot, I would head off towards it without taking my eyes off it. Not easy on rough ground! I was often well off the mark.

We only had a few lapwing (three or four pairs each year) and so the nests were always marked to remind ourselves where they were and also to warn everyone to stay away so that they had minimal disturbance. Our lapwings were long suffering. Predation by gulls or crows was extremely common and they usually made several attempts to breed, even then often ending in complete failure. It was a good day when eggs survived long enough to hatch and we were able to ring the chicks before they left the nest. They were some of the prettiest, newly hatched chicks I had ever seen; balls of amber fluff, dappled with dark spots, with a ring of white down round their necks. They were quickly mobile and left the nest soon after hatching, as do most waders, because that made feeding more effective in energy terms for the adult, and probably it was safer too. That meant that to ring them we had to be quick because, once away, they were very clever at hiding. The ringing session was often the last we saw of them.

I continued as if to skirt Purple Cove and avoid the temptation to scramble down the springy turf on to the rocky platform below. But the chance of finding a piece of wood or some other useful object jammed in the rocks was too tempting and down I went. Squinting into the blackness of a tall, narrow cave at the head of the gut, I saw only a small, white fisherman's buoy wedged in a crack at the back which was definitely not worth the effort of retrieving. It was a different world down there, hemmed in by towering walls of dark purple daubed in pale streaks of a leached material. Looking up at the walls with the clouds rushing fast overhead, it seemed as though they were about to topple over on me! The surf pounded into a deep cleft below and sent echoes booming back from the cliffs; it felt like a powerful and primeval place. I found it strangely alluring and sat for a while drinking in the solitude that seemed to magnify itself there. But I wasn't completely alone because there was the ubiquitous rock pipit scurrying over the rocks in its relentless search for food.

After that the indented coastline was confusing and I had to struggle yet again with the map to sort out Fossil Bay, Nell's Bay and the Oven with their various Points. Two crows hung around Fossil Bay where they had begun to build a nest on a convenient ledge for viewing (at least I thought it was convenient in those days). It was the very nest that the ravens had robbed. I didn't watch the crows for long, they lacked the charisma of their larger cousins and failed to capture my attention. Instead, the small groups of razorbills sitting around on the sea demanded that I continued my count. They belonged to various scattered breeding sites along the west coast, all of which were easy of access and would be on the agenda for more frequent visits later on. There were no guillemot ledges along there.

Noting the mat of bog pennywort leaves beneath my feet, I squelched my way across Windmill Gully and began to climb to the top of the Bluffs where a large raft of auks were congregated offshore. That was the largest, single colony on the island, with roughly forty-five sites to check in the future. There the razorbills nested mostly under boulders and many of the adults had been ringed by Clare, making it worthwhile for me to continue both monitoring and ringing. Climbing down to the remains of her rustic observation hide, I settled down for five minutes to recount the birds and scan the sea, by now quite wild in the vicinity of the Wildgoose Race. Offshore, a line of gannets flew downwind. Four of them beat their wings in synchrony and then melted languidly into a glide. They became etched on the sea like a string of white crosses, their black wingtips merging with the dark water. Close behind them came a three year old, with black secondaries exaggerating the forward curve of the wing. Angular and pointed, they were superbly designed for diving, but I would have to wait for rougher seas and mackerel shoals to enjoy that spectacle, or else a trip to Grassholm.

Then I stood on the top of the Bluffs again and there I looked back along the west coast to admire what must be the finest cliff panorama on the island. Much was still in shadow but it was striking enough. My eye absorbed the structural detail of the bays making up the coastline I had just traversed. They were composed on their northern sides of a series of planed surfaces tilted at the same steep angle and meeting the sea with a straight edge. The picture struck me as a classically beautiful record of an age-old earthly drama, in which strong colour and abundant wildlife played a vital role.

Warden's Rest (some warden's hideout perhaps?), Wildgoose Bay (who knew what goose?), Head Bay (another mystery) were skirted and the count continued, finishing up with more razorbills off the Quarry. I counted carefully because among them were a few guillemots, nearly overlooked, although hardly any bred along that stretch. Ever hopeful, I looked down on the tumble of scree inside the quarry, a black redstart maybe or the elusive ring ouzel? But it was not to be. The only life among the stones was yet another rock pipit picking about on a large slab of sandstone, the flat, red surface of which was streaked white with thin veins of quartz, the crystals opaque and glittering. The rocks were sharp and angular, of all sizes and in jumbled heaps, so that there were whole networks of cavities and recesses making ideal nesting chambers for razorbills, a few puffins, shearwaters and hundreds of storm petrels. Ronald Lockley cut his roof tiles for the Wheelhouse there and surely that was where our large flagstones came from.

My count was over, with nearly three hundred razorbills to be added to Ray's smaller count on the other half of the island. Next stop before heading back down the track was the lighthouse for tea and a chat. I passed the Table (a big flat topped rock) and headed for a grassy track. I had to be careful with my feet; the ground felt like a sponge, but a precariously fragile one in which thousands of shearwater had burrowed, some of which could have been already in occupation. Paying careful attention until I gained the track, I suddenly came upon another group of island inhabitants. The ground had sprouted horns! The goats were as startled as I was and far more alarmed. Full of panic, they scrambled to their feet and ran in a long line across the track, keeping to the path as they always did. I stared after them wondering what kind of a mean winter they had endured.

CHAPTER 5

Early Days

When the Heligoland traps were repaired and running, when tanks, cookers etc. were clean, and when the various special bird study programmes like shear-watering and counting auks were underway, we became involved in a frenzy of painting and decorating inside and out. There were no work parties in those days! Everything had to be made ready for our visitors who began arriving any time from the end of March onwards, and then continued to come in small numbers until the end of June when we began to fill up, although in some years there were visitor-free weeks in April and May. The biggest painting job was Snowcemming the Wheelhouse or the Cottage; they were done in alternate years and we would have to choose a fine day to do it. Out would come the huge tubs of weatherproof paint, brushes and long ladders. We would don our oldest clothes and then it was a race against time in case of a change of weather. It was not unheard of for a lighthouse keeper to lend a hand and one in particular, our friend 'Twiggy', was one who volunteered. Everything and everyone would become spattered in Snowcem for days to come. Our splendid, glossy black chickens were too inquisitive for their own good and soon became daubed and speck-led in hard, gritty, white blobs that stuck fast to their immaculate feathers and defied all preening attempts to clean them off. We boasted lavish, blonde highlights for days to come because the limey mixture would not wash out properly. Ray wore his white woolly hat in an attempt to cover his ample locks, and the streaks of Snowcem that soon annointed it showed how dirty was the rest of it. It didn't matter of course, our appearance wasn't important because we dressed for the weather and the task in hand. It was hard work but fun, and what a view we had from the roof, not only of our island surround, but eastwards across the sea to the Dale Peninsula and St Ann's Head, and northwards over Broad Sound to Skomer, Jack Sound and Wooltack Point. We would stop sloshing on the paint now and again just to gaze seawards and contemplate the everchanging light and colour. I loved to watch the tiny, dark shadows of cotton wool clouds scudding across the sea and over the island plain; it was therapeutic, like watch-ing waves on the shore. We paused often to identify a bird flying on to the island, it was part of the job after all!

The buildings looked bright and clean at the finish and, although I usually have a great dislike for white-painted buildings in a wild landscape, on Skokholm it only seemed to enhance their homeliness and charm. The outside doors and windows were painted black after a good sanding down to stop the paint blistering in the strong sun. There were a couple of benches outside for resting tired legs, one in the walled yard next the Wheelhouse and the other against the high east-facing wall by the Cottage. They were painted green and in March were brightened further by clusters of white narcissi and yellow daffodils that had been planted around them years before. We had ongoing battles with invasive stinging nettles that competed with them and surreptitiously stung our legs from within the daffodil leaves. They grew prolifically in the yard and we periodically gave them a good bashing with our ancient but efficient scythe, once we had learnt how to use it. Elsewhere they were left as foodplants for the tortoishell, peacock and red admiral butterflies. Large stands of nettle, such as those at the back of the Wheelhouse marking the sump, provided cover for small birds. It was quite usual to find chiffchaffs and willow warblers skulking among them during migration. Unfortunately for one schoolboy, they virtually concealed the sump and he had a rude and smelly awakening as he incautiously leapt over them in an attempt to dodge his pursuing comrades. Dozens of lime-loving *cepea* snails in stripey shells concealed themselves in the nettles that grew against the painted walls, and were eagerly sought out by our chickens.

Inside the Cottage, the common room and the guest rooms were painted after a good application of fungicide had removed any patches of green algae brought on by the damp winter conditions. It was the only time in my life that I ever saw anyone paint around a picture hung on the wall! Forgive me Mike for telling!

On the north side of the building were two single rooms each with two small windows and a door that led into the central common room, one on either side of the hearth. Those rooms were especially favoured by elderly people coming over on their own. Peeping through the windows in the early morning, you could watch rabbits cavorting outside on the meadow or the wheatears that nested in the garden wall picking about for grubs in the closely cropped turf. And then, by night, came the strange cries of the shearwaters homing into their breeding colony on the Knoll, immediately behind the Cottage. There was also a long room on the south side, joined on to the common room, which accommodated two people, and upstairs was a loft room with an open-beamed ceiling, affectionately known as the Angel Loft. This slept three. I believe visitors can no longer use this room because of fire regulations. Entrance to the loft was via an open stairway of oak said to have been salvaged from the *Alice Williams*. The rooms, especially when furnished with the newly laundered, yellow and orange curtains, looked bright and cheerful although they were obviously very basic. The concrete floors were scrubbed and sometimes painted. Old fashioned, wooden washstands, some with marble tops, were equipped with bowls, jugs and a water carrier for the convenience of the guests. The stands were cleaned and painted ready for use.

Blankets were provided but visitors brought their own sheets and pillowcases or sleeping bags. Many people told us they enjoyed the basic living conditions because it reminded them of the simpler way of life they had experienced in their youth, whilst others relished it just for novelty's sake. Whether they would have wanted to live like it permanently is another matter. Perhaps some of them would genuinely have felt quite comfortable with it, as we did.

Access to the common room was through a door to the left of the north-facing entrance lobby. Opposite the main door was the ringing room where we kept strings of different sized aluminium rings, spring balances and metal rules for weighing and measuring the birds, cloth bags, card indexes, log books etc. In this room the trapped birds were processed and enthusiastically admired by all those who happened to be around. Many photographs were taken by visitors and ourselves of birds in the hand, particularly the rare vagrant species. In that room we learnt plumage details and vital statistics that revealed the age and sex of individuals as well as general identification features. Plumage, state of moult, skull ossification, wear and tear of feathers were some of the key factors which had to be meticulously recorded. For example, a gentle blow to fluff up the crown feathers of the tiny, migrant goldcrest will reveal a tuft of fiery orange feathers beneath the yellow ones if it is a male. Differences involving the number of emarginated primary feathers in the wing of the willow warbler distinguish it from the very similar chiffchaff. There may be other subtle differences, for example leg colour is generally darker in the latter, but there is sufficient overlap to counteract this as a positive identification feature in the field. Song is often the main criteria to distinguish many similar species, but migrant birds don't usually sing. A skull that is not fully ossified signifies a young bird, just as the pale edging on wing coverts often provides clues to age, and this last character is not always visible in the field, especially among small birds. Many rare migrants and vagrants were caught during our years on Skokholm giving rise to great excitement and some of these are noted later on.

The ringing room became a small shop in 1977 after ringing ceased, selling reports, maps, postcards etc. A door led from it to another small room with a west-facing window. This was for odds and ends like mist-nets, first aid box etc., but was also used when we were overflowing with visitors to accommodate helpers or shearwater slaves, the duties of whom are described in a later chapter.

To the right as you entered the Cottage was one of two communal toilets, the second one being in a small annexe attatched to the western side of the cottage. This latter was once used to house a sick gannet which we fed with fish, laboriously caught by volunteers. Unfortunately, at a grand launching ceremony on the rocks at South Haven, it keeled over and died! The toilets were complete with elsans, cans of elsanol and months' supplies of toilet rolls. One of the jobs of the assisant warden (or a helper if we were lucky enough to have one) was to empty the interior bucket each morning whilst the visitors were eating their breakfasts. It was an unsavoury task but a necessary one obviously. The idea was to do the job discretely and this was normally easily accomplished. A broom was placed diagonally across the doorway to deter the errant visitor who might have risen late from depositing anything in the plastic holding-frame whilst the bucket was being emptied. Only once did the system fail and that was due to the lack of the barricading broom by a young lad who was too trusting! I don't know who was more embarrassed, the boy, the visitor or us!

Just inside the entrance lobby beside the toilet door was a wide shelf in front of a small, north-facing window. This held the Tilley lamps. We had roughy fifteen, some of which were usually out of commission awaiting spare parts or general servicing. Spare parts came to order from an amazing hardware store in Haverfordwest run by Archie Griffiths. Half an hour or so before darkness was considered to be lighting up time, and one of us would take our place before the rows of lamps, remove the filler caps, top them up with paraffin and then prime them by decanting methylated spirit into the little wells fixed on the stem of each lamp. This we set light to with a match. Some of the older lamps had removable asbestos collars that needed soaking in a jar of meths and clipping on for the priming procedure. When the stem had heated up and the meths was nearly gone, a few hard pumps would force a jet of paraffin up inside it which in turn ignited the delicate mantle in the glass lantern. The trick was to pump at precisely the right time or else the whole lot would erupt into a flaming mass, the smoke of which blackened the glasses. Visitors coming through the door were often startled when they were confronted with a small inferno and a fractious assistant warden! It was quite an art to get them all going at the same time and for a long time I was quite nervous of them. However, I soon got the hang of it. The lamps were hung on hooks fixed into the beams in the common room. They were distributed evenly around the room and gave off a strong, white glow that threw soft shadows around the walls. The light from the lamps was easily good enough to read by. Every now and again a lamp would splutter and dim and someone would jump up to give it a quick pump. Many tall people received a good crack on the head when they rose abruptly from their seat; they soon learnt! There were always enough of them for one to be taken to each room as people retired to read or sleep. Ray was rather good at tightening the pressure cap so that they were impossible to loosen. Many times, dear old ladies in nightdresses (and sometimes nightcaps!) would appear in doorways to plead with Mr Ray to please turn off their lamp!

Entering the cottage, one stepped on to a floor of large red flagstones, unpainted in those days. It was just as Lockley found it in 1928 and was the floor of the old pantry. Lockley had lovingly renovated this dwelling house for himself and his bride to be,

Doris. He was no builder or carpenter but turned his hand to all these tasks with much help from his carefully selected companions. A quote from one of his books runs as follows: 'I had no need to be particular with my building operations; the house was already so quaintly built after a whimsical manner, as Fenton in his *Tour through Pembrokeshire* (1800) remarks, "that my own improvements and unconventional methods could not be but somewhat in keeping with the inimitable style of the whole."' One assumes that he means features like the unconvential style and lack of uniformity of the floors, windows and doors. The cottage and the farm buildings were built in the 1760s, the former on the site of an original dwelling that was used by ferreters as far back as the 1300s when the islands were held by the Crown. There are references in 1387 to two shilling for repairs to the houses on Skomer and Skokholm! It was quite something to

Ray and Pippa in the common room

think back, whilst reclining in one of those armchairs in the common room, to the coarse life of those ferreters an incredible six hundred years ago as they wrested a scant living from the land and the sea, and most likely slept in that exact spot inside what must have been an exremely primitive dwelling. There are documents right back to 1387 referring to the 'ferreter's storehouse' and that probably stood right where the cottage is now. Lockley's companion, Richard, the old man who trapped rabbits for him and is described in *Dream Island Days*, must have been the last of these characters to have resided on the island, albeit temporarily.

When I think of the cottage now, I think of social evenings spent in the common room made bright and cheerful by the soft incandescence of many Tilley lamps. Staff and visitors are gathered there, sitting on the primitive orange sofa or on Parker Knoll chairs grouped around a small table in the centre of the room. Unlucky individuals would have to make do with the rather uncomfortable oak settle underneath the east window. If the weather is wet or cold, a fire of salt-impregnated driftwood crackles brightly in the hearth over which hangs a painting of shearwaters on a stormy sea, superbly executed by Keith Shackleton (a similar print hangs in my study here in Cornwall). On the opposite wall is an aerial photograph of the island in monochrome.

The polished oak floor shines around the edge of a thick, high quality, red-patterned rug. Two bookshelves house an excellent lending library, most of the books kindly donated by island visitors. Naturally, books on birds or islands dominate in the hard-back section. Few people are reading seriously, it is hard to concentrate because of the lively conversation dominating the room. Animated voices rise above the hissing of the lamps. First, the day's events and bird sightings are discussed and then the conversation becomes more general, often terminating in the early hours when the world has been put to rights, unless any nocturnal expeditions are on the agenda. On the table lies the annual log, its stiff maroon cover enclosing the daily record sheets filled in nightly by the warden at the appointed hour of nine o'clock. A tray has been set on the table, complete with all the necessary items for tea and coffee making, with biscuits or left-over cake to fortify any would-be night adventurers. Soon someone, usually the cook of the day, will arrive with the steaming kettle.

Running through the daily log was always an event of great significance and interest as visitors waited to make their contributions and to hear of other people's sightings. All bird species regularly recorded on the island were listed and called out, numbers or estimates were considered by the warden before he made the entry, as were claims of rare birds which in any case required a full description to be fowarded to the rarities committee. Needless to say we did occasionally get claims of rare sightings which were not terribly convincing. Those were handled as sensitively as the situation allowed so that no one was offended. It was easy to fake a mark in the log book with a quick flick of the pen! Some of the records were thrown out by the rarities committee, and I myself was much put out when a rufous bushchat we saw in 1978 was rejected by them. The bird stayed on the island for several days and we were able to approach it very closely. It was the first record for Wales and a good one too. Not long after that a rufous bushchat was found on Skomer and stole the title. I now realise the folly of not taking a photograph and believe it was rejected because it was the first record I had ever sent to them. All previous records had gone in under Mike's name so that I was an unknown quantity to the all male committee.

There was an ongoing debate as to whether we could include magpies that were spotted on Skomer (roughly two miles away) with the aid of a telescope! The same went for their ground breeding woodpigeons and short-eared owls. All these had already been recorded on Skokholm itself and we, rightfully I think, discounted them.

Incidentally, a magpie which turned up on the island in 1964 was the first proper record for the island and there have been eleven records up to 1996, including one from us in 1975. With regard to woodpigeons, it is interesting, but perhaps not surprising in view of their increasing numbers, that they are now attempting to breed on Skokholm.

Seals, butterflies and cetaceans were all dutifully recorded. As already stated, two species of bat had been seen on Skokholm but each was rare and the only one we saw was a lone pipistrelle. Another column in the log was for the daily total of shearwater corpses. These last were heavily predated on by gulls, particularly great black-backed gulls. The slaughter took place on moonlit nights and often all that was left of the bird were the wings and breastbone. These were disposed of down the cliff or left in a pile in the yard so that they weren't counted twice. Some visitors showed a morbid delight in collecting the highest numbers of them and I often wondered if they cheated and picked them up from down the cliffs! Such are the vagaries of a competitive spirit.

Visitors brought the corpses back to the yard and left them in a pile. They became used to trailing these sad remains around with them, but I'm not sure Mike became used to the growing pile of dead birds by his door! Sometimes we would find more complete remains where the torso of the bird was turned inside out (a typical method adopted by great black-backs) and somewhere in this grisly bag would be the legs and feet, often with a ring attached. We wanted the ring number of course, much to the dismay of squeamish visitors. There was a column in the log entitled 'any other corpses'. This gave rise to a few unavoidable jokes, and for our part we used to say that, in the case of a serious injury, visitors would be heaved over the cliff and recorded in the column. What really would have happened of course was a fast run to the lighthouse, a call to the coastguard and a helicopter or lifeboat rescue (either the Angle or the St David's boat). Nothing happened while we were there, and thinking back we were very lucky.

Shearwater corpse

Another trick we got up to when calling the log was to insert very unlikely animals and one of our favourites was walrus. This would be read out in its turn with us looking as serious as possible while we allowed the statutory pause for a response. One week it took three days before someone meekly enquired 'where exactly may we see the walrus?' The chance would be have been a fine thing!

In this way we kept a record of migrants as well as our own breeding and non breeding birds. The oystercatchers gathered to roost on the rocks at high tide and the flock was counted every day. It diminished as breeding got underway leaving only the younger, non-breeding birds roosting together. Later on the failed breeders joined the flock and then finally adults with young, and numbers rose again. In this way patterns were built up corresponding to the activities of the birds. The high water, roosting flock of purple sandpipers and turnstones were also counted daily, and reports for the previous fifteen years showed the annual fluctuation in numbers, particularly of the sandpipers. In some years there were between five or six birds only and in others flocks of up to thirty-two. I suspect that some of this may reflect the effort made in finding them. Again, enthusiastic visitors competed with each other for the highest numbers. They were present on the island all year, apart from in the high summer when most of them departed for their breeding grounds.

After the log, preparations were made for any nocturnal expeditions. These involved either shearwaters or petrels, and in the years up to 1976 it meant catching them too. Not until 1977 did we simply go out and look. Those experiences will be dealt with later on in detail, as those birds, particularly the shearwater, took up lots of our time and energy.

There were other buildings in the farm complex, some of which were used for accommodation and therefore needed attention before visitors arrived. The middle block of buildings comprised from east to west, a single room used in our first year by razorbill student, Clare, and later by lucky visitors. Lucky because, for those who like it, it was a room well apart from the others and so it was quiet, being not within earshot of the common room unlike all the rooms in the Cottage. It also had the tremendous asset of a large east-facing window that gave a fine view down Home Meadow and across the sea to St Ann's Head. Thus you could sit in the window and observe. People walked by of course, on their way between the Cottage and the Wheelhouse, or even sat on the stone patio outside waiting for the dinner gong, but that could be interesting too because you could hear what they were saying! I discovered the only possible disadvantage to this room when I returned with the new wardens in 1979 and spent three weeks in it. When it was rebuilt, after the old stone-built cook's cottage that it replaced had been destroyed by the weather, it was built of corrugated asbestos. Hence, when a gale was blowing, particularly an easterly or a southerly with rain, the noise was so great it was easy to imagine that you were about to take off, never mind the chances of going to sleep. I loved the noise of wind and rain on my window pane at night, but I liked to sleep as well.

Across a small hallway from this room was a door leading into our laboratory, a long room with windows running the full length of the south wall. It was occasionally used by schools for project work and by us as a lecture room when we started running courses in 1977. Other important uses were as a greenhouse for tomato and green pepper plants which were a great success, particularly the former. We did produce green peppers, but they were no great size. It was also the brewery where Ray concocted a strong, nourishing beer to keep up our stamina as well for occasional revelries! The fermenting liquid was kept in blue plastic dustbins underneath the benches, and one day one of our best brews was given an extra boost by the addition of several ripe shear-water corpses donated by a well-meaning visitor. Well, a dustbin's a dustbin!

In that lab, I spent many hours setting moths on a board for a Skokholm collection (this shows how I have changed because I wouldn't kill them today). Meadow brown but-terflies, caught for a population study, were treated with more dignity. They merely received a blob of paint on their wings and then were set free, but more of that later. Suffice to say that the laboratory gave us a useful space with ample light for these kind of activities. Also, it gave us the desperately needed floor space when we were descend-ed on unexpectedly by a film crew and the buildings were grossly overcrowded.

Next to the lab was the warden's quarters, first occupied by Mike and then by Ray and myself. It was a small flat consisting of a bathroom (with no bath, toilet or show-er of course!), a study and a bedroom with no bed! We were happy to sleep on the floor and were not even perturbed by mice taking short cuts over us to reach the other side of the room. It was separate from the rest of the accommodation, a great advan-tage for we needed our space (and somewhere to hide the chocolate!).

The flat and the lab were prefabricated, but adjoining us at the extreme western end was a little stone building used as a workshop. That is it housed the tools, paint, wood, longworth traps etc., and it was occasionally used for small construction jobs, although it was really too small to work in. Once or twice it was used to house a goat. I believe it has gone now and the whole arrangement of the middle section is altered.

The remaining guest room, which I have barely touched on, was the dormitory to be found at the western end of the northern block, the Wheelhouse being at the other end. This room housed a wardrobe in which I was forced to seek refuge one day as we shall see later. There were six beds in it for visitors of equal sex. This meant that we had to do a quick assessment of gender as we scrutinized our newly arrived group each Saturday while they waited to be assigned their rooms. It may sound straightfoward, but it wasn't always. Mistakes were made, both to our and their embarrassment. We couldn't inspect them like we did our trapped birds – we had to go on superficial char-acters. Thus the dormitory was usually a place for the men as they nearly always out-numbered the ladies. Today there is no dormitory accommodation so there must be fewer complaints about snoring too. In this spacious room the warden and his wife now live a life of relative luxury compared to the old days.

All those additional rooms had to be prepared as well as our own which, for the first four years, could be found squashed between the dormitory and the Wheelhouse store-room. There we stayed until we were promoted to wardens. At least we never had to share our quarters with anyone else unless you count the odd goat of course!

In the cottage garden we decided to create a vegetable patch, so that we at least had a limited supply of unadulterated, organic vegetables. Although familiar with the warn-

The vegetable garden

ings in Rachel Carson's book *Silent Spring*, it was not that we felt the amount of concern about pesticides in food that we do today, it was more a question of wanting a taste of the 'good life'.

Creating a garden sounds like a straightfoward task, but it is far from it on an island with a rabbit population that peaks at ten thousand. We could have done with a five foot high stone wall round it, like I have surrounding my garden in Cornwall. All we had was wire netting, scraps of wood and muscle. We made several naive attempts, first with a simple, wire netting fence turned out at the bottom to deter the rabbits. We soon realised our folly, rabbits can get through the tiniest of gaps. We then sunk the netting into the ground for a foot or so, again turned it outwards to stop them burrowing underneath, but rabbits dig deep and don't give up easily when faced with a row of succulent lettuces behind a wire screen. It was definitely a case of something being greener on the other side! They found a way in somehow by going deep underground.

Next, with the help of Mike's brother Nick, Ray dug a huge square pit a couple of feet deep which he lined with the netting, overlapping it carefully in case they surprised us from below! This, joined up with the fence, was ultimately sucessful, and from then on we were in production. Our vegetables would have won prizes for size and taste, and the most likely reason for this, as well as lavish dressings of seaweed and compost from vegetable spoils at the end of the season, was that we dug up the old elsan pits by the pigsty, and carted sackfuls of the rotted contents down to the garden. In this way we tempered the soil and it was soon a rich and friable loam. Overwinter, the earthworms did their very important (and too little appreciated) work. Thus natural decay and a little lime filched from the lighthouse ensured that we had a fine rich tilth for our spring sowing. Such carrots we grew, there was no sign of carrot root-fly or any other disease for that matter.

There was always work in the garden tending vegetables, and it was a great help to us when visitors volunteered to help with the digging or weeding. I suspect that some of them missed the regular sessions in their own garden. To be self-sufficient in vegetables was an impossibility with all those people to feed, but we made a big contribution. Ray was a good and keen gardener and welcomed the task. Soon we had another plot on the outside of the wall that joined the Wheelhouse under cultivation as well.

The arrival of the chickens in the spring of 1974 pleased me almost as much as the arrival of the auks. Except when I was too young to remember, I had never lived with chickens before and wasn't aware of the the therapeutic quality of watching those gentle, simplistic creatures scratching around in the yard. Terry arrived one Saturday with some lively hessian sacks tied loosely with baler twine. Our meat was always delivered fresh, but not as fresh as that! Terry had ordered some 'ready to lay' hens for himself from Letterston in Wales and, as we had agreed early in the season, he included six extra birds for us to keep on the island. They were a breed called Arber-acre and perfect for what we wanted, hardy, good layers and good looking too. Mostly they were glossy black with a green sheen, but each had a variable number of gold and orange feathers on the head and neck so that individuals were easily reconizable. Even now I have not come across a breed that I like better. It was an ideal way to make use of the kitchen scraps that we didn't compost. The hens had free range of all the land around the buildings except for the vegetable gardens, and beyond that if they wanted. Only one, a bantam that was given to us, took advantage of that. Fortunately for us, the rabbit proof fencing round our vegetable plots proved to be ninety-eight percent chicken proof. It was a joy to watch the hens foraging around and enjoying the benefit of the sun that so many chickens are deprived of. The pleasure they elicited from dust baths was enviable. Judging by the attention they paid to them, our visitors enjoyed having the hens around as much as we did.

I was disproportionately proud of the chicken house that I had built from scraps of driftwood. It was stong and lasted many years. It was also my greatest achievement with hammer and nails to this day! It was small, but there was enough room for a strong perch at a good height from the floor to accommodate six roosting hens. It was weatherproof too, with carefully designed overhangs on the roof, and it had a lift-off door that was fixed each side with a long nail sliding through two staples. For bedding I would go out into the island bog once a week armed with a rake and some sacks, and from there I would collect the dead Molinia (purple moorgrass) from the previous year's growth and cart it back to heap on the clean wooden floor. The latter was detachable so that it could be pulled out and scrubbed.

Just as each morning I would relish the moment of waking and stepping outside the door to breathe the fresh ocean air, so would the chickens make a mad scramble for

Ray and Nick de la Brooke creating the rabbit proof vegetable garden

freedom as I released the hen house door. I would hear from without their agitated cackling as they directed their impatience towards each other with much noisy squabbling. Their mash was prepared the previous night and they would race with me across the yard to the feeding bowl. It was chickens first and then visitors as far as breakfast was concerned. After a while, when the weather was fine, I used to leave their door open so that they could come out when they liked and then I could hear their early morning chortling outside my window before I rose.

It was intriguing but sad to find that when these five-month-old hens first arrived they merely cowered in the back of the hen house refusing to come out for two or three days. They were obviously quite unused to any freedom of movement. Gradually the bolder ones among them began to approach the door and finally to step outside, thus encouraging the rest. From then on they never looked back. I was as delighted as a child when, a week or two later, I found the first perfect, shiny brown egg. The nest boxes were placed in the store shed near to the wheelhouse, and we encouraged the hens to lay in them by shutting them in the shed during the early morning laying hours for the first couple of weeks. They occasionally laid eggs out in the bracken or in the hen house, but we generally discouraged them. During a busy period, one hen hatched a brood out in the bracken and the first we knew of it was when she proudly led them across Home Meadow into the yard. The dearest and the tamest of them, called Brown, because of her brown ring (see below), presented an egg to a visitor on her bed one day. I suspect it may have been a return of favours, something to do with the biscuit tin!

We even took advantage of them to teach our visitors some of the finer points of bird behaviour. The six hens, although fairly easily identified by their plumage, were each given different colour darvic rings and a chart was pinned on the wall to establish the pecking order. Visitors were asked to fill in who pecked who. Thus they acquired their names Blue, Green etc. It worked out to be no simple order from top to bottom either, for at the top we had a very definite triangle of pecking. One of the dominant and most aggressive hens was Orange and she, not surprisingly, turned out to be the best mother when the time came. Brown was at the bottom; she was the tamest and it was she who befriended our visitors most. I learnt something of the cruel side of nature too when I watched with great anguish the hens persistently attacking one of the flock who was sick. The pluckier ones among them would rush at any gulls or jackdaws that came into the yard, something which neither of our cockerels would do when they joined the flock. Male valour had no place there!

It wasn't long before we, and possibly the hens too, wanted a cockerel among the flock. We soon found a superb specimen of a Rhode Island red whom we called Rooster. He looked just wonderful as he perched on the high west wall and treated us all to his dawn salutations. Few actually saw him then but all heard him! I think not many visitors were disturbed by this after long nights filled with the cries of incoming and outgoing shearwaters, followed at first light by a chorus of screaming gulls. When Rooster took to crowing from a windowsill in the yard he fortunately chose ours, conveniently located between the Wheelhouse and the old dormitory.

He came from Oxfordshire where we bought him over the bar in a pub for five pounds. We were off the island at the time for our winter break and were visiting Clare. We were delighted with our purchase and Rooster was conveyed back to our winter residence in Hampshire where he was introduced to the island flock before he began tuning up for his role in the avian chorus of Skokholm. Later he was replaced by 'Pathe News'.

Jackdaw

When we returned for our third season, the hens and Rooster travelled in their own purpose-made boxes, one for the former and a separate one for their new male escort. The birds were able to pop their heads through holes we cut in the top of the box, from where they could view the countryside as we drove along the main roads to west Wales or the huge ocean swell from the boat. Few chickens have the chance to see that and probably wouldn't care to either. We once had one escape on the outward journey; a bewildered, half-drowned bantam, namely the adventurous Mary Cluckins, had to be plucked from the sea. How she must have envied the puffins their waterproof feathers on that brief but freezing immersion. Due to our variable cargo of livestock over the years, we were never able to go to the same car hire firm twice on the journeys to and from the island, especially after a haulage of goats!

With a little help from Rooster we were able to increase our family of fowls, and it wasn't long after he first arrived that we heard the cheeping of tiny beaks. At first this event didn't happen in the normal way. I had been so anxious to acquire some chicks that for an experiment I put out twenty-one eggs in gulls' nests, replacing their clutches of three with the same number of brown hens' eggs. They obliged me perfectly, not surprisingly, as I later learnt that gulls will sit on almost anything including a rubber ball! The replacement clutches were staggered by twenty-four-hour periods. Nineteen days later (the incubation period of a chickens' egg) saw me out first thing in the morning to check the first one before the chicks hatched and wandered away from the nest. To my utter delight, there in the nest were three tiny balls of fluff, two golden and one black. They were placed in my woolly hat and rushed back for immediate sustenance. Not a thought was given to the poor deprived gulls.

Once their plumage was dry and fluffy, the newly hatched chicks were so beautiful, coming in all shades of gold, white, brown and black. This daily episode was repeated every day for a week with a hundred per cent success rate! I didn't expect that, and what with some of the hens also hatching chicks, we soon became inundated.

Fortunately for me the broody hens accepted considerable extensions to their families and not all the chicks came under my wing! To see a mother hen leading them round the yard, clucking and fussing was a sight that delighted both myself and our visitors, especially some of the schoolchildren from the cities. One hen had seventeen to look after and she made a wonderful picture as she brooded them, with tiny beaks and feet sticking out all over the place. Some of the children had never seen such a sight and it was often difficult getting their attention away from the them. We soon realized the need for special brood-pens so that the chicks were safe from other hens, over enthusiastic visitors and the cockerel, who would sometimes go for them if they strayed away from mum.

I loved to see Rooster greeting the hens as they emerged in the morning. He would dance round them, leaning on one side with one drooping wing spread out like a fan. From his beak would come a bubbling chortle. He was very seductive, and a gentleman too, looking after them very well and always allowing them access to the food first. He would gather them together if danger threatened, even if it was always one of the hens who chased the intruder away!

A pair of muscovy ducks joined the flock later, and they even had a small pond built for them in the wheelhouse yard. Their wings were clipped at first but they soon settled and could later on be seen on flying jaunts around the farmhouse, even venturing over North Pond once but never landing there. One day the duck amazed us by appearing on Home Meadow leading a long line of twenty-two ducklings, and very sweet they were too. We found her nest in the old woodshed on the other side of the wall that ran along behind the cottage bench. It was totally covered in a thick layer of down which hid and kept warm the eggs when she left for food or exercise. We had noticed her prolonged absences but stupidly had not put two-and-two together, which she had done very well! This duck was once absent for days and was found locked inside an empty visitor's room; she was fine but very hungry.

Sometimes, to Mike's consternation, a hen would have a scratch about among the shearwater burrows on the Knoll. Naturally he was concerned about it, but I don't think they did any real damage in the end, otherwise it would have been deportation in favour of the native species! Another annoyance was when a hen was seen running about with a slow-worm dangling from its beak. That was a real prize and she was usually pursued by the whole flock, including Rooster, and finally with me bringing up the rear! Fortunately, I was usually in time to rescue the unfortunate creature. Round the buildings we had purposely left sheets of corrugated iron under which the slow worms concealed themselves, and that meant we had them close by to show to our visitors. No doubt, the hens cleaned up the yard of many would-be garden pests and I'm sure the slugs, snails, ants etc. contributed much to the excellent flavour of their eggs!

We kept an eye on the welfare of the island goats, first at a distance for interest's sake. We were under the impression that there was a dominant billy in our herd and occasionally there was a fight for male leadership, but it never came to much. Once, after a fierce battle of clashing horns, the herd split into two groups temporarily, some with the old leader and the rest with the contester. Otherwise, it was only when nannies left the herd to kid that their numbers were depleted.

We heard several stories about the goats from various sources. One of them referred to Mike Harris's billy goat called Llewellyn. Located in the centre of the island was the Bog, a damp area dominated by purple moorgrass which had been the main breeding area for a large population of lapwings in the past. It was also the goats' favourite browsing ground. A hide, called Rob's Hide, had been built there and it was rather a crude structure raised on stilts (when we arrived it was still there but in a very derelict state). It is said that two old ladies on their first week's visit to the island were in the habit of taking a break from their perambulations inside this hide, where they could sit in relative comfort and watch the goings on of the various island fauna all around them. They were evidently unaware of the nervous and timid disposition of the goats generally because as soon as they spotted the roving, long haired, horned Llewellyn coming up behind the hide, they froze to their seats and would not, or could not, budge. How many hours they were incarcerated in the hide isn't known and would undoubtedly be exaggerated if it was. Fortunately the alarm was raised at the next mealtime, when cook was found to have two spare meals. A search party was assembled and they were rescued in due course, none the worse for wear. Llewellyn, reputedly harmless, was also said to have butted his master playfully into the sea whilst they were down on the landing steps!

Some of the nannies were not good mothers (notably the younger ones) and they would often leave the newborn kid (occasionally twins) in a discrete hollow or sometimes in a rabbit burrow for long periods. Sometimes they became stuck and these misadventures led to our adoption of several kids over the years.

Baggins was brought to us in 1974 when he was a tiny, limp thing hanging weakly over a visitor's hand. He had been found stuck fast in a burrow, deserted by his mother. He was pathetic and terribly thin, but we fanned the little flame of life that was left in him and coaxed him into accepting milk from a bottle. Anyone who has reared a young lamb, goat or a human baby for that matter knows what that means. Our bedroom became the goat nursery and every now and again in the night came plaintive bleatings from a box by the bed demanding the next feed. We didn't need this extra mouth, especially one with anti-social habits, but he won us over (especially Ray who was partial to anything small and hungry) and one of us would reach out for the bottle of milk. However, tiny limp things don't stay that way if they are well fed as we soon found and Baggins began to get bigger and hairier every day and so, in the end, did his playful butts! He had light beige and dark brown markings on his body and a cute face with a curly forelock. As he gained strength he would leap into the air on his gangly legs, twist round and drop down facing the other way; his life was a continual playtime. His frolicking was much enjoyed by our visitors who loved to have mock fights with him, encouraging him to rear up on his sturdy hind legs and whack into their clenched fist with his head which soon sprouted stumpy, little horns.

But horns get bigger along with their owners and Baggins didn't like being ignored. Unfortunately, one of our lady visitors, the only one we ever had who didn't fit in well with the company or the island, wore a stunning pair of bright yellow trousers. Baggins was unable to resist them and they soon became the chief object of his attentions. He would wait in the yard until Yellow Trousers appeared; then his eyes would roll, his head would go down and he would canter into attack from the rear. He was just the right height for a knee-buckling shove, so by the time cook responded to her screams, Yellow Trousers was folded up on the grass. As if this wasn't enough, the chickens joined forces with the goat and pestered her as she sat enjoying (we hope) tea and biscuits in the yard with the other visitors. Maybe it was the way she sat, or maybe she just happened to like the right type of biscuit, but it was always on to the arm of her chair that the hens fluttered and her biscuits they snatched. The lady was more than a little disgruntled when she left. Perhaps the animals sensed our unease with her and clubbed together to make life uncomfortable! It transpired that she had been coerced into coming to the island by her bird-watching husband, who also showed signs of being ill-at-ease in her presence, but who nevertheless enjoyed his holiday.

Baggins didn't get big enough during his short stay on the island for tossing us into South Haven or any other major mischief. Perhaps his worst was with Yellow Trousers, but he was capable of minor capers like clambering up on to the cottage roof via the wall when he was shut out. Up there he would stomp around making a loud din on the tiles, protesting against his exile. He spoilt a birthday cake one day, whilst cook was being inattentive, by putting his foot in it, literally! There can't have been many birthday cakes perforated by genuine hoof marks, but fortunately small hoofmarks can be filled with icing sugar and a few people just thought they had extra icing!

It was with some amusement that we watched Baggins attempt to make friends with the chickens. He did this by nosing them gently while they were much too occupied with eating or indulging in dust baths to run away. They received his dubious attentions with suspicion and remained aloof like a band of indignant old ladies. However, when the time came to transport them all down to Hampshire for our short winter sojourn, things were different. When released in their new environment, they stuck to him like glue, hanging around his legs for several days as the only thing familiar to

Baggins in his new paddock in Hampshire

them. When Baggins was taken on this long journey, he rode in the backseat of our hired car, sitting upright and looking out like a royal personage. In traffic jams he was inclined to gaze out of the window at the astonished faces outside and in other cars, several times tempting me to reach back and raise his hoof in a goaty wave.

Soon after our arrival at Titchfield Haven, our winter quarters with warden Barry Duffin, a photograph of Baggins appeared in the paper which claimed the attention and admiration of a Chief Inspector of the Hampshire Police who adopted him. This man was large (as most Chief Inspectors I know are), large enough to control Baggins's rough and tumble games by the use of rugby tackles. He built a paddock for him on the edge of suburbia and the following year he took over Pippa, a little brown and white nanny goat that had been found deserted and whom we also reared. She seemed happy to join Baggins, by then a superb, mature billy goat. In his bachelor days, Baggins had again got himself into the local newspaper when he escaped from his paddock and joined a bus queue! I wonder where he was trying to go?

After Baggins and Pippa, came an unfortunate experience with a nanny goat which we had tethered on Spy Rock. She became entangled and strangled herself much to our intense dismay. We were responsible and felt distressed for days afterwards. It taught us to be more careful when tethering animals.

Many people were of the opinion that the island would be well rid of the goats for various reasons. It was considered that nothing could be encouraged to grow, particularly in the way of small trees and bushes, because of their capacity for eating virtually anything, and it was also said whilst they moved round the island they broke through the delicate and friable earth over the shearwater burrows, although nobody claimed to have seen this happen. The former was certainly true to a degree, but, with such a large rabbit population and a high degree of exposure, it was difficult to get anything to grow anyway. Furthermore, anyone who watched the goats moving from one area to another could see that they followed well-defined paths except in the browsing areas which were well away from the shearwater colonies.

So it came about that we were instructed to begin a cull and, accordingly, given a rifle. Some unpleasant incidents followed because none of us were cut out for the business and, in the end, it was called off. Another way of reducing numbers had to be found. Thus began the famous goat chases intended to capture and ship off a few animals each year. They involved both staff and willing visitors and were relatively successful. I will not attempt to describe in detail the chase, suffice to imagine a large herd of agile and sure-footed animals being chased by a group of clumsy-footed humans on an island bound by two hundred foot cliffs, accessible to the former but not to the latter. There was much hilarity, a great deal of heroics by some of the male contingent and plenty of drama. The poor goats got a bad deal of course, and, as well as losing one or two members of the group, the herd was split up. Very often they didn't reunite for many days. Once a billy went missing and was located a few days later at the bottom of Calf Bay. Mike descended the cliff in a rescue bid and that was all that was needed. Up leapt the billy, clearing a ten foot chasm in the rock before scrabbling up a near-vertical cliff face which was more than any of us could have done.

Similarly we went to the rescue of three goats stranded down Dip Gully, armed with Ray's special goat ladder (he must have been under some misapprehension there!), ropes, bored lighthouse keepers and sundry other aids. The goats thought it was hilarious, let us play around and risk a few lives and then walked up the cliff on their own! For a graphic account of a goat chase read *The Islanders* by John Lewis, 1997.

When we left in 1978 there were still goats on the island, about nine or ten I believe, but they were all removed eventually. I was well aware that goats had been (and still are) very destructive on islands around the world, but we enjoyed them nevertheless and so did many of our visitors. They had provided milk for Ronald Lockley, but never had we tamed a nanny enough to give up her milk, even though Mike once caught a nanny and kid together. She gave a few drops and dried up. I don't blame her.

I respected those goats living as they were, independent of humans. They had retained the dignity that animals are entitled too and which so many are deprived of today. They weren't true wild animals, but they deserved their temporary freedom and I was sorry to learn that they had gone. I was sorry too that I hadn't thought to ask Ronald Lockley when he visited us in 1973 what he thought about them!

One daily task which should not be omitted because the results were relevant to some of our studies was the weather recording. Every morning from the first day onwards, either Ray or myself would break off whatever we were doing at ten o'clock each day to take readings for the meteorological station at Bracknel. This is how I came to be well practiced in the art of guaging wind speed. The methods were primitive, especially wind speed and direction: the mythical Met. men required us to venture out on to Met. Heath where our thermometer screen was and toss a small piece of vegetable matter (was that where the heather went!) into the air to see which way it blew or whether it fell at our feet. Four canes were stuck in the gound to mark the four compass points and from those markers we guaged the direction. For wind speed, various charts were available; there was a chart of sea state relative to wind force (white horses, horizontal white streaks on waves etc.) that we could conceivably use, and another that described the motion of the trees which wasn't quite so good when applied to the sycamore tree. My own method was the degree of discomfort out on the heath. In gales you could hardly stand up, in hurricanes you couldn't get out there, and if it was calm you couldn't find the piece of lichen you'd just dropped! One bad day, I set off to do the duty only to find that the met. screen, thermometers and all, had blown down and everything within it was smashed. There was no weather that day which would have surprised anyone who was out in it! I was quite taken aback as it was a sturdy structure and wondered if the big billy goat had a hand in it, or rather a head, as he had been seen giving his nape a good rub on its solid base.

Once a month I would hide myself away and spend an hour or two filling out the weather chart, a mammoth task in my mind because we hardly had any paperwork to do in those days. Average monthly temperatures, max., min., wet bulb, dry bulb, ground min. all had to be worked out with no calculator at hand. I'm sure it kept some part of my brain exercised. I know I felt a great relief when it was done.

CHAPTER 6

Spring Migration and the onset of Breeding

The annual migration of hundreds and thousands of birds of many different species is a phenomenon which can hardly fail to fascinate any serious naturalist. The whys and wherefores aside, it was a unique privilege to be living on that small and beautiful island and to witness at first hand the arrival and departure of regular migrants, as well as the added bonus of rare birds and vagrants. We also welcomed the arrival of our summer residents, some of which we knew as individuals because they wore rings in certain colour combinations or with large numbers and letters. March and April saw the departure of the last of the overwintering robins and wrens. We always hoped that some would stay to breed, but they always left. Robins had bred twice before, many years ago, and have bred since we left too. Wrens also began to breed after our departure, although previously it was thought that there was too little vegetation on Skokholm. Funny how we always think we know so much and then are proved wrong later on! The origin of our overwintering wrens and robins was a bit of a mystery. The only ringing recovery of either that I can find is of a post-juvenile robin that was ringed on Skokholm in April 1968 and recovered in France in December 1970.

The spring passage generally brought fewer birds than the return migration in the autumn because there were no young birds to boost numbers. Previously, ornithologists found this hard to understand because they could not believe that juveniles could migrate south on their own. Migration north in spring was also a more concentrated affair with birds eager to arrive at their destinations and get down to the serious business of breeding. Many birds return by a different, more direct route than that used during the more leisurely return migration southwards. Indeed, when weather conditions were very fair for a long period in April and May, migrants were few and far between on the ground because they passed high overhead unobserved.

It was worth the effort of getting up very early in the morning (which meant excessively early for the cook) to walk round and see what the day offered. It has to be said that the birds didn't always seem to be early risers and there was generally little activity from the passerines before eight o'clock, probably because both they and their insectivorous food were still in the process of warming up for the day's activity. Many keen visitors had completed the rounds by seven thirty, only to find that the goodies turned up after breakfast. Many early birds caught no worms!

Before our guests began to arrive, we had the place to ourselves and that was indeed gratifying; it also induced in us a certain posessiveness which is probably unavoidable when living on a small island. After all, does not a place belong to whosoever is most familiar with it and takes the most pleasure from it? I think so. We enjoyed the company of our visitors but we relished the quiet weeks before the season got going, and later on when it drew to a close. However, without the careful searching and critical observation of our visitors, many birds would not have been seen at all, and during our busiest time we relied on them to complete our daily records.

Early spring days were highlighted by the arrival of the first migrants. Ring ouzels often arrived as early as March, and in 1974 there were no less than eight in one day. It was always a great thrill to see these close relatives of the blackbird on their way to their breeding grounds in the wild uplands. Most striking were the males sporting large, white bibs and grey panelled wings. They favoured the half tumbled down walls around the Observatory and many were trapped and ringed in the Wall Trap. Black redstarts were early arrivals too, and if we were lucky so were hoopoes. Favourite places to find them were Green Heath and Gull Fields. One day we had no less than three hoopoes on the island, two of which displayed in front of our newly arrived visitors who happened to be signed up for a 'birdwatching for beginners' course. They got full marks for identification and immediately questioned the rarity of this seemingly exotic species! One lady became over enthusiastic and later in the week she led me slowly down Home Meadow to look at her hoopoe which turned into a piece of twisted metal! I struggled to break the news as tactfully as circumstances allowed. In 1974 we had the first hoopoe on the island for nine years.

Around mid March, wheatears began to arrive, some passing through and others staying to breed. Males always arrived first and Mike was delighted when his colour-marked birds returned to the island wearing their striped trousers, a little faded by the African sunshine. Larger birds, believed to be of the Greenland race, turned up more usually in the autumn. The next long distant migrant, after the wheatear, would usually be an early sand martin homing into the island from its coastal flyway. Only a speck in the sky at first, but the erratic flight always a giveaway. A few martins and then the first swallow would herald the hirundine invasion which went on into July, with the house martins being generally last to appear. Swifts, bringing with them nostalgic thoughts of sleepy English villages and austere, grey church towers, first arrived in April with numbers building up in May and June. How I welcomed the first glimpse of those arrowed wings slicing through the sky. Mixed streams of swallows, martins and swifts always seemed to come north with a light following wind, but would home on to the

Hoopoe

island against it. I have clear memories of standing at Wallsend and marvelling at a continual stream of swallows and house martins skimming over a choppy sea and then winging their way up Windmill Gully to flash by me, dark, agile and hurried. One of our swallows ringed early one year was recovered in Cape Province, South Africa,

Early records of some species like goldcrests, stonechats, linnets and others probably represented short-distance migration or dispersal movements. Chiffchaffs started to arrive in late March, but the origin of these early individuals was uncertain since some of them winter in Britain. Recoveries from our ringed passerines were few and far between, but the information gleaned from those that were retrapped (controlled) or picked up dead was highly significant especially in the early days of ringing. In 1965 for example, a chiffchaff ringed on Skokholm in April was caught alive in Morocco the following October and released again. So those olive-coloured warblers skulking in the nettles took on a new significance as I became more aware of just where they might have spent their winters. The same can be said for their look-alikes, the willow warblers, arriving on the island a little later in April, with an ongoing passage all through May. Many of them sought the scant cover inside the Heligoland traps and left the island bearing monel rings. Over two hundred willow warblers were processed each year, with nearly five hundred in 1975. There have been a few autumn and winter recoveries of Skokholm-ringed birds over the years from Spain and Portugal. Chiffchaff numbers were consistently about a fifth of the total of the willow warblers.

The bulk of the migrants came through in April and May, and I soon learnt about the 'falls' that occur when low cloud or fog suddenly descends on what begins as a clear, starry night. The disorientated birds are forced down on to land as the stars and moon (their navigational aids) are obliterated, and many perish on the sea. Such is the case when they are attracted by, and home into, the brilliant white flashes of certain lighthouses. In the Skokholm library at that time was a copy of a book by Eagle Clarke, written in 1906, that gave vivid descriptions of birds dashing helplessly into the glass lanterns of various lighthouses in Britain, France and the Channel Islands. There were also graphic accounts of hawks chasing pipits round lighthouse towers at night. Migration in those early days must have seemed an unfathomable mystery and indeed certain aspects of it still are today. We are now at least some way to understanding how a bird as tiny as a goldcrest can undertake a long and hazardous journey over land and sea. Incidentally, the above mentioned book disappeared from the island years ago; a sad reflection on someone's character.

At the first indication of a fall we would be out whenever possible to see what we could find. Whitethroats, sedge warblers, blackcaps arrived each year without fail, generally flitting around in the bushes or other low vegetation. Later on, migrating flycatchers, stonechats and whinchats were much more obliging, perching out in the open on sycamore branches, walls or the tops of bushes. Spotted flycatchers outnumbered their more strikingly marked cousins, the pied flycatchers, and were often caught in the garden trap. Over the years there have been recoveries of Skokholm-ringed spotted flycatchers in Morocco, Nigeria and Portugal, and a juvenile ringed in August 1966 was recovered in Germany three years later. Whinchats pitched on the walls, flicking their wings and cocking their tails just like stonechats, but easily distinguished from them by the pale eyestripe which can be exceedingly bold in the male. Stonechats, which are partial migrants in Britain, always arrived earlier and were more numerous. How we wished they would stay to breed as they had done for Lockley back in 1928 and 1932. In *Dream Island Days* he remarks that they did not breed after he had fired the heather, implying that they nested in it. In those years, the sedge warbler had bred too, and it is interesting to note that they are once again breeding on the island. This comes as no great surprise as many times we listened to the bright, rasping notes of singing males issuing from the tall clumps of hemlock water dropwort inside the Heligoland and hoped that they would breed. Whitethroats also bred in Lockley's time (it seems that they ousted the sedge warblers!) and there were nesting linnets too. The disturbance caused by constantly running the trap may have deterred some of these small birds from breeding.

Less common warblers passing through in spring were garden warblers, reed warblers, lesser whitethroats and grasshopper warblers, the last heard but rarely seen unless trapped. Other less common migrants were redstarts, tree pipits and the four wagtails (white, pied, yellow and grey). A very scarce or rare bird could turn up at at any time, like a wryneck, a melodious warbler or, as in 1975, a beautiful male bluethroat which was caught in the Winch trap, although we had nothing quite as rare or stunning as the white-throated robin of May 1990 which was only the second record for Britain and Ireland. Such rarities would often disrupt breakfast, but in our case 'cook' would join the rush to the ringing room rather than be left holding the frying pan! One morning in June 1975, Mike declared at breakfast that, as far as migration was concerned, the day was good for nothing except perhaps a rustic bunting. He promptly went out and found one; and caught it! However, 3 June one year brought a woodchat shrike, seen by Ray, caught later by an excited schoolboy and retrapped seventeen days later in Suffolk, making it Britain's first woodchat shrike recovery.

We had our share of birds escaped from captivity and, during my visit in 1971, I had learnt not to cast doubt too readily on visitors' tales of exotica when one morning someone rushed excitedly into the Wheelhouse, whilst the rest of us were enjoying our breakfast, with tales of a bird – blue, yellow, red, purple etc. – in the garden. Although he was considered of sound mind, it was with great scepticism and on account of much persuasion that the warden (Barry Chambers) disappeared and returned with a paint-

One of our more unusual migrants – a Wryneck

ed bunting in his hand. Was it out of a cage or a passenger on a passing Venezuelan tanker thankful to see land again? There have been several records from Skokholm of red-headed buntings, a commonly kept cagebird, but we missed out on that one. A snow goose on South Pond in 1975 was tame enough to allow us to read the ring and confirm that it came from Slimbridge.

Cuckoos arrived in April and called to each other from the walls and rocky outcrops; some were caught in the wall trap. Our meadow pipits seldom gave them any peace and we did record juvenile cuckoos on the island but we were never certain of their origin. Collared doves and turtle doves graced us with their presence. Glancing back through old Skokholm reports, the decline in turtle dove totals is sadly noticeable and reflects the relentless persecution they face on the continent. Currently there is concern over the persistent shooting of this species by Italian hunters who are pursuing their hobby in Hungary because of the tightening of the laws in their own country. This beautiful dove with its stippled, chestnut back, white trimmed tail and finely striped, black-and-white neck patch could soon be no more than a wavering memory. I was mortified when one day I flushed a turtle dove from the bracken in which it had taken refuge from a fierce gale, when instantly a peregrine appeared from nowhere and snatched it from the air before my very eyes. It was a terrific spectacle, but should I have felt guilty? Well, I did.

Rustic Bunting

Wading birds dropped in to rest and feed on the sparse muddy edges of our pools, but there was little to attract large numbers. The occasional dunlin, knot or redshank would provide entertainment from the hide at North Pond, but they were more likely to drop in during the late summer or autumn as stray juveniles. Common sandpipers frequented the rocky shore in ones and twos, bobbing nervously and flying round corners with a curt whistle. Whimbrel were regular visitors, alerting us to the flock by a short flurry of whistles. Occasionally there would be a godwit or two among their number. They very often joined up with the curlews, of which considerable numbers used the island as a roost during the autumn and winter. The flock, often several hundred strong by the time we left the island in November, had decreased somewhat by the time we returned in March and continued to do so into the spring and summer.

We had few crakes or rails during the spring passage, but one April day in a raging gale, a friend Dick Jones, and myself flushed a bird from the bracken which was unfamiliar to me. It had chestnut flashes on its rounded wings and my friend, fresh from a stint on North Uist in the Hebrides, immediately shouted 'corncrake'. It dropped down not far away but was never seen again. My first record, an authentic but very brief sighting.

Early spring usually saw a merlin or two dashing about the walls hunting unwary pipits. Pitching on the walls, they gave us splendid views through the island's telescope and I remember noting the flatness of the head for the first time when comparing one

Mike holding a cuckoo

to a kestrel. These latter came over to the island also, but more in the autumn. Most exciting was a male red-footed falcon, discovered by Mike in May 1975, which had flopped down exhausted on the Neck early one morning. At the time I was in bed, down with a particularly nasty influenza virus, but nothing save imminent death was going to stop me seeing that bird. I did see it and it was worth every ghastly minute of the struggle. It was a first for me and for Skokholm. Three weeks later, a hobby turned up, only the second one recorded there.

Generally, the spring brought us few rare birds compared with the return autumn migration which is dealt with in a later chapter. In no way did our resident breeding birds get second place. They needed counting too and, in some cases, monitoring, both of which occupied a lot of our time.

'A fine sunny morning in May finds me comfortably settled in a bluebell-filled hollow beside Alice's Knoll staring aimlessly at the sky, or so it would seem. The puzzled look on my face and the bubbling song of the bird on high gives away the nature of my task. Where is it? Then, somewhere in the blue void over my head, I would locate the bird descending, slowly, slowly, with wings quivering and tail cocked, still singing. Down, down, down it would come, the notes getting louder, richer and clearer by the second. Satisfied, I put another cross on the skylark census map marking the point where it lands. Several hours of watching from various vantage points has produced a map showing tight clusters of crosses. Each cluster represents a singing male and hence a territory.'

This short extract provides an example of the nature of some of our work, work of the most pleasurable kind! We didn't do a skylark census every year unfortunately as the population seemed stable at thirty-five to forty pairs, and is reported to be much the same today. However, with the severe decline in skylark numbers throughout Britain, this could alter. Incidentally, Lockley in *Dream Island Days* noted only two skylarks singing, and in the early 1960s twenty-five to thirty pairs were reported implying that there has been a gradual build up over the years to what appears to be the optimum number of pairs for the island.

Meadow pipits were censused in much the same way except that they were easier to see. One could note the position of singing males on a general walk around the island. They may be rather plain to look at but I was charmed by their jubilant display; they would rise up slowly to no great height and then descend like little parachutes to claim territorial rights or to show off to their mates. During our six years, their numbers remained stable at around thirty to forty pairs, but more recent surveys have revealed a minimum of sixty pairs. Meadow pipits also occur as passage migrants, and neither were our Skokholm birds necessarily resident all year round. A nestling ringed on Skokholm in 1965 was recovered in Portugal. British meadow pipits are known to migrate down to France and Spain as well.

Nearly every cove boasted a pair of rock pipits. They nested way down the cliffs in cracks or holes, and were easy to census from above as they displayed in a similar manner to the meadow pipits. Their nests were very well concealed and I stumbled on one only once and that was whilst searching for razorbill sites. It was in a dark, damp crevice concealed behind a decorative clump of sea spleenwort. It gave me a special kind of thrill because of the cryptic and beautiful location. They numbered roughly thirty-five pairs and figures from the early 1960s suggested that there had been a slight increase.

Reed buntings, a species now causing concern among conservationists, bred in spaced out localities on the island. They had first bred in 1960, then again in 1967, and stayed from then on as a steady four pairs. They were unobtrusive little birds singing out their few plaintive notes from tall bracken stalks. Bad feelings arose amongst ourselves and a well known photographer who selfishly subjected our East Bog pair to continual disturbance in order to obtain photographs. Recently they have ceased to breed. It is just one of many species suffering from lack of winter stubble and habitat loss, and it is sad that this attractive bunting has disappeared from the island.

Obviously, little effort was required to census the reed bunting and the same applied to our blackbirds and dunnocks both of which were restricted to a few pairs only. Blackbirds, which bred only very rarely since 1928, did so with us from 1975 onwards and in recent years have increased to about a dozen pairs. In an early chapter I have expressed how much we enjoyed listening to their melodious singing when they first came to breed, and the more so because Skokholm lacked the sweet singing of our familiar garden birds. Six or seven pairs of dunnocks were present and they too increased to between eighteen and twenty-two pairs in 1996. Our dunnocks struck me as retiring and unobtrusive with their thin, lisping song hardly inspiring, but they were friendly, endearing creatures. It took me a while to recognise the song simply because it has nothing particular to distinguish it.

The wheatear count was left to Mike. His special study followed up work done by Peter Condor in the 1950s from which he produced a monograph. About nine pairs bred during our time, a decrease since the late sixties (from about twenty-five pairs). More recently, in 1996, the population increased to a healthy thirty-two pairs. We were not to escape involvement in Mike's intensive research programme and we found the work both enjoyable and interesting. Undoubtedly it would have been more so if we had been a little less busy with routine work. Since the cook rose well before seven, it was decided that he or she might as well rise before five for an early session in the hide to record visits of male or female bird, feeding times, prey items etc. Try identifying a mangled fly straight after dragging yourself out of bed at some unearthly hour in the morning and you will see what I mean, especially if you have been out catching shearwaters for a large part of the previous night! The saving factor was that most of the watching was conducted just outside the cottage where a pair nested conveniently in the garden wall. Wheatears have two broods so they kept us busy! We were greatly privileged to be able to view all the goings on at the nest from only a few feet away in Mike's portable hide; wheatears are markedly handsome, particularly the boldly marked males, and so bright and alive in their movements. The hide was a homemade affair built so that Mike was able to move it by wearing it! It was a simple, pitched frame covered with a sky blue material and quite became him when he was inside it, setting off his dark hair and sunburnt face. Typically, Mike's natural reserve meant that he never told the visitors or ourselves of its imminent arrival on the scene and so while it was being tested there were many strange reports coming in ranging from strange aliens to deranged lighthouse keepers. Such reports were quite normal to us.

Wheatear

Similarly jackdaws were designated one of my special projects. In collaboration with a student on Skomer (Andy Richford), I was to locate all the nests and monitor the success of the accessible ones. Jackdaws have a youthful wickedness about them, a look of blatant mischief in their beady, ice blue eyes. They looked as if they would try anything once and they did, attempting to take over puffin and shearwater burrows, stealing eggs and even arriving in the yard in time to share the chicken feed. I grew fond of them and was quite sad when I found the eggs or young chicks had disappeared and a puffin was in attendance. For my cheek and intrusion, I would receive a hefty bite from Mr Puffin as I reached in to check the jacklets. The shiny, turquoise blue eggs of the daws delighted me just as they did their proud owners who also weren't beyond giving me a nasty peck for my trouble!

It was generally thought that our breeding jackdaws were an overspill from Skomer where the population had stabilized at two hundred pairs as a result of the general increase throughout Britain in the post-war years. From 1965 they had colonized the island with increasing numbers until, in 1974, I was dealing with fifty-five pairs. My census technique was straightfoward; some birds simply flew from their nestholes, flushed out by my arrival. They were alerted by the vocal abuse and general mayhem created by the local herring gulls. They were most obliging. Others were not and I would need to sit some distance away and watch for their entrance into a hole with nest material. There was a concentration of them at Hog Bay (around 19 pairs) and an accurate count there involved making a sketch of all the various holes and cracks followed by prolonged watching from a good vantage point on each side of the bay, in fact from South Haven for some of them. Once I was satisfied that they had all been located, I would spend some time scrambling around on the earthy cliff to monitor progress in the accessible nests. That kind of detailed recording work was very rewarding in that you gained an intimate knowledge of the private life of a wild bird without causing them any harm. I also discovered the passive enjoyment of using intense and sensitive observation techniques. I was learning all the time.

Jackdaws had a low success rate on Skokholm. Virtually all the eggs hatched but many of the nestlings used to disappear mysteriously one by one almost daily, even when they were growing fast. There was already fierce competition for burrows on the island between rabbits, shearwaters and puffins without the arrival of yet another hole-nesting bird. Certainly some of them were ousted by puffins. Our razorbill student, Clare, estimated that, between 1971 and 1974, sixty per cent of razorbill egg loss was due to jackdaw predation and concluded that they did affect razorbill breeding success on Skokholm. They have also been seen entering shearwater burrows, pushing out the eggs and eating them. Jackdaws peck a clean hole in the egg and suck out the contents, whereas gull-predated eggs are cracked apart and split into two or three pieces with the spilt contents scooped up. Control measures had been taken on Skokholm between 1965 and 1968, but the population continued to expand; obviously there were surplus birds around. It seemed to me to be inevitable that losses would occur where jackdaws mixed with auks on remote islands.

Andy Richford began a special study of jackdaws on Skomer in 1975. He was responsible for the sporadic appearance of some oddly coloured birds on Skokholm; each adult jackdaw that he could get his hands on flew away bearing wing tags of flourescent green, orange, pink etc. We received reports of strange, tropical black birds flying in from who knows what distant land. Sometimes we went along with it for a while too!

The Jackdaw population rose to sixty pairs, colonizing all but the extreme south-western end of the island. I note that they were back down to thirteen pairs in 1996.

Crows were relatively easy to census, there being only eight or nine pairs, each building a large nest of sticks on the cliffs. Most were half concealed on a cliff ledge, but occasionally they were very cunning in their choice of site and without some scrambling about they could easily be missed. I learnt from the crow census that I always walked in an anticlockwise direction around the island without thinking about it, and neither did I look behind me. One day a visitor showed me a crow's nest, easily visible but only if you happened to be walking clockwise. Habits die hard!

We had but one pair of ravens as described already. There remains little more to say except that, one year, one of their chicks was the object of a dramatic rescue attempt. The said chick had mysteriously remained on the nest after its sibling had left. A curious visitor noticed that a length of thin nylon fishing line, which was well woven into the nest, had wrapped itself tightly round one leg of the overgrown chick. It was literally tied to the nest and there was nothing we could do about it because of its inaccessible and dangerous position on the ledge, at least nothing short of summoning a helicopter. So we did. The official reply from HMS *Brawdy* was a definite 'no way, not for a bird!' but the unofficial answer from the boys in the air was that it would be good training practice for them, so out they came. We rushed to the cliff and waved directions to the hovering monster which nearly blew us over the cliff! Clad in protective gloves, a bold young man swung on the end of a wire and with much difficulty got himself beside the nest. Sadly the huge bird was too much of a handful and when he cut the line it plunged down on to the rocks below to die instantly. It may also have been in a weak condition from not having been fed. Still we were much heartened by the effort they made. We had done all we could. It only happened that once, and generally the ravens did well, although never as well as in 1996 when they apparently raised six young.

The buzzard method was my main tactic for conducting the stock dove census. They were always reluctant to leave their holes in the cliff and so I would look around to see that the coast was clear and then slowly raise my arms up and down, creating merry hell among the gulls. Out came the doves and more crosses were added to my map, totalling around sixty pairs. I thought them attractive and gentle looking doves, smaller and more graceful than woodpigeons and it is a great shame that, for reasons unknown to me, they no longer breed on the island. Indeed, they have declined in Britain generally. Most of their nests were out of reach, but I once found the pure white eggs of a pair in Seal Bay whilst out climbing. When they hatched, the nestlings seemed to be much too ugly to grow up into those beautiful doves. Adults flew to the mainland to feed and life must have been all the more difficult for that. They were first time breeders in 1968, so they colonised for a very short period only.

A small starling population had built up on the island since Lockley's sojourn, when they were only recorded as non breeders. They were distributed around the island and bred in small holes and cracks in the cliffs. We had no significant spring or autumn movements of starlings, although I note from past reports that large flocks of over hundred or so had been recorded in March and April in previous years. They were most likely remnants of a large overwintering population from Europe.

Lapwing numbers were low, so that a census required little effort. The method has been descibed already. It was relatively simple to reckon on the number of pairs (amounting to between four and seven), but it wasn't so easy keeping up with their progress, or lack of it. We often didn't know exactly how they fared, but more often than not their nests repeatedly failed. They had been more numerous in the past with up to twenty-seven pairs in the 1960s and with autumn flocks of around two hundred and fifty. They must have been a fine sight swooping low over the centre of the island. The cold winter of 1962 caused heavy losses but they recovered from that. In Wales generally lapwings have decreased alarmingly, giving great cause for concern. From around seventeen thousand pairs they have dropped to less than a thousand pairs, with none breeding in Pembrokeshire today except on the offshore islands (Skokholm, Skomer and Ramsey). Only a few pairs remain on the island but, with virtually no breeding success, it seems they are destined to disappear. The island bog will seem oddly deserted.

Lapwing

You could hardly walk anywhere on the island without getting a torrent of abuse from one of the many pairs of oystercatchers, of which we had around fifty pairs each year. First of all, as you unwittingly approached a nest, you would catch a glimpse of one of the adults silently running away, head bowed and bill pointed downwards, and then the aerial attacks and screaming would begin. There was much individual variation and, as with most birds, some were very aggressive, whilst others were silent and unobtrusive, leading you to think that perhaps they didn't have a nest. We were the least of their problems considering the number of marauding gulls, as well as opportunistic crows and jackdaws, although disturbance by humans obviously made them more vulnerable to avian predators. One day Lord Hailsham and the Earl of Pembroke arrived for a visit, escorted by Dillwyn Miles from the Trust. Awestruck as I was by these eminent persons, I remember being more concerned about the welfare of the oystercatchers nesting beside 'Alice' when they strolled over to see her. The birds piped frantically and flew in tight circles over their heads whilst I tried to control my anxiety. I think they got the message.

We had a well marked oystercatcher population on the island, most of them decked out with multi-coloured rings and, with so many being faithful to their territory, it wasn't difficult to keep track of their breeding attempts, despite the many cases of repeat nests following egg losses. Sometimes the colours on the rings faded and it was hard to tell what it originally was, for example if the pink you were registering was supposed to be brown or red. Mike retrapped some of the birds at the nest using a wire-framed trap that was moved closer each day to the incubating bird until, eventually, it was actually placed over the nest and was triggered by the returning bird. The eggs were temporarily removed to avoid any harm coming to them. Oystercatcher ring reading with the Nikel telescope was a most enjoyable relief from domestic work. No tripods then, we would simply drop down on the ground, preferably against a rock, and rest it on a raised knee. I continued for a while like this on the mainland before I discovered the luxury of a tripod!

Oystercatcher nest

The oystercatchers, like the lapwings, found it a struggle raising chicks on Skokholm, with many falling prey to gulls or crows. All nests were marked with a white-tipped cane placed ten yards to the north and then we kept away as much as possible. Since reading about the crafty and intelligent behaviour of corvids, particularly crows, I now wonder about the wisdom of marking the nests with canes. Individual corvids have been seen investigating objects on the ground after they have witnessed humans paying particular attention to them, and it may also be possible for them to learn to associate objects with food such as sticks? Ravens, for example, will follow a man stalking with a gun in the highlands in anticipation of the grallochs (deer innards). Hopefully, our canes were placed far enough away from the nest to counteract this and some kind of warning telling people to keep away was perhaps a safer option for the birds.

To find the shallow nest scrape on the side of a rocky outcrop was always a great thrill. It was often lined with tiny, chippings and decorated with a sprig or two of vegetation, and in it would be a clutch of three or four olive, blotched eggs with the perfect background of red rock and bright cliff flowers. Other birds used a simple scrape on the ground. Curious visitors often found nests for us, and elusive nests were tracked down using the telescope in a similar way to the lapwings.

The oystercatchers were colourful and entertaining, enlivening the island with their loud piping displays and energetic defensive behaviour. It was upsetting to see nests fail so often. Nevertheless, their numbers have remained fairly stable for many years, although there is the suggestion of a substantial increase since the nineteenth century in a report by Lockley et al. in 1949. He himself made efforts to encourage them by burning the heather.

Ringing studies once again had revealed that the population was by no means resident and indeed most of the birds moved away from the island after breeding. By the time we left in November the counts had diminished and evidently remained low throughout the winter. Birds ringed on the island have been reported from France, Spain, Portugal and Morocco.

Before embarking on the seabird census, here is a brief resumé of some of the island's sporadic breeders, many of which did not breed with us. One that did though was the moorhen. One day on 1975, I was making my way along the partly-collapsed wall on the west side of South Pond, when suddenly at my feet were nine of the cutest, blackest chicks that I had ever seen, and ushering them along was an adult moorhen. Overcome with surprise, I only just got round to counting them. The surprise was more due to the fact that they were there at all, nesting right in the middle of a huge colony of lesser black-backed gulls. Needless to say no chicks survived the ordeal. In 1973, one pair tried and failed, but they had attempted to breed in most years since 1967 (not always unsuccessfully).

During the twilight hours between April and June in 1976, an unfamiliar, diminutive lump appeared on the side of Alice's Knoll. It was Lockley's 'silent, evil little owl'. The previous year there had been an April sighting, but this particular bird stayed and, as far as we knew, there was only one. It was a stranger to us; we never saw it properly, only heard its ringing 'kew' call, but we had misgivings in case there were two and they bred, as they did in Lockley's time. They weren't native and were known for their predation on storm petrels. Lockley found a nest of four eggs laid on ninety-eight petrel quill feathers, and also a nest with two chicks and a larder of nearly two-hundred petrel corpses. Needless to say he got rid of them by one means or another because he 'preferred the petrels'. The owls bred or attempted to breed again right up until 1954, with several birds being deported in an effort to control them.

Buzzards had bred in years past and they have done so since, but not always successfully. We were treated to regular visits throughout the season. It never occurred to me that they might have bred because of the persistent harassment they suffered from the gulls, so what a pleasant surprise to find they had built a nest in North Haven when I revisited in 1980. It was well worth sacrificing swimming trips there in order to leave them in peace. In 1989, peregrine falcons took over the site and the buzzards moved to Hog Bay. Once, back in the 1930s, peregrines had bred in Dip Gully. How excited we were in the 1970s to see this falcon dashing across our skies, scimitar-winged, leaving a trail of confusion in its wake as it stooped long and low over the nesting birds. Recently, the buzzards moved away and the peregrines have bred in Steep Bay. Once again the old association of ravens and peregrines crops up, with the ravens next door in Twinlet in 1996. Buzzards, it seems like to keep their distance from both, which is perhaps why they once used Crab Bay as a nesting place.

Swallows and pied wagtails are both sporadic breeders on Skokholm but they never bred in our time, although both have done so since. Many times we saw swallows investigating the lighthouse coal shed, but evidently it wasn't quite right for them. One or two pairs of pied wagtails have bred in various island bays or in the walls around the Observatory over the years, but they didn't nest with us. We, at least, saw many of them on migration, with white, yellow and grey wagtails in lesser numbers. Similarly, both early and late in the season, we regularly disturbed snipe during our walks across the middle of the island. They were on passage or overwintering but, before our time, breeding had been suspected in 1927 and 1965. Shags we saw everyday and up to two pairs of them nested in the 1930s in Mad Bay. More recently a pair raised two young on the Bluffs. Cormorants were often recorded but they have never bred, although they are well established on other Welsh islands. To distinguish them from shags was something I learnt quickly. Difficult at first, but once you had the hang of it you wondered how you could ever have mixed them up. Shoveler and mallard ducks have also bred and our Muscovy ducks claimed the title of first breeding pair. In 1999 both shelduck and Canada geese attempted to breed.

CHAPTER 7

Of Auks, Gulls and Fulmars

The razorbill I am holding barely struggles. I have its head firmly but gently wedged under my left arm, whilst my left thumb and forefinger hold the right leg of the bird with the ring in place. The wings have been folded into the body and the bird is restrained by my clasping it against my middle. With the pliers in my right hand, I close the ring and then check that it moves freely on the leg without chafing. Soon I will replace the bird and watch it scuttle back to its chick, now crouching at the back of the cavity in the boulders, peeping softly. The chick is less than two days old and still has an egg tooth. Already it can stand, flap and preen itself. It will be brooded only for the first three or four days of its life and after that, although one adult may occasionally remain in attendance, much of the time it will be left completely on its own. On open ledge sites, one adult is always present, those chicks being more vulnerable. This adult has opted to stay by its offspring whilst I intrude and thus I have

Myself ringing a razorbill chick in the Quarry

been able to secure it and replace the worn monel ring with a new one made of a chromium nickel alloy which is more resistant to abrasion on the hard rock. These rings are three sided, specially designed to fit the flattened tarsus of a razorbill and the full number is engraved on each side rather than round the ring so that no figures are obscured by wear on the bottom. It already has a yellow darvic ring bearing a single, large letter and two large numbers etched in black, identifying it as an individual. The idea of the inscribed darvic ring is that it can be read easily through a telescope from a considerable distance when the bird is out in the open. It enables recognition without disturbance. I know from the rings on this bird that it is the same one breeding in this site as last year, and chances are that it has the same partner because Clare's figures show that nearly three-quarters of the birds retain the same mate in successive seasons.

This razorbill is particularly docile and very tolerant of handling, others are not and struggle for all they are worth. The position of the head means that if I am not careful I shall get bitten around the waist area, and I'm well aware that razorbills can hold on tight with their strong beaks, gripping like a pair of pincers, shaking and pinching the flesh viciously. You can't blame them; how are they to know that the knowledge gained from our studies may help in future conservation measures. If it does bite me, it'll be case of grin and bear it, because pulling away will only mean tearing the flesh,

Razorbills

my flesh! It is possible to prise apart the mandibles but then they have a way of lacerating the fingers! The rings are tough and springy and are more difficult to close than the old monel rings so that, after the last few days of ringing, the pliers have caused blisters on my hands. This doesn't help with the cooking.

Because the cavity is deep, the razorbill has been extracted with the use of a long wire hook fixed into a stout cane. The hook was eased gently beneath the bird, while it was crouching at the back facing away from me, and then looped round the leg joint. It was then pulled slowly towards the entrance, growling in protest, until I could get my hand round it to pull it out. Its body feels plump and firm, the feathers slightly oily, as they must be to prevent chilling in the cold water. The eye that looks into mine is soft and brown; and it is this eye, hidden in the dark feathers of the head, that must show well in a good razorbill photograph. The gape flashes rich, egg yolk yellow, a startling colour to be concealed within the shiny black, silver striped mandibles. Not surprisingly, it is used during displays of aggression against rivals or would-be predators. Do these bill stripes really emulate sand eels and teach the chick in its dark nesthole to peck at the bill? If they do, what a fantastic evolutionary feat!

Now I release the bird back into the cavity and watch it shuffle back to the chick. This latter is still a ball of fluffy, grey down, much paler on the head, and it is not yet ready for ringing. I shall need to come back here in a week or so, which I don't mind at all. The Bluffs are my exclusive territory, being otherwise out of bounds for the sake of the birds. Soaking up the sizzling June sunshine, I sit on the rocks and watch a group of non-breeding two and three year olds loafing on the rocks below me, with a few guillemots in their company. One razorbill has fish, it is most likely a breeder, but non-breeding loafers have been seen to carry fish. I look closely at one bird which lacks a white bill stripe. It has no monel and no plain coloured darvic ring to tell me in which year it was born. It is most likely a two year old because no one year olds have been recorded on land up till now, even though they have been seen very rarely on the sea. Plain colour rings have been used on the chicks since 1968, a different colour for each year, to give some idea of survival rates. Among the loafers, there may also be off duty birds with mates still incubating eggs. I study them again and try to detect differences in head size and thickness of neck which can be used to sex individuals in a pair. I can see differences but that means nothing because the birds are unlikely to be paired off.

Never does this task seem like work, even though it lasts for five or six weeks. I enjoy it immensely. My oil-stained, bleached smock gives off a strange odour in the intense heat, but it is not at all unpleasant when mixed with the salt air and general earthy smell of the island. The cobalt sea sparkling below, warm red, guano-splashed rocks, yellow ochre lichens, whirring wings of black and white; it all goes to my head and I say to myself in all honesty that there is nowhere else in the world I would rather be.

Razorbill ringing was not always like those diary notes of mine. Sometimes the weather was foul and the cliffs slippery and treacherous. There were occasions too, whilst climbing to reach birds that were nesting on open ledges, when I found myself in situations where I would (almost) rather have been anywhere else in the world than where I was. I began those more adventurous solitary climbs after looking at the razorbill chicks in Head Bay and wondering if it was feasible to try to reach them beneath their precipitous overhang. The rock was solid with several places to hold on to, but by then I loved a climbing challenge and reached the birds with no great difficulty, although with a wildly beating heart and a surge of adrenalin. Going out along the cracks to ring razorbills at the top of North Lighthouse Point, a sheer (150ft) slope with a long drop, had become a gentle stroll, so I could cope with heights all right.

In those places, it was a fairly safe bet as the rock was solid and secure, which is more than could be said for a foolhardy venture at Little Bay Point where the rocks and soil were loosely bound. Again, the chicks were ringed successfully, but I had gone down the cliff the wrong way, working on the basis that it was easier to get up than down. Not always so! For about forty minutes I sat petrified on a narrow ledge of soil not being able to go up nor down like a crag-bound sheep, heart thumping and knees weak, not a nice feeling when you are alone. The problem was that the loose material on the cliff gave no hold at all. In the end by digging my fingers in almost to the palms I literally clawed my way up, collapsing in a heap at the top with great relief and gratitude to whosoever controlled my destiny. That was probably my closest shave, not counting a fulmar-ringing expedition at the top of Twinlet which involved dangling on the end of a half-rotten rope held by Mike who was grinning facetiously. It must be said that at times our relationship was tricky and I am glad he didn't take advantage of that situation!

To render some assistance with the chicks that were impossible to reach without proper climbing gear, Martin Garnett and Euan Dunn came each year from the Edward Grey Institute at Oxford University. Those were excellent times, we scaled all the difficult places for razorbills and guillemots – Twinlet, Guillemot Point, Purple Point, the Jags etc., not to mention some recreational climbing and abseiling. We would dare each other to climb unaided the thin, vertical cracks on North Lighthouse Point, first with bare feet and then wearing wellingtons!

An expedition to the Stack razorbills was organised annually with Martin in the lead. His long legs enabled him to jump the channel, as the tide raced through below, in order to fix a rope and carabina for the rest of us to go across. No mishaps occurred, but looking at some of those sites several years after ringing had ceased, especially those I visited alone, filled me with horror. However, it was not just in the interest of science, as I enjoyed myself immensely!

For the razorbill census itself, a thorough egg count was undertaken usually in the first or second week in June when peak laying had occurred and when few eggs had been lost. The precise timing depended on whether the season was early, late or normal, but it was roughly about a month after the first egg had been laid (or at least found). It involved much scrambling around, a little climbing and an evening boat trip to count incubating birds in the few places where we could not see them. Mike had brought over to the island a very small boat with a one-and-a-half horsepower engine, not an ideal craft for the waters around the island! We were reluctant to go out in it on account of that, and also his inexperience. He was not deterred and went out several times, spinning out of control in the Wildgoose Race on one occasion and, on another, finding himself unable to return to South Haven because of the strong tide race off the aptly named Devil's Teeth. He survived both events unscathed. One day he set out to sea for an interview on the mainland in thick fog, simply pointing the boat in the right direction and depending on a compass he clutched in his hand. A suit and tie were neatly packed beside him in a plastic bag. We never thought we would see him again and began to plan our take over, but he survived that too, even attending the interview. I believe he acquired a little seamanship after a while and we felt more confident about accompanying him to count the hidden razorbills. I could never decide whether he was intrepid or naive. On reflection, I would say he was both!

The razorbills occupied a variety of nest sites – boulder scree, open ledges and even two enlarged rabbit burrows on the earthy slopes of Crab Bay overlooking the puffin colony. Lockley even found an egg laid among the coal stored on the cliff after the wreck! Scree sites required a thorough search until all the eggs were found. This applied especially to the massive tumble of boulders that lay in the base of the Quarry. Clues to the whereabouts of the sites were given by the accumulation of guano on the boulders around them. Sometimes, an occupied site where an egg had been lost could be identified by the amount of guano in the cavity. Ledge sites were easily monitored, one simply counted the incubating birds as we did from the boat. Evening was best as only incubating birds were present then, non breeders and off duty birds having left the ledges for the sea. They stayed at sea all night, the breeding birds returning to change over in the early morning. Clare had established this, and lots more data, like the number of changeovers per day, by undertaking night visits and dawn to dusk watches. She would set off with a bundle of sandwiches and drinks for a long sojourn in one of the hides.

After the first year (1973), which involved many visits to study the progress of eggs and chicks, I became familiar with all the study sites, just as Clare had been, making census work and monitoring the following years much easier for me. Fortunately, the visitors were able to share our enjoyment of the razorbill and guillemot colonies at

Razorbill chick

Twinlet and Guillemot Point, where they bred in good numbers on open ledges and could be viewed without causing disturbance.

The eggs of razorbills are white with varying amounts of brown or black blotching on a background of white, buff, even pink sometimes, and they are about twice the volume of a chicken's egg, making them proportionately large for the size of the bird. They are pointed like guillemots eggs and pivot a little. The shape was thought to have evolved to prevent them rolling off when knocked or pushed around accidentally by non breeders struggling to find a position on the ledge, but current thinking (Tim Birkhead 1997) is that it is more to do with the shape and positioning of the brood patch. Often there are small chippings and fragments of vegetation placed around the egg which may play a role in stopping them rolling around. Birds' eggs are undoubtedly one of nature's finest works of art, with a tremendous variety of exquisite markings and subtle colouring within and between species. Although the pattern of individual razorbills eggs differed from one to another, Clare showed by a series of photographs that each bird produced a similarly patterned egg each year. That way she was able to tell, after a couple of years, when the female of a pair at a certain site was a different bird to that of the previous year. The finding of a new razorbill egg always thrilled me, and each and every one was nearly as precious to me as to the birds themselves! The incubation period was long, at around thirty-five days, but Clare's figures showed that thirty per cent of eggs fail to hatch, some predated, some chilled and some simply disappeared. However, she acknowledged that her activities around the breeding colony may have caused a slight increase in egg loss, as perhaps did mine.

An interesting feature about razorbills is that they have two brood patches, one on each side of the breast. This is why they appear to lean over when incubating, with one wing drooping over the outside edge of the egg. Does that mean that they once could raise two chicks? Most of the double clutches recorded had been eggs laid by two different females or a replacement egg laid beside a chilled one. No two-egg clutches from one female were reported. However, in view of the mystery of the double brood patch, Clare experimented by giving some birds an extra chick. The twinning experiments showed that in very few cases did both chicks survive to fledging, although feeding did not appear to be a problem. Something must have changed since a long, long time ago.

Those kind of experiments raise ethical questions. How far should we go to satisfy our thirst for knowledge when there is no conceivable advantage? Similar questions arise with egg and chick swapping experiments to find out whether the birds recognize their own eggs and chicks.

My census figure from the egg count was around 425 pairs, with slight variations over the six years. The population had peaked in 1948 at 730 pairs. An auk wreck in winter 1969/70 caused a significant decrease from six hundred to below four hundred. There was a drop in 1990, but in 1996 the figure was again over five hundred pairs. They do not appear to have been directly affected by the *Sea Empress* oil pollution incident in February 1996, when 72 000 tons of crude oil and 360 tons of fuel oil were lost after the vessel grounded outside Milford Haven. However, only time will tell, as they and many guillemots were observed perilously close to it. It may be reasonable to expect a temporary decrease.

Whilst counting the razorbills on Northern Rocks, I would peer cautiously over the wooden barrier on to the ledges mentioned in Chapter Four, by then packed with breeding guillemots, some of them crouched or huddled in to the cliffs, incubating eggs. The guillemot ledges were often close beside or among the scattered and less dense razorbill colonies so that they could be counted at the same time. You could hear their distinctive crying from some way away, a kind of contented cawing interspersed by more rasping cackles when conflicts occurred. Guillemots were fascinating and all-absorbing to watch because of their intense social activity, nesting as they do cheek-by-jowl in a confined space. Greeting ceremonies, between pairs, appeasement postures and aggressiveness towards the all too curious non breeders could all be observed simultaneously. They were always bowing, especially those new arrivals wanting to avoid harmful physical confrontation. I considered the time well spent when watching guillemots; entertainment was guaranteed.

Their eggs were very variable in colour; I saw them a lovely turquoise blue, green, cream or white, that is if you could see the colour because they were usually lying in a bed of stinking guano. Guillemots ledges are notoriously filthy, but how could they be otherwise in such crowded conditions. Chicks were usually smeared in guano and so were we after a ringing session! In winter the muck was cleaned off the ledges by heavy rain and winds. The central part of a guillemot ledge was apparently the most protected from predators and was occupied by the older, more experienced birds. This seems to be the general rule for colonial nesting or roosting.

Around 110 pairs of guillemots bred with us, a slight increase on fifteen years ago. They appear to have increased more than twofold more recently. Not that long ago, the eggs of razorbills and guillemots were taken as food by fishermen and rabbiters whilst they worked or sheltered on the island.

The auk studies go on, but are now centred on Skomer. Intense behavioural studies have revealed other interesting facts, like a high incidence of extra marital copulation resulting in up to five per cent of guillemot chicks having other fathers than the accepted mates. Trapping on Skokholm and Skomer has revealed that auks from other colonies (e.g. Saltee, Bardsey and east Scotland) visit the Pembrokeshire Islands from time to time, although few stay to breed. However, a little immigration is needed to bank up the gene pool. It has also come to light that whilst some guillemots breed at four years of age, others will not breed until they are ten years old; and the same probably applies to razorbills. Much of this recently acquired information comes from studies supervised by Tim Birkhead, our one-time colleague on Skomer and now a professor.

It is a June afternoon in Crab Bay hide. There is constant bustle and activity from hundreds of puffins gathered around the rickety wooden hide. It is an enthralling spectacle, enough to make our appreciative visitors forget about their precarious position, perched low down on the steep, grassy slope of the bay. There is barely room for three of us, but the birds make it worth the discomfort of being cramped up inside. The bay is literally buzzing as dozens of puffins wheel round and round in large circles, some breaking off and coming into the land against the wind, using it skillfully as a natural brake. Bright orange legs and feet spread, reaching down for the flower-studded turf, and with a neat bounce they are grounded. They stand, immaculate in black and white feather, brazenly flaunting the bright colours on beak and face, the winter grey of which has turned a clean white. Their soft, red-brown eyes with scarlet orbital rings are set in a triangle of slate giving them a quizzical expression. Close by, a bird nibbles gently at its mate's yellow rosette, fixed like a little badge at the base of the mandible, and then induces a mutual clashing of bills which delights us. The green sea below is flecked with pied bodies bobbing on the choppy sea and through binoculars we note a small group facing each other, cocking bills.

Now that the disruption caused by our arrival has settled down, more puffins come in to land and stand about singly and in groups. Established breeding birds often dive straight into their burrows. Others, probably adolescents, are hesitant on landing and remain with wings upraised for a moment or two awaiting acceptance into a group. A bird plucks a sprig of sea campion and disappears into a deep burrow to greet its mate, sitting tightly perhaps on the plain white egg. A peace offering or decoration? Clouds of soil and dust erupt suddenly from another burrow, a bout of earth shovelling. We can now see orange feet kicking frantically; a puffin doing his (or her!) housework?. Great excitement! Out come the cameras as the first bird arrives with a beakful of fish, arranged in a head to tail pattern. One theory as to how this comes about is that the puffin swims forward into a school of fish turning its head from side to side as it snatches each one from the water. Ridges on the mandible and tongue hold the fish in place.

Puffin

There is silence here, save for the surf swishing on the rocks below and the occasional groan of a puffin. But now, a commotion arises on the far side of the bay, a puffin audience gathers to watch two birds fighting, bills interlocked, grappling together in frenzied activity until they start to tumble down the slope. They roll over and over until they reach the edge where they finally separate in mid air and head down to the sea.

Once in a while, a puffin launches itself and flutters, moth-like down to the sea: it is a display that often goes unnoticed. We see too, a razorbill, from a burrow at the top of the east cliff of the bay, fly down with exaggeratedly slow wing beats, a display called the 'butterfly flight'. Above the point where the razorbill flew from stands a herring gull waiting, we think, for the chance of snatching an easy meal from a puffin returning with fish. That individual is a specialist in kleptoparisitism, we recognise it from a small dark smudge on its face. The gull soon learns where to wait for a meal.

A distant puffin struts around wearing a pale green darvic ring with inscribed letters, one of the few remaining individually marked birds from a study many years ago. We attempt to read it with a telescope as this will contribute to our knowledge of adult survival and longevity. It is only just possible as the lettering has worn. Indeed few of them nowadays have these darvic rings, used in the 1960s. We return with just one colour ring number, but hopefully it will be a useful statistic.

The puffins had strongholds on the island, the largest colony being Crab Bay where they monopolized the seaward edges of the cliffs. There were other places where they could be found in high densities around the cliff tops, for example around Peter's Bay and Dumbell Bay on the Neck, and also around North Haven. A walk round the neck when the puffins were massing, highlighted many a fine June evening. They strutted about like crowds of little people, full of self importance, but always ready for a quick exodus down to the sea if you tried to get too close. The yellow light shone on their breasts and mellowed the black feathers on their backs to a glossy sepia. The golden green, sun-lashed turf was a dazzling contrast to the monochrome bodies and coloured beaks, and it worked brilliantly on camera.

Elsewhere puffins were thinly distributed around most of the periphery of the island, in many places overlapping with shearwater colonies. There was evidently competition between the two, and this was ably demonstrated by student Ruth Ashcroft on Skomer. She showed that it was possible for each to oust the other from a burrow. By creating a series of artificial burrows in an area of overlap, she showed the tendency of puffins to dominate those near the cliff edges and of shearwaters to monopolize those further inland.

How did we count the puffins? We didn't! To do an accurate census was impossible. Ringing and recapture techniques like those used for estimating shearwater populations were out of the question as puffins bred more or less round the whole island. Occupied puffin burrows could be identified by a ring of guano splodges around the entrance (shearwater burrows tended to have a long squirt of guano), but to attempt to count them was not feasible and anyway some of them nested deep in scree. The figure that had been quoted for many years was somewhere in the region of 2,500 pairs, a big decrease from Lockley's estimated 20,000 pairs. The total counts carried out by ourselves and other wardens early in the season, hopefully would serve as useful figures for comparison by which any significant increase or decrease would be noticed.

We made some effort to ring puffins, but the main study was taking place on Skomer. Sometimes we strung a mist net across Crab Bay on calm afternoons and had some success, catching a dozen or two on good days. We felt guilty when birds with fish flew into the net and lost their catch, but that didn't stop us collecting them and having whitebait or sand eels on toast later on! Incidentally, there is an average size difference between the fish caught by the three species of auk, although there is an overlap. Whilst they are held horizontally in the bills of razorbills and puffins, the thinner-billed guillemots hold fewer, larger fish lengthwise.

Ray handling a well grown puffin chick

Other attempts were made to catch the puffins with long-handled nets and elaborate noose systems (aimed at legs not necks) laid over the rocks, but I don't recall much success, at least not when the time spent made the effort worthwhile. It was more of a challenge than anything else!

The thousands of gulls nesting on our island gave me much pleasure, and even today I find the raucous cry of the herring gull a highly evocative sound that takes me back to the cliffs of Skokholm and bluebell-scented ocean air. Right at the beginning of the season, herring gulls were standing around on territory, always earlier than the more migratory lesser black-backed gulls. Save for the hours of darkness, there was seldom a time when a gull could not be heard crying somewhere. They are all undeniably handsome, singly and *en masse*, although some people would dispute that because they fail to see anything beautiful about anything so common. The fact that gulls can live alongside us, taking advantage of our buildings for nesting, and our careless rubbish disposal, always goes against them.

Herring Gull

We had a dilapidated hide at Bread Rock; this latter so named because islanders used to light a fire on it if they needed bread desperately. It overlooked a large lesser black-backed gull colony and had been used by a research worker. I spent some time there just watching the behaviour of these colonial birds. They were very regimentally spaced, hundreds of them standing or sitting in the bracken and bluebells, the lush green and blue background setting off their immaculate charcoal grey-and-white uniforms and formidable yellow beaks. It was a fine and lively composition effected by nature's whim. I was inspired by a book written by Niko Tinbergen and became fascinated by the language of postures and visual signals, soon realizing that there was more to a gull colony than a noisy mass of birds. Let the clamour die down and give them time to settle and the birds will interest and amuse you as they perform their various antics during the different stages of the nesting cycle – territory holding, pair bonding, nest building, incubation and chick rearing.

Gull census techniques were rather arduous because every nest had to be counted for each of the three species. For the cliff-nesting herring gulls we divided the island into three coastal sections and took one each, counting both empty nests and those holding clutches of two or three olive brown, blotched eggs. Sometimes we would find a nest with two normally-coloured eggs and one completely plain, usually of the palest, chalky blue. Then followed a few hours of up and down, in and out, along your section, counting all the way and never mind the screaming mass of gulls around your head. Wave your cane at them – they won't go away but it might stop that vicious one splitting your skull! They dive bombed you continually, and much more when they had chicks, but some were definitely worse than others. One herring gull from Spy Rock used to come out to meet us when we walked up the track and menace us with its persistent dive bombing until we were half way to the lighthouse. If you were alone, it was worse. Once, while ringing razorbills in Wreck Cove, I came away with a deep cut in my head. With blood running down behind my ear and down my neck, I felt angry because it had attacked me while I was ringing an adult razorbill and so was unable to fend it off. On reflection, who could blame it, it was only trying to defend its chick.

Whilst searching for nests on the cliffs, one often came across all kinds of odd bits of rubbish brought over to the island by the gulls. Plastic arms, legs and heads from dolls, tiny toy cowboys from cereal packets, rubber balls etc. Sometimes a gull would be seen flying around with an empty lager tin stuck on its foot! One of the strangest things I found was a six inch rubber worm, very fat and anaemic looking. It was bad enough picking it up anyway, but when it wriggled as I touched it, I jumped back and dropped my binoculars on a steep slope running down to the cliff edge. Throwing myself down to save them sliding down, I almost went over. Who would have known what had happened to me if I had, and if anyone did guess when they found me clutching the worm, I wonder if anyone would have tried to sue the manufacturers in this age of litigation! Wickedly, when I regained my composure, I decided to put it in the fried rice to give someone else a heart attack! That it nearly did. Such an innocent toy!

We arrived at totals of around 1250 herring gulls for the years we were there. From over 700 pairs in 1963, the population had risen and then stabilised since 1969. Not so the lesser black-backed gulls; they had increased enormously to around 3000 pairs spread over large areas of the interior of the island. The 1963 report states that there were only 200 birds present when records began, which presumably was when Lockley was in occupation. The increase had been fairly rapid since 500 pairs were recorded in 1963.

How did we count them? By taking advantage of fifteen energetic schoolboys who regarded it as a welcome break from drawing limpet movement graphs or searching for elusive topshells on the beach! We fed them mountains of chips beforehand (the boys, not the gulls!) to build up their energy levels. They took part with great enthusiasm and much hilarity and, apart from water fights, I don't think they enjoyed anything on the island more. They were spread out in a line along one edge of the largest colony in the middle of the island and marched forward to the other end like a military invasion, except that the purpose was more innocent (smaller colonies were counted by ourselves later). The boys were kept on a level with each other to count nests, pointing at each one so that their neighbours didn't include it in their total. Naturally there was a great commotion among the gulls, which hung in a great, screaming cloud above us and made sure there was much washing of clothes to be done on our return! They even bickered amongst themselves and stole each other's eggs in the confusion, flying in to snatch them, then dropping them and spilling the ghastly contents on the ground. Their cannibalistic tendencies were both surprising and sickening to those people who had never witnessed that kind of extreme behaviour directed at one's own kind (excluding man of course). This predation was generally considered a good thing as their rising numbers had been giving cause for concern. Indeed, along with the Skomer wardens we were asked to conduct some control measures, like egg pricking and nest raking, but whatever we did (and it was very labour intensive), the same numbers returned every year.

Each year, we collected hundreds of eggs from the lesser black back gull colonies to make delicious omlettes and cakes. We did that brandishing a bucket and a stout cane! The chosen plot was first cleared of eggs and from then on we collected daily. The gulls laid up to twelve eggs before they finally gave up sometime in late June. The eggs were placed in a bucket of water to check that they were not developing; as long as they sank to the bottom they were OK. The spectacle of one of our visitors setting out with great determination to collect eggs for us, wearing a metal colander on his head and with a stick wedged down the back of his shirt supporting a rattling lager can, lingers in my memory. We did a good line in eccentrics! The farming of gulls eggs was not a necessity for us, but a luxury! When Peter Condor was warden, chicken's eggs were rationed and they were highly valued.

Great black-backed gulls were easy to count. They built their nests on isolated rocky outcrops like the Devil's Teeth, the Tabernacle or the Stack, and in any case there were only around eight pairs each year. These gulls do however nest colonially on other islands. Under instruction, we attempted to control them, either by taking eggs (which gave me an excuse to climb the Devil's Teeth) or, I hesitate to say, by shooting them. I am ashamed to say I participated in the latter. My aim was good, but perhaps my principles were not so good then. Up until then control seemed to have been the pol-

Herring Gull nest

icy, but not now for numbers have risen and it appears that many chicks fledge each year (52 from 37 pairs in 1996). Prior to 1973, even with control measures, the population was more or less stable, although back in 1940, the island held 60 pairs. As large predators, they took puffins, shearwaters and rabbits regularly and some were fish eaters. Judging by my examination of the debris lying around the nests, each pair specialised in particular prey items. Very often we watched one swallow a small rabbit whole. Its throat would become hugely distended and it would gulp several times as if it was choking. Sometimes the grisly remains of chicks were found in their pellets complete with rings, or even a whole shearwater head!

Gull chick ringing was quite intensive. We advanced through the colony of lesser black backs with five or six hundred rings each year, and it could not really be described as a pleasant task and nor were we a pleasant sight at the end of it. It was inevitably a hot sunny day, the chicks would be hidden in family groups of two or three in the bracken, half feather and half down, quite ugly and squarking miserably as we held them. Only the very small ones were pretty, with fluffy, greyish gold down spotted with black, particularly around the head. Overhead the screaming parents would dive down relentlessly and aim their well-directed excreta over our crouching forms. We ended up smelling worse than a guillemot ledge. In July and August each year, a few chicks became prematurely separated from the adults by storms, or by some kind of misadventure, and then they would turn up weak and emaciated around the buildings. They rarely survived and were often in such a bad state that it was kinder to put them down.

Herring gull chicks were sought out on the cliff slopes in a similar way and picked out of rocky crevices to be ringed. We had to take special care that they didn't inadvertantly leap off the cliff because of our sudden appearance. Herring gulls and lesser black backs occasionally interbred, but as there had been egg swapping experiments in the past, we were never sure it was a natural occurrence as the chick would have imprinted on the wrong parents. The two species did indeed mix where the lesser black-backed colonies reached the cliff edge. A few hybrids were seen on the island and one that paired up with a herring gull produced chicks. The hybrids had intermediate coloured backs and legs that were neither pink nor yellow, but the best way to tell them apart was that they had blue rings! The two species form part of a genetic cline and some researchers maintain that they should not be treated as separate species.

Another time when I enjoyed watching the gulls was rubbish-tipping time, when our dustbins were full. The chickens ate the food waste, vegetable waste we composted, and miraculously we hardly had any plastic waste. Not even any plastic bags or wrapping on the vegetables! Life was almost plastic free and the better for it. What we did have was lots of discarded tins that needed dumping and they went into the sea where they corroded and we hoped, disappeared. A convenient tipping place was off the end of the iron gantry just round the corner from South Haven. We would take the dustbins there on the dumper, and then carry them one by one out to the end and tip them over. It's surprising that we never went over with them! The gulls knew long before we arrived what was going to happen and assembled very quickly for any titbits that lurked among the general rubbish. Below us, hundreds of them would swoop down over a light green, froth ridden sea; it became a kaleidoscope of dark and light grey wings, white heads grabbing and stabbing for a share, yellow bills tussling over a morsel of mouldy bread, pink and yellow legs dangling and clawing. Their clumsy, shallow dives amused us. In their midst would be one or two greater black backs, bullying and driving away their smaller cousins, their wings longer and blacker, their cries deeper and their manner more imperious. Juveniles and sub-adults hung around on the edge of the throng awaiting their chance to grab. I tried to photograph it, thinking it inspiration for an abstract painting, but it has never been put to the test.

Fulmar petrels have been mentioned in a previous chapter. We had little option but to count the chicks on the ledges. It was the only way to be certain of breeding because there were so many sub-adults sitting around on ledges looking just like breeding pairs. In any given area, one always had the impression that there were many more birds breeding than there actually were. They sat so tight that it was impossible to see if they had an egg or not. Fulmars have to reach the age of at least eight years before they are able to breed. Possibly, some of them lost eggs and escaped our notice. The chicks were comical lumps of white down to begin with, and then they grew on to look just like the adults by the time they fledged in September/October time. Twelve to fifteen pairs bred with us. Their spread south has already been commented on, but for the record they first bred in 1967, albeit unsuccessfully. In 1968, five young fledged from five pairs. Before 1967 they had prospected the island for no less than thirty years.

CHAPTER 8

Night Birds

Night was falling fast. Tilley lamps glowed in the windows of the Cottage whilst a babble of excited voices issued through the open door. Torches were thrust in pockets and the night's expedition was ready.

Fog enveloped the small group of figures as they set off down the track towards the western end of the island, their lamps throwing gross shadows across the ground. Outcrops of rocks were amplified by the fog and loomed up in the Cutting like monstrous ghouls. Pale patches of lichen shone out like weird disfigurements. From the waist-high bracken skirting the road and open places came anonymous scufflings. No moon interfered with the intense darkness and the fog obliterated any trace of starlight. These conditions were paramount to the success of the expedition. The night was ideal and they could expect hundreds, if not thousands on such a black night in July.

On they went, footsteps crunching in the gravel, excitement mounting with each little distance covered. Rabbits scuttled away nervously and a frog, the colour of the red earth, squatted by the track soaking up the damp air. Queer-shaped outcrops of pitted red sandstone marked their steady progress, and fragments of ancient walls spoke of past husbandry.

Through the murk came the mournful wail of the foghorn, but it was still some time before a subdued flash of red light foretold the proximity of the lighthouse. The sweet aroma of campion flowers hung in the air and mingled with the smell of the earth. From below came the ominous sound of waves crashing on to the cliffs hinting of wild seas, jagged rocks and shipwrecks.

Suddenly a devilish cry pierced the darkness, followed shortly by the thud of a body hitting the ground. Shouts of 'there! over there!' accompanied the random flashing of torches exploring the ground. Then gradually more cries came until the air was filled with a cacophany of demoniac wailing and choking. Soon the densely burrowed earth was littered with softly feathered bodies, shuffling, scrabbling or else just crouching. The Manx shearwaters were in. Some made straight for the safety of their own burrows, others, the adolescents, loafed on the surface with no burrow to retreat to and became mesmerized by the bright torchlight cast on them. Pigeon-sized, their black and white bodies glowed with an oily lustre and their dark, alert eyes were bright as an ocean's reflection. It was their island; they had colonized long ago and outnumbered the human occupants by tens of thousands.

Manx Shearwater by torchlight

Their other home was the Atlantic Ocean, north and south, where they were in their true element. From the island on a rough day, they could be seen gliding, banking and shearing the waves on long, narrow wings adapted for long distance flying; now black, now white, wheeling and turning, skilfully making use of updraughts generated by the air flow over the water. The rougher the sea, the better they mastered it. Earlier that evening, before the fog had blotted out the mainland, rafts of many thousands had been seen gathering on the sea between the islands, waiting for darkness in order to make their landfall. In this way they avoided the attentions of marauding gulls. They floated in idle serenity; a great dark cloud on a silver sea, until one of their number rose languidly, inducing wave after wave to take to the air until the whole mass were winging across a rose-tinted sky. Several times they rose and settled again whilst circling the islands.

They were ill-adapted for movement on land, with legs set far back on their bodies for swimming, but allowing only a clumsy, shuffling gait on the ground. They were even unable to adopt the common upright stance of most birds and tended to topple forwards, making them especially vulnerable to predation. Their wings were spread for balance and support when they needed to climb to rocky summits to launch themselves on windless nights. This was achieved with the aid of sharp claws to grip the rock and hooked bills to haul them up almost vertical faces. Wall Rock was an excellent launching pad. They were also capable of using their half opened wings to 'fly' underwater in pursuit of fish. The elliptical shape of the tarsi was thought to minimize water resistance. It was imperative for them to come onshore to breed, and remote islands like Skokholm and Skomer were relatively safe since they were without mammalian predators (rats, cats and mustelids). No harm was meant by those spellbound observers, they were only there to watch and wonder. The birds would be quite safe until the dawn broke.

The bedlam continued; they filled the night air with their weird wailing - 'cocklollie cocklollie', each call slightly different to the next. The listeners discerned easily the higher pitched, clearer call of the male birds in the air as against the throaty and less commonly heard female voice. Some birds called from burrows, single males hoping to entice prospecting females to visit their newly acquired burrows. Their strange cries were somewhat muffled by the earth and it is no wonder that stories are told of workmen coming to the islands in the past and being driven mad overnight by this unearthly chorus, believing it to be the spirits of devils. What stranger would know that a bird was capable of uttering such supernatural sounds?

The watchers had chosen the time of their visit well; they knew that on moonlit nights few birds came in, and those that did were adults come to relieve mates, hungry after several days incubating, or to feed their solitary chicks. No torches were needed on such nights for the moon set the sea shimmering and the black outline of the mainland was clearly visible. There was silence then save for the occasional whirring of wings cutting the air.

By midnight, birds were calling from every quarter of the island. A group of upturned faces gazed at the flying forms caught momentarily in the red, rotating lightbeams. The observers were gathered on the track taking a final look round before making their way homewards guided by the dying light of the Tilley, all feelings of tiredness and hunger masked by their high spirits.

Above is a typical account of our visitors' experience of the main shearwater colony at night after ringing had ceased in 1976. Before that however, things were rather different. The ongoing ringing programme meant that we were actively involved in working with them, and this was both useful and rewarding. Ringing studies had already provided a means of estimating the population size, but it also brought to light much interesting information that may help to benefit the species in the future. From our point of view, it gave us a real insight into the shearwater's life history, while at the same time raising many questions, as we shall see.

The difficulties of a census are obvious. There was no question of counting burrows, even though they were sometimes recognizable by the guano splash outside, or by the well-defined tramlines made by shuffling feet. Burrows often formed a network of tunnels with chambers leading off which could have been occupied by rabbits as well as shearwaters. One entrance could have been used by more than one pair of shearwaters, and what of the ones that nest in scree? Simple ringing and retrapping data was unreliable because non breeders were caught more often. Lockley first estimated ten thousand birds and later amended this to ten thousand pairs. Later, two separate statistical studies were carried out, first by Mike Harris and then later by Chris Perrins, both in the 1960s. The first was based on the ringing of fledglings and the daily recovery rate of ringed corpses, and the second involved the retrapping of fledglings ringed in their burrows by day. Incredibly, both gave a rough figure of thirty-five thousand pairs. Chris Perrins held that this was more due to coincidence than accuracy, and that view was supported by Mike Brooke. However arbitrary the figure, and it certainly had to be regarded as a vague estimate, it seemed to signify an increase since Lockley's day. Certainly, in the days of ploughing there would have been less opportunity for burrowing and, even now, shearwaters are sparsely distributed in the old fields. The fact that the age of first breeding rose over the years suggested that the population had reached saturation point, with territory a limiting factor. Indeed, Mike's research into burrow competition suggested that this was a contributary factor to limiting the population size. He recorded territorial fighting, persistent attempts to re-enter blocked burrows, several incidents of egg laying by two females in the same burrow and a great readiness to occupy artificially created burrows by probable first-time breeders. Rabbits compete for burrows, starting to breed just as the shearwaters return. All these facts indicate that it is not easy for a Manx shearwater to acquire a breeding burrow on Skokholm. No new population estimates, have been forthcoming, but this is pretty well an impossibility with the current lack of ringing, since nocturnal burrow nesting birds are the most difficult to census. Overall, there was thought to be a general increase in North Atlantic populations.

Thus, on a good night in July, a phenomenal number of shearwaters must have been present. The estimated number of pairs breeding was in the region of thirty to forty thousand, and many would have had chicks in burrows at that time. Thousands of non-breeders were also present including two, three, four and five year olds. The age of first breeding was between six and nine years. All first-summer birds remained at sea. These figures imply that there could have been somewhere in the region of 100 000 birds present on such a night.

For four years of the six we spent on the island, as many birds as possible had to be procured and ringed, or re-ringed due to salt water abrasion of the original ring. That meant that we readily accepted help from our guests who were mostly very willing. For ringing adults and sub-adults in July and again for the chicks in August and September, we had help from two or three shearwater 'slaves', some of them fresh from Oxford. Martin Garnett and Euan Dunn were annual stalwarts and we welcomed them both for their work and for entertainment value (banjos and handstands come to mind!). I have visions of Euan standing with a sweaterful of thirty odd birds when his trousers suddenly fell down. The birds had their revenge! Indeed, 'shearwatering' was a regular and popular occurrence, almost nightly in fact when the weather and the moon (lack of) allowed. In wet weather the reason we abstained was for the sake of the birds, not ourselves!

'Shearwatering' was ongoing from the beginning of the season, as some birds had already arrived by mid-March, and it lasted nearly to the end, with the last chick leaving in mid to late October. However, it is with great nostalgia that I look back on it, as do perhaps many of the visitors for whom it was certainly a novel experience. Those long nights spent in the company of birds were hard work, but stimulating. It seemed a long trudge back to the buildings, sometimes as late as three o'clock in the morning, and although we were tired and ready for bed, food and drink were first on the agenda. 'First breakfast' we called it and it was often pretty substantial, like beans on toast. There is something very special about being out at night working with wildlife; it is a world that is closed to the majority of people, and we were privileged.

As to the method, the Observatory possessed a number of head torches, worn in the manner of mining lamps, and fixed on to the head by means of a piece of thick elastic. The torches were good old fashioned metal, not plastic, and I have a scar to prove it where the metal band slipped on to my nose cutting it deeply! They were run on batteries contained in a metal box which hooked over the waistband or was put in a large pocket. Maximum production was expected from staff and the following is an account of how we achieved it.

We would don the biggest, baggiest sweater that we owned, preferably one that was three times too large, and then tie a string around it at waist level. It needed to have a loose neck. It only requires a little imagination to work out the rest. Arriving at the main colony (sometimes we limbered up in Crab Bay first), we would stealthily approach a grounded shearwater whilst dazzling it with our head-torch. If it stayed put, we bent down slowly and then made a grab for it with one hand, keeping the wings folded against the body so as not to damage it. The bigger your hands the

Myself 'shearwatering'

easier it was. To coin a phrase we then stuffed them up our jumpers! Or rather down them via the neck. The number it was possible to collect depended mainly on the capacity of the jumper, plus your agility and experience. The birds came to no harm in there, indeed they probably thought they were inside a crowded burrow. Some sat quietly, others shuffled around. Most of them behaved perfectly, provided you were well padded beneath the sweater! My cousin accidentally put one inside his shirt and, on returning home, had a hard time explaining to his wife all the scratches on his chest! Rarely, adult shearwaters regurgitated the semi-digested fish meal prepared for the chick, but when they did, never mind the unpleasantness, you couldn't help feeling guilty about the effort of collecting it being wasted. It was possible to carry fifteen birds comfortably, thirty was the record, but for most people it was a lot less. We must have looked very strange indeed judging by the faces of newly recruited lighthouse keepers looking on. Oversize, squawking birdwatchers with heaving, gyrating stomachs!

The full load was taken to the ringer (usually Mike) who sat by the lighthouse shed and received the birds for processing. Someone was delegated to write, usually a person who was no good at catching. Mike had to work quickly on a good night, either ringing, re-ringing or reading retraps. Sometimes Ray or myself disappeared into the lighthouse for a breather, but Mike was an astute judge of time and we didn't push our luck. Lack of sleep crept up on us, and while at first we were very keen, we soon prayed for rain (or a big moon) to stop play.

The following morning one of us would be in the ringing room with Mike to update the card index for the previous night's catch. A great proportion of the birds were ringed already and so it was a time-consuming business, usually conducted between bouts of yawning. Even by 1963, nearly 90 000 birds had been ringed on the island, beginning, of course, with Lockley's pioneer studies in the 1930s, although they were curtailed by the war and the rings quickly became worn and lost. Monel which is a tough alloy was first used for rings in 1958. With the involvement of the Edward Grey Institute in 1963, there was a huge ringing effort concentrating on fledglings and, between then and when we arrived on the island, 86 000 had been ringed. The kind of information that has come out of this intensive work includes such complex issues as population dynamics, mortality rates for adults and chicks and age of first breeding. In conjunction with studies on Skomer, Mike has been able to show that most males return to their natal colony (Skokholm), but half the females which survive to breeding age emigrate to Skomer. Over there, the population is several times that of Skokholm, making the actual recovery of Skokholm-bred females a rare occurrence. For the record, the oldest known Skokholm shearwater was at least thirty-two years old in 1976, the last year of ringing and retrapping.

The incubation period for the egg was long at fifty-one days, and this was followed by an even longer period, seventy-one days, between hatching and fledging. Just prior to fledging which occurred after desertion by their parents, the chicks spent several nights sitting around on the ground outside their burrows giving us plenty of time to find and ring them. During this venture into the outside world, they stretched their legs and flapped vigorously, sometimes moving many metres away from their burrows.

Shearwater chick ringing was an intensive operation and we tried for as many as possible. Their breeding was not very synchronized and fledging extended over a period of many weeks, beginning roughly around 20 August. One night, over 1000 shearwaters were ringed. We started in Crab Bay, made our way to the lighthouse, spent most of our time in the main colony and then worked our way down the west coast to North Haven. Even the Neck was searched sometimes. Incredibly, you could tell a chick by the way it felt, plump, soft and fluffy, even though it looked just like a neat replica of the adult. They actually weighed about half as much again. Research has shown that heavier chicks are more likely to survive. Some of them found outside the burrows still had small patches of grey down on the neck and head like a ruff, or else a patch in the region of the vent. Their plumage was very fresh, the feathers being in perfect order, the black very black and the white (save for dirt), very white. Shearwater's legs and feet are basically a fleshy pink colour, which looks very new and bright in the chicks. There was no risk of displacement with collecting these fledglings because they had plenty of time to find a burrow in which to conceal themselves before daylight. We left any that had appreciable amounts of down as they were probably still being fed. Nearly 7000 were ringed in 1973 and a few less in other years.

Whilst handling these young shearwaters, I was always acutely aware that they were about to undertake an immense journey southwards across the Equator to the South

Atlantic where they wintered in the coastal waters off South America, and these chicks went alone since the adults had already departed. From the confines of a dark burrow, across thousands of miles of sea to the opposite hemisphere; that certainly added a sense of awe and wonder to their life cycle, fascinating as it already was. Why did they go that far? It has been suggested, and it seems likely, that warmer seas south of the temperate regions offer little feeding opportunity and the shearwaters need to go further south, as far as Brazil, for their food requirements to be met.

Ringing has shown that it is possible for the young bird to complete the journey of over 9000 kilometres in an incredible thirteen to fourteen days. That they had been deserted, left to go hungry and find their own way to the sea, is food for thought, but that they should inherit or acquire the navigational skills required for such a rapid migration is phenomenal. Were those lonely nights spent under the stars really a mechanism by which the celestial pattern became integrated into a complex navigational system? If they were, then such journeys to and from their natal colony and wintering grounds became feasible perhaps, but no less incredible. Many researchers now believe this is the case, but accept that other aids such as the sun and the earth's magnetic field are likely to play a part. Following homing experiments by Lockley earlier on, Geoffery Mathews in the 1950s conducted some field research using breeding shearwaters from Skokholm. He demonstated clearly their homing ability, and also showed that the sun was a useful factor in the reorientation of the birds when they were released inland in fine weather. A colleague, who was present at one of his lectures, remembers being told that the birds were first placed on a record turntable to disorientate them! Thus true navigational ability in birds was first properly tested and verified using shearwaters from Skokholm. Incidentally, because these experiments involved taking incubating birds, the hatching success which followed, demonstrated the remarkable resistance of the egg to chilling.

There had been many recoveries of ringed birds from Brazil and Argentina over the years, and they continued to come in during our years there. Other places of recovery had been the Azores, Bermuda and Ghana in Africa. The African recoveries imply that they follow the eastern Atlantic seaboard in their migration southwards before crossing to the South American coast. Recoveries also came from as far away as the Bay of Biscay during the early part of the breeding season, proving that some birds (mostly pre-egg laying females) did go that far to feed on the sardine shoals which migrate northwards as the summer progresses. Most exciting are the recoveries implying that Skokholm birds have been involved in the colonisation of Middle Lawn Island, in Newfoundland, starting in 1976–77.

While some chicks achieve their journey to the sea by flying, most travel over the ground and we used to find many gone astray on their way, unable to find a burrow to hide in. They would be picked up from corners around the buildings in the daylight, poor lost things, confused and huddled up against a wall from which they could find no escape route. One day, I found one of my chickens gazing down on one, and well it might for a domestic chicken's life is a poor one in comparison. We would place the bird down a burrow as near to the sea as was convenient and be certain it would leave safely that night.

The chick's normal introduction to daylight is on the morning after fledging when it is well out to sea, but there was another more insidious reason for a fledgling to be abroad in daylight and that was the prevalence of a mysterious disease called 'puffinosis'. Nothing to do with puffins – more to do with *Puffinus puffinus*, the Manx shearwater. The afflicted birds were a sorry sight with badly blistered feet, possibly conjuntivitis and generally in bad condition. Many exhibited partial paralysis, but it remains uncertain whether this is due to puffinosis or whether it is a symptom of another disease. Only the birds nesting in certain areas seemed to get affected and the worst areas were in the centre of the island. More recent research on Skomer has indicated that the disease is prevalent in damp areas, and indeed that seemed to be the case on Skokholm. Sometimes the birds were found dead; we didn't ring the sick ones as the disease appeared to be fatal. Few adults and nestlings appeared to catch it and, so far as is known, it is only birds from those two Pembrokeshire islands that are affected. As yet no agent has been found for transmitting the disease, but research points to a pathogen being responsible. Bracken mites have long been suspected to play a host role, but that has yet to be proved. We suffered badly from being bitten by these invisible little devils ourselves and checked our feet regularly for blisters! It is not considered that the mortality caused by puffinosis is a threat to the population.

The shearwaters suffered predation by other birds. Ravens, peregrines and buzzards took their toll, but it was mostly the gulls which were responsible for the corpses we collected. Over 1000 corpses were picked up each year, with the numbers rising in September every year as the fledglings emerged. The total annual figure included around 900 adults which, according to statistics worked out by Mike, represents ten per cent of the annual mortality rate and, in a stable colony, he concludes that this is not likely to adversely affect the population.

Clearly, adopting the nocturnal habit is likely to reduce the risk of predation considerably. But how did the birds find their own burrows as they flew in to the island? Our efforts mostly went into ringing, but there were times in those latter years when we had more time to watch them and ponder these questions. On the blackest of nights, birds were seen to land within a few metres or less of their burrow, to scuttle straight towards it. Whether they used visual clues, smell or some other unknown sense seemed an

Burrows in the main Shearwater colony

absolute mystery to us in those days, but some of Mike's experiments shed a little light on the matter.

One day his enthusiasm for decorating seemed to have gone beyond the bounds of common sense. He was seen squatting outside his room avidly painting a number of cardboard boxes with white emulsion. We decided to leave him be and await developments. We noticed tunnel-shaped holes had been cut in the boxes. Soon they appeared scattered about in the shearwater colonies, placed upside down over burrow openings. The mystery deepened, but Mike's sanity remained intact and we guessed that it had something to do with testing the bird's use of visual aids for burrow location. If this was the case, at least some of them would be caught in traps placed inside the boxes when, some time later, they were moved a little way away from the entrance. A significant number did indeed get caught that way, and so the results suggested that vision was at least one factor involved. Birds did not always call from burrows, so attraction by a mate's call was ruled out and experiments by other students more recently have shown that smell has no role in burrow location either. Mike's boxes raised many comments from visitors and led to interesting discussions taking place at the dinner table. Has anyone taken up his theory of the possible use of proprioception (the sense of registering the use of limbs over a familiar pathway in the dark) I wonder?

Things changed dramatically for the birds (and for us) when ringing stopped. Basically they were left in peace, there was no need for any handling apart from rescuing a bird or lifting a sod to show our visitors a downy chick. I felt by then that enough was enough and it was for the best. Certainly the ground had become very eroded by trampling, indeed parts of it were virtually bereft of any vegetation at all, and no-one could help falling through burrows either. Similarly, it has been shown by a student on Rhum that the disturbance caused by frequent visits to study burrows leads to a higher incidence of eggs being abandoned. However, they are hardy, and as long as the island ecology is fairly stable (rabbit populations etc.) there seems to be no threat to the birds at present. Neither do they suffer badly from flooding as do the shearwaters on the Hebridean islands where rainfall is higher. They are safer in fact on Skokholm than they were years ago when they were netted on the cliff edges for lobster pot bait! This practice was curtailed in 1880 by the passing of the Wild Bird Protection Act.

Skokholm must be one of the most densely populated islands in Britain as regards wildlife. The shearwater burrows are more dense than on Skomer, although the latter's population is considerably higher. Skokholm is teeming with life in the summer months, and not far off it during the winter as you will see in a later chapter. A story is told of a gravid rat that leapt from a boat on to Skomer but was killed by a very accurately aimed pebble. If that story is true and the rat had not been killed, that island, and perhaps nearby Skokholm too, may have suffered the same fate as the Calf of Man where the shearwater population was decimated by the introduction of rats in the late eighteenth century. Other burrow-nesting birds would have suffered a similar fate. Islands plagued with rats, cats or ferrets are always ecological disaster zones.

Out of his work on shearwaters, Mike acquired a PhD and also produced a splendid monograph on the Manx shearwater published by Poyser (1990). Much of the technical information in this chapter was taken from this book which I recommend for further reading.

Another exodus would take place on the first fine evening in May, this time just as dusk was falling and before the arrival of the shearwaters. We did not go far; we would stroll only to the gateposts just beyond the Knoll, which was all that was necessary, to see the first storm petrel of the year. Eerily silhouetted against the twilight sky, the gateposts were said to mark the grave of two elderly folk who lived and died on the island. They were reputed to have been so fond of the island that they wished to be buried on it.

This time no unearthly cry was to herald the arrival of the first petrel, indeed there was normally no sound at all save perhaps the distant surf. Our eyes were directed upwards at the sky, alert and searching for tiny dark wings flickering against the fast diminishing western glow. We were looking for a mere sprite of a bird, homing in to a familiar cavity in the wall, where the previous year it may have left a full grown chick to find its own way to the sea. Its flight would be erratic like that of a bat, and then with a low swoop it would silently disappear into a crack in the wall. If we stayed we might be lucky and hear its fairy-like chuckling. It is another sound difficult to describe; a long series of bubbling notes rising and falling, and impossible to forget. I can close my eyes anytime and hear it, as I can a shearwater.

How fanciful were these small petrels, flying in so secretively from the ocean in order to breed on our island. We would try to catch one in a torchbeam so that our visitors could glimpse the elusive white rump, which surely provides visual contact in the night or on the dark background of the sea. They were often no more than a black, flickering shadow no larger than a swallow, a nightime will-o'-the-wisp.

Arriving about the last week in April, their numbers increased until they peaked in July and August when many sub-adults came visiting. Between five and seven thousand pairs were estimated to breed on Skokholm, a figure drawn from the ringing studies undertaken by Derek Scott between 1966 and 1969. It was a much larger population than had previously been thought. It always seemed an incredible number to me, and it shows the value of ringing when no other census technique is feasible. Never in all those years did I see a storm petrel on the sea from the island during the day, although Mike once saw one off the Stack in a gale. Since living in Cornwall and seawatching regularly, I understand the difficulty of picking up these tiny birds in a rough sea even with a good telescope of thirty-times magnification. You have to work hard at it, harder than I realized then.

The best and most exciting place to see petrels at night was in the island quarry where many hundreds nested in the piles of rocky scree. We would lead our visitor group to the lighthouse, and then across a grassy track between shearwater burrows to a cryptic pathway going down through the boulders into the quarry. No health and safety rules in those days! It was a great adventure to them, and once there we would sit in a group with our torches out and wait for the 'flight of the storm petrel'. This happens to be the title of a most excellent book written by Ronald Lockley. As darkness fell and the gulls ceased their cackling, the line of white surf crashing on to the rocks below would take on a luminescent quality. Ghostly red beams from the lighthouse searching the inky skies didn't interfere with us, and served to enhance the novelty of the experience for most people. They spoke to each other in whispers and looked about anxiously lest they were to be disappointed, but they seldom were.

Soon the petrels were in, flying round and round in large circles, some alighting on the rocks and pattering quickly into burrows, others returning to the ocean. Never did they sit around in the open like shearwaters, giving us a chance to see them properly. It was safer for these smaller petrels to conceal themselves immediately from potential

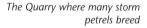

The Quarry where many storm petrels breed

predators. Neither do the chicks sit around before the night of fledging. On some nights in July and August there were dozens of them in the air, flitting and swooping around our heads in an aerial ballet. Sometimes you could hear a faint whickering sound as they chased each other round, but mostly they were silent. We would watch for a while in the darkness and then try catching them in our torchbeams. They had a pleasant oily smell about them, which hung faintly in the air with a hint of sweetness. The oil is derived from their planktonic food and may serve purposes other than water-proofing the plumage, such as location of burrows and mate recognition. The odour emanated strongly from the entrances to the nest cavities, deep in the stones, giving away their secret occupants. Even the chicks were fed on a regurgitated oily soup. Most nests were several feet in, and it was seldom that you could look in at a sitting bird.

In the early years of ringing, we would set up a mist net across a level area in the quarry and many storm petrels were caught and ringed. There was a special recess in which we hid a Tilley lamp so that it didn't interfere with the flight of the birds, and in there they were processed and handed out for release. Storm petrels sat quietly in the folds of the net and were no problem to extract. The only problem was to keep your balance on the rocks whilst taking them out! Some of our nervous visitors were horrified the next day, when they saw in daylight where they had been taken the night before. We were lucky, we had no accidents during those nocturnal forays.

One June night in 1976, we heard a strange clacking call echoing around the quarry, one that we had not heard before. The bird was evidently in flight and was identified as a Leach's petrel by someone familiar with the sound, but we only actually saw a silhouette. It was south of its normal breeding range. The first one caught on the island was in 1966, but Lockley described hearing one among the storm petrels many years before that. It was exciting for us, but I never saw this bird properly until my sea-watching days began in Cornwall.

Such was the unusual atmosphere in the quarry that I took my sleeping bag there on several occasions and stayed the night in order to see the birds leave in the early hours of the morning, and also just for the experience. It was very hard to find a niche among the stones in which to be reasonably comfortable, but it was possible, just. Once, at first light, I saw a great black-backed gull ominously hanging around, hoping to catch the late-goers perhaps? I also saw gulls wandering in the shearwater colony on my way back, peering into burrows for chicks lingering near the entrances. In one case it was an adult gull with a juvenile alongside it learning the trade!

It was not necessary to go far from the buildings to see a storm petrel, as they were widely spread across the island. Just a few yards from the Observatory, an exceptionally tolerant petrel nested each year in a nest box placed in a wall at Coal Corner. The

Storm petrels

door could easily be removed to expose the bird, or later the chick, for the benefit of our visitors, if they hadn't seen one otherwise. Mostly we kept it quiet. Several of those boxes had been put in the walls by a student, but apparently they were unsuccessful. We also went petrel hunting in North Haven and in Crab Bay where they nested in scree beneath the cliffs. Visitors never flinched about descending Crab Bay because, as with the quarry, they couldn't see where they were going! Whilst mistnetting in Crab Bay there was always a chance of meeting a puffin chick on its way to the sea as a bonus, but this was an exremely rare occurrence.

The fledging of puffin chicks was a bit of a mystery to us. We hardly ever saw the fully grown chicks make their solitary, nocturnal exodus, even when we tried at all hours of the night to find them. Mike tried very hard one year to find and ring some, but with a very low success rate. In fact we hardly ever saw the chicks at all, their burrows were mostly too deep to see down or to reach into, and they didn't sit around prior to fledging either. Apparently puffin chicks are not deserted by their parents before they leave their burrows. We did try the 'arms-down-burrow' method, again with only a little success. If there was bird in there, the trick was to tap the fingers on the floor as far down as possible to get the bird to peck you and then, holding on to the bill, gently pull it towards you. Usually we ended up with a shearwater!

Young puffin chicks, when you did see them were extraordinary, clownish looking balls of grey down, not unlike shearwater chicks. The chicks had fledged and most of the adults had gone by the end of the first week in August, and we had many disappointed visitors during that month who expected to see hundreds of puffins still around.

There is no doubt that the presence of thousands of nocturnal birds added another dimension to the island. We talked jokingly of going to the West End for an evening out or, more boldly, the Red Light District, not everyone's idea of an evening well spent!

Chapter 9

Island of Flowers

In spring and summer our island was festooned with a wonderful array of flowers, many of which flourished in the extremely salty conditions. The rabbits held the grasses in check and allowed the cushion-forming and low-growing plants to dominate. We were able to demonstrate to interested visitors that grazing was the dominant factor governing the vegetation by building rabbit proof exclosures. Grazing was the all important factor, over and above exposure. For example, on the very exposed west coast, a long, lush mat of fescue (Festuca sp.) replaced the tight cushions of thrift (Armeria maritima) and excluded all else. Rabbits did not graze the latter, but they nibbled the grasses that came through between the plants. Thrift withstood the salt spray and the dessicating effect of drying winds better than most of the other plants, save some of those that grew on the cliff face itself, and so it was the dominant plant on much of the west and south coast fringes. Its deep rooting system and peaty, moisture-holding base enabled it to survive in the heavily burrowed areas which dried out quickly. It survived there very well, along with deep-rooted sea campion (*Silene uniflora*) that grew in the sheltered hollows formed by the hummocky terrain. Indeed, rabbit grazing was ultimately responsible for the particular variety and beauty of our flowers, and together with the exceptionally high degree of exposure to winds and salt spray, it played a vital role in the overall ecology of the island. Without the rabbits, much of the coastal area, where the shearwaters and puffins burrowed, would have been similar to the vegetation on Grassholm i.e. a thick mat of fescue. Grassholm is similarly exposed and is of a different rock type. Burrowing would not be easy in such conditions and there would be no rabbit holes to exploit.

The rabbits were therefore responsible for the most spectacular aspect of our island flora, which was the mass flowering of the cliff-loving varieties. By June, drifts of sea campion and thrift turned the Western Plain into a softly undulating sea of dappled pink and white bloom. I have seen the plain blazing with a carpet of thrift so densely flowered that barely a green leaf could be glimpsed between the composite flowerheads. And it was no even coloured carpet, for the tone varied from a pale silvery pink to deep rose. Most stunning was the illuminating effect along the west coast during a sunny summer's evening, when the intense yellow light shone through the dried flowerheads and lit them like thousands of little beacons. I thought the deep red buds as attractive as the flowers; they shone as if coated with wax and the red extended down the stem to the base of the sheath. The darker bracts with their light, papery margins made attractive, chequered patterns when the buds were swelling.

Neither was any year the same because the island vegetation underwent a cycle of change according to several different factors, most importantly drought, storms and intensity of rabbit grazing. Thrift appeared to be thus affected but, during our years there, it continued to dominate in places of most extreme exposure. Lockley once described the Neck as 'glowing with flames of thrift'; we never saw it like that, but once it was glowing rusty red with broad swathes of fruiting sorrel. Indeed, many people imagined that the flowers would have been the same every year. That was definitely not the case. No two years were ever the same because of the fluctuating nature of the environmental factors. Each year brought unexpected delights and disappointments. To a lesser degree the same applies to mainland plant communities, but on small islands where pressures are extreme and where one probably becomes more familiar with the detailed distribution of plants, the changes are more pronounced.

Sea campion is less tolerant of exposure than thrift and it is not eaten by rabbits. Whilst completing a revised map of the vegetation, it became evident to me that it had spread since the last survey by Goodman and Gillham in 1954. Stephen Warman and Carol Hellawell, in a 1981 report, suggest that this could have occurred gradually since the removal of the large flock of Soay sheep, which apparently showed a preference for this species. Being tolerant of heavy manuring it was common among the puffin burrows on the Neck, on the sides of Crab Bay and in several other places. It provided many a picturesque backdrop for photographs of puffin groups. The loose white flowers with their dusky anthers were at their loveliest when they grew in isolated clumps

Sea Campion (Silene uniflora)

cascading over the sandstone rock. Some of the campion flowers stood out from the rest, having pale yellowish green calyces without purple veins.

Plants associated with the cliffs were naturally of the greatest interest to our visitors, as the majority of them lived far from the coast and were unfamiliar with them. Thrift and campion were the most obvious, being the dominants, but there were many others, some of them quite as colourful and adding much pleasure to cliff top rambles. On rock with little soil, there were patches of pink rock spurrey (*Spergularia rupicola*), and wild thyme

(*Thymus polytrichus*) sprawled carelessly over the fractures. Lemon yellow kidney vetch (*Anthyllis vulneraria*) and golden bronze bird's-foot trefoil (*Lotus corniculatus*) lit up many green hollows, while mauve buttons of sheepsbit with sugar-pink anthers grew from crevices on Spy Rock, where the rabbits couldn't reach it. Nearly always it was associated with cushions of pearly pink stonecrop (*Sedum anglicum*). Like little lavender stars, spring squill flowers (*Scilla verna*) dotted the green turf in soothing contrast, its short, grass-like leaves lying curled and close to the ground in a bid to evade trampling feet and browsing teeth. A perennial growing from a tiny bulb, it undoubtedly benefited from rabbit grazing. I was charmed on my first acquaintance with it as I watched the first buds unfold their dark striped petals and reveal a ring of powder-blue anthers. It was new to my questing eyes, then only familiar with the flowers of the Hampshire basin. Because it was confined to the west coast of Britain and new to many of our visitors, we were often asked to identify it.

On the upper cliff face, below the thrift and campion, grew some really hardy plants that were able to tolerate extreme exposure to salt spray, but which were palatable to rabbits and therefore confined to inaccessible places. These included sea plantain (*Plantago maritima*) and two edible species - sea beet (*Beta maritima*) and rock samphire (*Crithmum maritimum*). We sampled each of them but, as is often the case with wild collected plants, they didn't seem to match the preferred taste of our cultivated vegetables. I have since eaten the beet in Cornwall and found it every bit as good, if not better, than spinach! My mistake may have been picking it at the wrong time. I have also tasted rock samphire pickled by a cordon bleu chef and it was excellent. It has a mustard like taste, but when I tried it chopped in salads on the island it was no great success. Nettle stew and Welsh laver bread (although I doubt if I prepared either properly) were both dismal failures. Common scurvygrass, disliked by rabbits, was edible and a great source of vitamin C, useful in the past to shipwrecked sailors prone to scurvy. I too would need to be shipwrecked before bothering with it. On the introductory walk around the island on a Saturday, I would point out the plants and particularly the edible ones. One day, I noticed one of our tribe picking off a sample of each and chewing avidly. Whilst I was becoming quite a good and confident botanist, I couldn't help imagining the result if I made a mistake, or if someone accidentally pulled of a snippet of hemlock water dropwort for their lunch, and from then on I refrained from imparting my dubious botanical knowledge.

While clambering around the lower parts of the cliff, below the samphire, to explore caves and fissures, it was always a thrill to find tufts of a brilliant green fern sprouting out from damp and shady nooks. The fronds were almost luminescent, as they shone out from dark cavities. That was sea spleenwort (*Asplenium marinum*), a favourite of mine on account of the secret and enchanting nature of the places where it grew. For example, I found it in the narrow entrance of a wide crack, down which you could crawl to a broad cavity opening on to a sandy bottom at low tide. At high tide, a pool of sea water glinted in the elusive daylight.

All the plants growing on and around the cliffs showed some kind of adaptation to exposure and/or grazing in the way of excessive hairyness, fleshy leaves and compact or prostrate growth form. I sometimes thought, after we had been there a while, that we had begun to develop some of these characters. Certainly our hair grew long, Ray sprouted a thick beard, our skin dried and weathered in the salt air and we were often seen in semi-prostrate mode when battling along against gales. Mercifully, we worked much too hard to become excessively fleshy!

Away from the exposed south and west facing cliffs, another mass flowering took place, if anything a little earlier than the thrift and campion. This time it was a plant more associated with woodlands than with coastal communities. Bluebells are undoubtedly among the most evocative of British flowers and, during the month of May, sometimes early sometimes late, acres of them spread a cool, cerulean carpet over the flat, central part of the island and down the slopes of the north and east coasts. Waterfalls of blue flowers trickled down gullys and oozed into the minutest clefts. It was a celebration of floral fecundity. Their presence, along with some other plants characteristic of woodlands like wood sage (*Teucrium scorodonia*), ground ivy, honeysuckle (*Lonicera periclymenum*) and primrose, has led to the suggestion that Skokholm may once have been wooded. There is no evidence to prove it, and as far as I know no pollen analysis of peaty deposits has taken place, so that it is merely an unsubstantiated theory. There is evidence however, that some of the treeless islands on the west coast of Ireland once supported woodland (oak and pine), and also that birch, pine and alder once grew on St Kilda, so that it is not as unlikely as it seems. Mesolithic flint flakes found on the island give evidence of a human presence, which in turn could have influenced the vegetation locally.

The dew-laden flowers of the bluebells would soak my legs in the early morning as I went down to North Haven for an early morning swim, but it was the heady scent which saturated the damp morning air that was so delicious. It set me up for the forthcoming chilly immersion, and there is nothing like a dip in the Atlantic to wake you up and recharge the appetite! Sometimes during the day, I would abandon my duties and steal away to the cliffs to relax in a flower-strewn gully near Wreck Cove, where bluebell fragrance mingled with the subtle sweet aroma of sea campion. This cocktail of perfume had soporific qualities, and once I well and truly succumbed. On that day I had ten minutes to prepare the same number of salads on returning (or was the salad a change of menu?).

My initial arrival in that gully would send the resident puffins whirring down the cliffs to gather on the sea below where they floated and fussed about each other, resentful

Thrift (Armeria maritima)

of my interrupting their domestic affairs. One by one they would return and, if I kept absolutely still, their natural curiosity drove them closer and closer until they were but a few feet away. They really did seem like little people, with their human-like manner-isms and condescending groans.

Large numbers of sheep once grazed the island. Lockley kept a hundred breeding ewes there in the 1930s and, in the 1940–50s, there were up to ninety-six Soay sheep. Lockley's sheep apparently ate bluebells. All those animals, together with goats and the odd horse and cow, must have had quite an impact on the island's vegetation as a whole, never mind the bluebells. Indeed, Lockley reported that the island was over-grazed during that time. Among other plants, violets and ground ivy were also favourites with his sheep. With only a small goat flock remaining on the island, the bluebells flourished for us, and the broad sheet of blue on the north coast was easily seen from Skomer. How tempting the island must have looked then to a nature lover on the mainland, although the colours on the island were always beautiful, even out of season.

Other major plant communities dominated the interior of the island, one of which was closely associated with the bluebells. Like trees in a woodland, bracken acted as their nurse in many parts of the island, and it also allowed for the early flowering of other plant species before its dense canopy cast a deep shade over the ground. Violets and ground ivy have already been mentioned, but there were also lesser celandines (*Ranunculus ficaria*), stars of gold strewn on the dark, bare earth. The mass of young fronds grew up with enviable vigour until it overwhelmed the fading bluebells and became all enveloping, in places reaching two metres high by late June. The fresh, lucid green delicately-textured foliage had a beauty of its own, but that didn't last.

With no large grazing animals to check its growth, bracken grew unhindered on the island where sufficient soil was available and where there was a lesser degree of expo-sure. The central and eastern parts of the island supported the largest and tallest stands. Somewhat stunted growth occurred in the southern and western parts of the island, where the exposure was greater, until finally it disappeared and gave way to pas-ture or maritime communities. Lesser black-backed gulls nested in sparse, low grow-ing bracken, where it was not too dense to impede their activities but where there was good cover available for the chicks to hide in. No doubt they had an effect on it mechanically, breaking it down by constant trampling and pulling about the dead stalks for nest building.

The first gales of autumn, often coming as early as mid August, gave it a merciless beating, and the deep green tones were scorched by heavy deposits of salt. The effect of the salt was heightened by hot sunshine following the storm and it had dev-astating results, so that spring or summer gales were very effectual. After a very severe gale, the most exposed bracken could turn brown overnight. I rather liked those early autumnal tints; they mellowed and made more attractive the jaded summer colours. By the time we left the island in November, the bracken was a rich tawny brown and most beautiful when it became saturated in mist or drizzle. Covered in glistening droplets of moisture, it acquired a ruby flush that was especially beautiful in a sea of grey mist. Often I would stop in my tracks to admire it. During our absence in winter, the gales played havoc with the tall, dying fronds, stripping them of their curled and brittle leaves and leaving thousands of naked sticks strewn around on the ground to lie and rot. The dead material faded to dull copper and blended well with the pastel green of the dormant turf. Thus we saw it when we returned in the early spring.

The bracken had its uses as bedding for the chickens when the supply of dead grass was exhausted, and also for goats when they joined our company. For all sorts of reasons - theories of bracken taking over from heather, gull increases etc. people had just begun to talk seriously about controlling it. Even Lockley had tried to keep it back by mowing it! There was no doubt that it had spread after the removal of the large flocks of grazing livestock. We started to do a little cutting back of the bracken/turf interface on Home Meadow and in Gull Fields, but as concern mounted, the Trust requested that we conduct an experiment with Asulam, a supposedly harmless and selective herbicide. We did not like the idea of using chemicals on the land, but eventually a block above the *Alice Williams* was sprayed. At that time, none of us had had any experience of monitoring plant communities with the use of quadrats or transects, and so, with very little time available anyway, we collected no quantitative data. However it was obvious that, although a double application did knock it back for a year or two, continual spraying or cutting would have been necessary for permanent clearance. Sea campion was one of the plants that grew prolifically after the experiment and golden rod was another. The area contained many burrows used by birds and rabbits and we little know whether or not it affected them.

There were some quite large belts of ling (*Calluna vulgaris*) in the central and eastern parts of the island, namely on Ishmian Heath, Met Heath, Green Heath and in Gull Fields. Bell heather (*Erica cinerea*) a common associate of ling, unfortunately became extinct in the 1950s. Whilst a little more tolerant of exposure than bracken, the heather was severely checked by heavy grazing and was in a degraded state in the 1970s, becoming even more so after we left, until it virtually disappeared in the 1980s. Bracken was quick to invade the receding edges. Currently, rabbit-proof exclosures are proving successful in encouraging its return.

Because of the wind effect, heather grew either in loose hummocks a few inches high or as a mat of prostrate stems barely raised off the ground. The hummocky areas we

'Rolling' heath

called 'rolling heath', because it did indeed roll across the ground like a gently undulating sea, but very slowly of course so that only by careful measurements could anyone have detected it. Shoots on the windward side died away leaving bare branches gnarled and twisted, and on them grew several species of lichen (*Ramalinas, Cladonias and Xanthorias*) giving the plants a wizened look. Healthy shoots on the leeward side grew on, but then were browsed and their growth checked by goats or rabbits. Lockley burnt the heather in an attempt to encourage oystercatchers and wheatears to nest in the open places, and the corresponding flush of new grass provided fresh grazing for his sheep. Even then, in his diary of 1928, he describes the heather in North Field as 'useless, thick, old and mostly dead'. Why it was in a state of degeneration then and right up until our time, could have been due to a variety of factors such as drought, bracken invasion, senility or climate change, as well as overgrazing. They all may have contributed. Mary Gillham showed that in sheltered conditions heather replaced bracken when the grazing influence was removed.

The degenerate heather was still lovely when it flowered; a sparse dusting of lilac would appear on the coarse, dark green foliage, catching the eye as one walked over

Green Heath to North Pond. Straddling the turf between the tussocks were yellow tormentil flowers (*Potentilla erecta*) and pert eyebright (*Euphrasia species*). Years ago, there would have been bright blue flecks of milkwort flowers (*Polygala serpyllifolia*) but that seemed to have disappeared. In the shelter of the tussocks, meadow pipits and skylarks raised their young, if they were lucky enough to escape the attentions of the crows. I soon learnt that it was foolish to search for their tiny, neatly woven nests, as the crows often found them shortly after I did. I soon stopped searching for them. When the birds had finished nesting and autumn was imminent, a sepia flush crept over the heather, a colour ripe and mature as suits the season.

The Pleistocene ice sheets left a large deposit of boulder clay spread over the central plain. Drainage was poor and rabbits generally kept out of the area. It was a favourite browsing area of the goats though, because of the long, lush grass. Purple moorgrass was dominant in some of the wetter parts, and that was where I raked up the bedding for our chickens. Tufts of Yorkshire fog (*Holcus lanatus*) and rush (*Juncus effusus*) were also common there. It was good to have a bit of bog that you could trudge through in wellingtons and pretend it was more extensive than it really was! Out there on the edge of the bog one year, there was masses of Ragwort (*Senecio jacobea*), a broad yellow flush that later became infested with hundreds of the orange-and-black-striped caterpillars of cinnabar moths. Ragwort cropped up in different places each year, but I don't remember seeing it covering the Neck as Lockley did. The main interest for me were those enchanting moths, whose wings shone metallic green and red.

In the proximity of the buildings and stretching out across Northern Plain, were several large, open fields, very heavily grazed by rabbits, stark reminders of the farming era. I liked these green spaces, they were pleasant to walk over and a complete contrast to the rough bracken-dominated areas and tussocky grassland. Furthermore, close examination of the cropped turf, particularly of Home Meadow, revealed more than a simple mix of dominant grasses (red fescue, *Holcus* and *Agrostis* species). There were many diminutive herbaceous plants that were relegated to creeping along the ground or forming tiny, compact rosettes of leaves tight to the ground. Pearlworts (*Sagina maritima, S.subulata* and *S.procumbens*), buck's-horn plantain (*Plantago coronopus*), sea stork's-bill (*Erodium maritimum*) and heath bedstraw (*Galium saxatile*) are a few examples. The three pearlworts were the hardest to identify and I spent some time looking closely at them whilst referring to the island's collection of Stella Ross-Craig's botanical handbooks which, incidentally, contained first-class, pen and ink illustrations. These tiniest of plants would most likely be overlooked by all apart from the serious botanist. The humble, white-petalled flowers, only a few millimetres across, are all but invisible in the turf and, to make matters worse, sometimes they don't even have petals. The close-grazed turf meant that we had an almost perfect cricket green on Home Meadow, but for the slope which sent balls rolling downhill to get lost in the dense bracken surrounding the pitch. Balls have been known to reach South Haven from there after a good slog!

What kind of farming took place on the island? This is fairly well documented and there is little point in repeating the details except in summary. A variety of stock (cattle, horses and pigs) were fattened, suggesting that there must have been good grazing in spite of the rabbits. The chief source of revenue in prosperous times was fat cattle and butter. The animals were swum or shipped across between the mainland and the island, a formidable task in itself judging by our limited experiences with goats and chickens. Seed corn was grown, but only to maintain the island's herd according to Roscoe Howells (see Skokholm report for 1968) who believed that Lockley mistook Skokholm for Skomer when he claimed that a quantity of first class seed was once exported from the island. There certainly was ploughing, because furrow marks are clearly visible in aerial photographs. This would have restricted some of the ground-nesting birds. Lockley claimed that the Neck had never been ploughed and offered the richest pasture on the island, but it was apparently fertilized for rabbit research in 1963. Due to its small size and inaccessibility, Skokholm was less viable than its larger neighbours, Skomer and Ramsey, but the pattern of farming still followed that of the mainland.

Lockley contemplated restoring the island farm, but was deterred by the difficulty he would have faced in acquiring manual labour, and also by the effect it would have had on the wildlife and the inherent charm that lay predominately in the wild character of the island. Shearwaters are breeding today in areas around the buildings that had been ploughed in the past. One of the advantages of restoration that he cites, is the sure return to the island of arable land birds such as the skylark and the grey partridge, and he considered the corncrake a possible colonizer too (a pair had bred in 1930). Ironically, all of these are in serious decline today because of modern farming methods. His attempts at ridding the island of rabbits by a multiplicity of methods, the most successful being that of gassing with cyanogas in 1949, brought about enormous temporary changes in the island's vegetation.

The beautifully constructed stone and earth walls are another legacy of the farming days. I saw them as works of art, even though many were in disrepair due to general decay and rabbit burrowing. They were built in the traditional herring-bone style of slanting the horizontal rows of thinly cut sandstone first one way and then the other, the overall pattern being overtly attractive. At about the same time as the Cottage and farm buildings were built in 1760, about half the island around the farmstead was walled in.

*Wall Pennywort
(Umbilicus rupestris)*

Rounded cushions of stonecrop clung to the crevices, and what delicacy of colour in those silver-pink, star-shaped flowers sparkling between the dark red stones. My discerning eye detected no such jewel-like quality in the clusters of shiny, round leaves of aptly named wall pennywort (*Umbilicus rupestris*), but I liked it for its simplicity of form and for the tall cream-coloured spikes flattened against the stonework. Reigning supreme, were magnificent foxgloves (*Digitalis purpurea*) that spiked the blue skies with purple, or lashed generous colour into grey foggy days.

One of the walls. Half-way Wall, with its corresponding dyke, ran north to south right across the middle of the island. Its course ran through an area which was bracken infested and heavily burrowed, making it difficult to negotiate by foot. There was a huge and formidable gull colony at the base of the Hills, which extended east and west of that wall, so that it was advisable to get through as quickly as possible. The wall was an ideal footpath, but not one on which you would pause to study the flora. Anyone walking across it in the summer would instigate wave after wave of gulls to rise up and fill the skies overhead with anxious clamouring. It prompted visitors, out enjoying their walks, to pause and gaze skywards, searching for a buzzard or pere-grine falcon. Vagrant herons had the same effect, and if it came to that, so would a gyr falcon, so it was always worth a look!

Around the island, many other plants species could be found. Gillham (1953 and 1956) listed 275 species of plants and ferns on Skokholm, with about five per cent introduced. A few have been lost and a few gained since then. Some have a special place in my memory for being abundant only in certain years. For example, one par-ticular summer, the slopes in and around the puffin colony in Crab Bay were festooned with a picturesque abundance of that tiny and most beautiful of wild pansies, com-monly called heartsease (*Viola tricolor*). Some were yellow and white, some purple and yellow, some plain purple and so on. They exibited such variety of colour and pattern that one could while away many minutes going from bloom to bloom inspecting every one. Why it favoured those slopes between Crab Bay and Gallery Rocks was a mystery to me.

One year, amid the gull colonies around Bread Rock, carpets of sea mayweed (*Tripleurospermum maritimum*) burst into yellow and white bloom. They were clustered on a feathery green mattress of leaf, thousands of them peeking up at the sun. The plant was thought to have been introduced, as its seed was found to be common in gull pellets according to Gillham (1955).

Over the moist soils on the edge of East Bog, and also in Orchid Bog, trailed the frail, ribbony stems of bog pimpernel (*Anagallis tenella*), with many pairs of tiny, round leaves neatly distributed on either side, and in summer studded generously with pale rose-pink flower cups that flaunted bright yellow anthers. In good years, the flowers were so dense that rosy patches appeared and caught the eye of even the most bird-orientated visitors. There was another pimpernel too which one year put on a brilliant display. Familiar to us already as a weed in our garden, the scarlet pimpernel (*Anagallis arvensis*) suddenly invaded a large area on Northern Plain within and adjacent to the gull colony. The enrichment of the soil by guano and the bare soil exposed by the birds' activities must have encouraged it, but why that particular year? Among the normal flowers, which were more brick red than scarlet, were some pale flowers of a delicate washed-out peach and also a few of the variety *azurea*, a dazzling gentian blue.

Another garden weed, common chickweed (*Stellaria media*) grew at burrow entrances because of the nitrogen enrichment. Anyone who has kept free-range chick-ens will know how much they relish this plant, and on my wanderings round the island I used to stuff my pockets with it. I never saw the hens eat anything green with such enthiusiasm, except when they scaled the garden fence and made free with the lettuce! Since then I have watched them eat garlic mustard (*Alliaria petiolata*) with equal gusto, but that was a plant which we didn't have on the island. Our hens deserved all those

Half-way Wall (Skomer beyond)

treats because they provided us with a continual supply of real eggs – perfectly fresh with rich, orange yolks, a different product altogether from the pallid, sloppy objects that pass as eggs today. They were a real treat for most of our visitors.

Some years were good sorrel years. I remember it dominating a large area around North Pond, with millions of tiny flowers and fruits forming a red haze that flared up in the glow of the setting sun. There were two species on the island - common sorrel (*Rumex acetosa*) and sheep's sorrel (*Rumex acetosella*), the former favouring more exposed places where the higher pH is thought to promote its growth. Sheep's sorrel seemed to like to grow in the shelter of burrows where it had the benefit of rabbit or bird dung. Both have edible leaves, but I found them sour. The sorrel shed a lot of pollen and brought on sneezing bouts and so I avoided walking through it. On Skokholm, although there was much relief from my rye grass allergy, easterly winds inevitably set it off. No anti-histamine there; the best relief I found was swimming. In a late season, the sorrel flowered while the bluebells were still out and often amongst them, and what a wonderful mixture that was: the orange feather-like sorrel amid the drooping bluebells,

Other plants were very special to us because they were rare or scarce on the island, and more so because I didn't know then how common some of them were on parts of the mainland, like the red campion mentioned earlier. On Skokholm, that campion was treasured, but now I can stand and admire thousands of them festooning our Cornish hedges. Always attractive of course, and no less appreciated, but just in a different way. We made pilgrimages to Wreck Cove to view our one and only plant of wild carrot (*Daucus carota* ssp. *gummifer*) but, because it grew in a crevice several feet feet down a precipitous cliff where the rabbits couldn't reach it, it could only be seen through binoculars! It was there in Lockley's day! At my home in Cornwall it is exceedingly common, but it still has a special fascination for me, not only because the lacy white umbels look so well in the seascape, but also on account of the difference in appearance of each one during the varying stages of its developement. By this I mean both the colour, which varies between white, green and pink, and the geometrical pattern of each one. It is a kaleidoscopic effect. If you don't know what I mean then you haven't really looked at them.

Sea purslane grew only in Obione Bay, and its fleshy, grey leaves seemed to glow with the salty lustre of the sea. It was not so rare in Britain but, nevertheless, it was of great significance in our small world. Neither did it boast large, colourful flowers like the next described. Pride of them all and isolated in enviable supremacy on the Stack, were a group of tree mallow plants (*Lavatera arborea*). The thin soil over the top of the rock was lavishly supplied with the phoshate rich guano of a pair of great black-backed gulls. Again, we had to admire the bright, velvety pink blooms through binoculars, and had

Red Campion (Silene dioica)

Tree Mallow (Lavatera arborea)

only tantalizing glimpses of the dark-veined, petals radiating from a deep purple heart. There was but one chance to study them properly, and that was during our razorbill ringing expedition over to the Stack. Again, Cornwall provides ample opportunities for encountering this most tall and stately of mallows.

At the other end of the scale, a patch of tiny, insignificant-looking chaffweed (*Anagallis minima*) was also of great interest, being confined to a damp corner near Alice's Knoll, and it only had a very localized distribution on the mainland too. We made much of it on our botanical expeditions although, not surprisingly it failed to arouse much interest among non botanists. Allseed (*Radiola linoides*), not quite so rare but also very small and slender, was another that grew in damp spots especially on the margins of the pond. They all had their place, the large and flamboyant, and the lesser, more humble varieties.

The irises in the Heligoland were a further source of wonder to me as I watched the yellow flags unfold their summer glory. Trying to photograph them, first with a vivid blue sky behind and then with a background of spiky green leaves, would involve contorting myself into ridiculous postures on the marshy ground, and I usually ended ended up wet and smelling of bog, not altogether unpleasant, I liked to think, on account of the prevailing smell of crushed water mint. The resulting photographs seemed first class then but, by today's high standards, they wouldn't even be considered good! The colour and shape of the figwort flowers, growing in that same marshy spot, were intriguing too. They ranged from, a deep burgundy red to purplish brown, stunning colours for a flower and such that are seldom seen. Deep red roses, black tulips, a certain red cosmos and the wild marsh cinquefoil (*Potentilla palustris*) are other blooms of an unusual red that I find irresistible. The figwort flower forms a small pouch and is mostly pollinated by wasps.

Our marshy areas and ponds were on a small scale, but they held concentrations of interesting, moisture-loving plants, increasing the plant diversity enormously. There were several common ones like the acrid smelling hemlock water dropwort, delicate, pale blue water forget-me-not (*Myosotis scorpioides*) and purple marsh thistle (*Cirsium palustre*). Woolly, mauve clusters of hemp agrimony flowers (*Eupatorium cannabinum*) erupted on tall stems that grew up from dykes and damp hollows on the sheltered northern and eastern slopes. They were greatly attractive to migrant red admirals, as well as our resident tortoiseshell and peacock butterflies. Tiny blinks (*Montia fontana*) grew prolifically in the damp, grazed turf around the well and escaped my scrutinizing eye for a long time. It had not got much going for it, apart from its humility, nevertheless it was a revelation when I eventually found it. The well itself was originally covered by Lockley because of the invasion of blinks and water-starwort (*Callitriche stagnalis*).

East Bog contained an interesting variety of moisture-loving plants between the larger communities of soft rush and stunted willow, including marsh St John's wort (*Hypericum elodes*) with its attractive, silver grey leaves, sprawling lesser spearwort (*Ranunculus flammula*) with pretty, lemon flowers, and shiny mats of bog pennywort (*Hydrocotyle vulgaris*). Lesser scullcap (*Scutellaria minor*) skulked beneath the taller vegetation, its pairs of tubular, pink flowers nodding shyly in the axils beneath the leaf pairs. Orchids grew almost exclusively in Orchid Bog but, from time to time, specimens cropped up in East Bog. The exotic, dark pink spikes, which I took to be southern marsh orchid, (*Dactylorhiza praetermissa*) was later identified as the hybrid D. x hallii (*D. praetermissa* x *D. maculata*). Orchid Bog lies to the south-west of North Haven and is now an exclosure, and it will be interesting to see whether the total exclusion of rabbit grazing will be beneficial or detrimental to the plant community there. It may be that a little light grazing is needed to keep open the sward. Orchid Bog rose from a spring that trickled downhill and spilled over the cliffs on the west side of North Haven gully. It was one of a series of springs that cropped up across a line of faults from North Haven to Crab Bay. Another orchid, the early purple orchid (*Orchis mascula*), was recorded by Lockley, but this is questioned by Dr E. Gynn and F. Bos in a plant list they compiled in 1981.

Lockley cut his turf for use as fuel around South Pond and marked it on his maps as the turbary, although apparently it was of poor quality. In *Dream Island Days* he claims that turf was first cut there over a hundred years ago. This practice must have altered the terrain, not least the drainage. South Pond and Winter Pond often dried out in the summer, but only during the drought of 1976 was there no water at all in North Pond. This last had been dammed and dug out to extend its boundary. After a wet winter it was extensive and I used to love its openess and the rippling, blue reflection of the sky. From its surface in summer rose armies of bistort stems (*Polygonum amphibium*) bearing oblong flowerheads of pale pink, whilst around the edges of the pond were the lax feathery blooms of water-pepper (*Polygonum hydropiper*).

We had little in the way of ferns, in spite of our wetlands, probably due to the very open nature of the island habitat. Apart from the sea spleenwort, I remember with affection the lady fern (*Athyrium filix-femina*) with its pale green, finely trimmed fronds growing out from a cleft beside the track. Several other species of fern had been recorded on the island, including the largest and most elegant of them all – royal fern (*Osmunda regalis*), but they were never refound in spite of intensive searching. After we left, the diminutive and very rare adder's tongue fern (*Ophioglossum vulgatum*) was found in East Bog by Fred Bos, a Dutch botanist. It was an excellent find because it is an extremely simple and inconspicuous plant, requiring close searching on hands and knees. It is with great embarrassment, that I either did not notice or have forgotten the rustyback fern (*Ceterach officinarum*) growing on the chimney of the dormitory. It is unlikely to have suddenly appeared after we left, and it was a gross oversight!

It remains to describe the very little we had to boast of in the way of scrub and trees. On the east-facing slope of North haven was a small patch of low scrub. It consisted of severely wind-pruned blackthorn (*Prunus spinosa*) and wild privet (*Ligustrum vulgare*) with a lacing of honeysuckle (*Lonicera periclymenum*) and ivy (*Hedera helix*). It grew on a very steep slope and there was no chance of ever imbibing the heavenly scent of the honeysuckle flowers. A pair of blackbirds once nested in its cover. We used to wonder why gorse (*Ulex europaeus*) didn't grow on Skokholm when we saw the brilliant blaze of yellow creep over the mainland cliffs opposite. We would have liked to have had it on the island, thinking it may have encouraged stonechats to stay and breed as they did in years gone by. Lockley wrote (presumably based on heresay) that gorse was plentiful on the island in the 1890s, but that he found only one bush in North Haven. Even though that bush was dying, a pair of linnets bred there for him. If indeed it once was common, the intensive grazing in the past may have been the reason for its demise. We tried planting some seedlings but they died, no doubt because the rabbits gained access to the tender young shoots. The other vegetation that barely deserves to be called scrub was the stunted creeping willow (*Salix repens*) which grew along the ground before Tattenham Corner. After the goats were taken off in 1982, this willow grew up to a foot or so in height. Other changes, as noted by Liz and Graham Gynn, included more bramble cover and more heather seedlings.

For anything that resembled a bush or a tree, we had to content ourselves with a few introductions, many of them around the buildings where there was some shelter. The garden containing our vegetable plot and the garden trap was surrounded by an earth and stone wall in which rabbits burrowed, wheatears nested and storm petrels purred. Within the wall many attempts had been made to plant trees, few of which survived, but one which did was a much revered sycamore, one of two specimens on the island. It actually grew inside the trap and attracted many birds. Purist conservationist as I was, I did appreciate the value of a tree or two on a windswept island, even if it was a sycamore. The other tree grew in the corner of the Wheelhouse yard. This one had reached the point where the top of the west wall met the roof of the middle block, and beyond that it encountered the full blast of the salty south-westerlies. Hence the young twigs withered away in their hopeless struggle to continue growing. I loved to see the new leaves of those trees unfold in the spring, delighting in the rich pinky-bronze colour and the gluey shine on the swollen bud scales, and would rush to get my camera as soon as the sun lit them up. There were also elder bushes planted inside the trap, although I don't remember them flowering as they are supposed to have done after the removal of the goats. It is certainly true that in the winter the flock spent much time in the vicinity of the buildings, judging by the generous piles of droppings scattered about the place. Also, after the goats were removed, elder bushes are said to have sprung up in places where they were not in evidence before. They were originally introduced to the island, according to Lockley. During our years there, and later on too, suckers from those bushes were planted around in an attempt to increase the amount of cover for the birds.

Mike Harris notes in the 1963 island report that some serious tree planting took place during his spell of wardening in the 1960s. Twenty-five sycamores, fifty Scots pines and ten stone pines were planted. Well, when we arrived we found only a poor specimen of Norway spruce (*Picea abies*), a stunted Bishop's Pine (*Pinus muricata*) and the two sycamores mentioned above. Later, a post-goat tree planting exercise by Graham and Liz Gynn took place and there was yet more elder planting in 1989. We tried to establish some *Fuchsia magellanica* cuttings brought over by a friend, so impressed were we by the way they grew around the farmhouse buildings on Skomer. We also tried black-currant bushes and tamarisk cuttings. Another introduction was horse-radish (*Armoracia rusticana*) that we planted in the Wheelhouse yard. This last was relished by visitors when served with Sunday beef (the plant survives, but probably there is no beef to go with it!). Previous introductions into the cottage garden were borage *(Borago officinalis)* and hydrangea, the former recorded by Lockley. It is with some trepidation that I read of the recent arrival of Montbretia (*Crocosma* x *crocosmiiflora*) because of the rapidity with which it spreads and the impossibility of eradicating it. It is a noxious pest in Cornwall.

Whilst the above is mostly a general account of the flora as it was in my day, it would be an omission if no mention was made of certain interesting historical records. There were many plants recorded by Lockley and others in the preceding years that were certainly authentic records but which have since disappeared. One such is the cowslip (*Primula verum*) said to have grown in the South Haven gully along with the primroses. Its presence was probably due to the practice of liming the soil. Marsh lousewort (*Pedicularis palustris*), lousewort (*Pedicularis sylvatica*), bugle (*Ajuga reptans*) and lords-and-ladies (*Arum maculatum*), the last two usually associated with woodland, had gone. The small fern, black spleenwort (*Asplenium adiantum-nigrum*) was recorded between 1947 and 1960. Red poppies (*Papaver* species), corn marigold (*Chrysanthemum segetum*), chicory (*Cichorium intybus*) and even the rare casual pheasant's-eye (*Adonis annua*) occurred as field weeds, and had predictably disappeared. Once, the creamy flowers of meadowsweet (*Filipendula ulmaria*) gave off their sickly sweet perfume down by the well, but I was not to know it until I moved to Cornwall. There were many more species and botanists should refer to the list mentioned at the end of the chapter for further information.

Real perfection is only to be found in an untouched landscape, but there is a haunting beauty to be found in land once managed but long since neglected. Skokholm has been altered by farming and all that went with it – ploughing, liming, fertilizing, grazing stock, wall building etc., but perhaps the biggest impact was man's introduction of rabbits. The self regeneration of whatever vegetation was there before this happened must have been severely curtailed and whole plant communities altered. What was there in 1973 was the sum of all those historical events left to itself but still at the mercy of the harsh conditions. What I enjoyed about it was that it was really left to itself; no fences, no fussy management, just a wild community, ever changing, dynamic. Only by understanding the complexities of the controlling elements (droughts, gales, altered grazing pressure and natural succession) could one begin to understand the bewildering cycle of events which took place among the plant communities. It seemed to me to be a very unique system in that it was primarily maintained by the rabbit. I hope it retains that special character always.

For a detailed scientific account of the flora of Skokholm, readers should refer to a paper by G.T. Goodman and M.E. Gillham to be found in the *Journal of Ecology*, 42, 296–237, published in 1954 and entitled 'Ecology of the Pembrokeshire Islands 2, Skokholm, the Environment and Vegetation'. For a detailed plant list, refer to the *Flora of Skokholm* by Dr Liz Gynn and Fred Bos (1981), taken from data collected from many sources including Lockley (1947), Mary Gillham (1953 and 1956) and the Skokholm card index (1960–1980).

CHAPTER 10

The Human Element

Distant shrieks of laughter came to me through the open door of the Wheelhouse as I stirred the 'Saturday soup'. The younger and more energetic visitors were indulging in a game of French cricket which I had initiated to keep them happy and occupied until the boat came. I glanced at my watch and then looked through the little window in front of me. There was Jack Sound in the distance, churning and spitting white water as the sea rushed madly through it. Thus Middleholm was separated from Wooltack Point on the mainland. To the left of centre was Tusker Rock, looking nothing like a boat to me although it tricked many an untrained eye into thinking it was one. Such a familiar profile; well and truly imprinted on my brain (so that I can see it still!) so many hours have I spent staring at it over the years, searching for a tiny speck that was the *Sharon* turned end on and coming towards us. Three or four times she crosses the sound to Skomer with day trippers before it is our turn, and on bad days she might not show at all.

I blinked, was that her? My eye had caught a white speck tossing in the waves. I reached for my binoculars. Yes it was, and she's turned towards us at long last, the lunch I had prepared would be for the new arrivals rather than be served up as the first of two sittings. We had about twenty minutes before she came into South Haven and so began the panic. I looked about me; tables laid, cooker turned off, boiler filled and lit. Grabbing a pile of mail, I stuffed it into a waterproof bag and ran out the door clanging the dinner bell on the way to announce the boats imminent arrival. Chickens scattered everywhere as I tore across the yard shouting 'boat's coming, be here in ten minutes'. People engaged in a last wander round the island headed back quickly, whilst the cricketers foresook the pitch and disappeared into their rooms to return seconds later laden with bags, 'enough gear to last them a year,', I used to think. One or two people looked anxiously at the sea, weighing up the prospects of an uncomfortable crossing and not feeling much reassured by Ray's rendering of 'Oh hear us when we cry to thee, for those in peril on the sea,' over breakfast, the only line he ever remembered from that well known hymn.

To my great relief, I heard the sound of the dumper truck approaching. Ray hadn't lingered too long over coffee at the lighthouse and soon his familiar form came into view, pitched on top of the red truck as he trundled down from the gateposts with ex-naval anorak billowing in the wind and loose curls flying from beneath his brown, woolly hat. Mike appeared at the same time in his dark red, holey sweater, brown baggies and wellington boots, clutching his letters. The dumper swung round, stopped on the meadow, and loading was achieved in a matter of minutes. Then off it went heading for South Haven with the brakes in good order, we hoped, for the steep descent. Someone usually hitched a ride by sitting on the box behind the seat or standing on a metal plate low down on the back.

A last minute check by myself inside the Cottage followed. Guest rooms were spick and span, the fireplace was clean and, most importantly, the common room looked delightfully welcoming and smelt highly of furniture polish. The oak floor gleamed, not for nothing did we pile on the polish and then skate joyfully around on rags! It was as good as it possibly could be. Off then to South Haven for the great weekly event. No headache yet, that would come later, all ex-wardens know about the Saturday headache!

A trail of people disappeared down the hill before me and I rushed to catch up to say a few words to newly acquired friends, sad to see them go but confident of their return in the future. Goodbyes, handshakes, back patting and promises passed between ourselves and our visitors while we waited on the landing. Yes, they would send photograhs, what did we want them to bring us when they returned? Whisky? Yes. Chocolate? Yes. Newspapers? Grief, no! Were we going to be here next year? Yes, definitely! Had they got the mail safe? and so on.

Sincerely hoping that we would see most (but not all!) of them the next year, we tried to chat and at the same time organize a chain to pass luggage down from the dumper to make a distinct pile, in order to avoid the chaos that might occur when luggage is coming off and going on at the same time. Valuables were clutched to bosoms, for fear of loss or ditching, no way was that man going to let go of his expensive camera, and I didn't blame him.

The bow of the *Sharon* appeared, and then the whole lovely shape of her emerged from behind the rocks that sheltered the cove. Terry turned her slowly into the landing, cautiously drawing her alongside as he reckoned with the slight swell that washed the steps. We acknowledged him and his crew, but their attention was concentrated on keeping the boat from banging against the steps. Rubber tyres served perfectly as boat fenders. I glanced at the new faces, I had seen the visitor list and recognized some names, although I couldn't clearly remember the persons associated with them. This was often the problem, so many people came and went that it wasn't until they arrived that you realized who they were. Yes, I did remember that gentleman, wasn't he the one who entertained us with stories of his bees? Should I ask about them? Later I did and he looked blankly at me. Oh well, you can't win 'em all!

At least today's landing was no hassle; no dinghy and no cliff climbing, a relatively easy step on and off the boat for our guests as long as they timed it right, and easy for us handling the heavy gas cylinders. Luggage transference, on and off the boat, went perfectly smoothly with our super efficient human chain. Greetings and news gradually passed between ourselves and Terry who promises us another bag of corn for our chickens and ensures that the long-awaited bundle of mail has been given to one of the visitors. Last farewells and the boat pulls out, everyone smiling but many not wanting to go, and who could blame them!

We waved until the boat was out of sight, the new visitors joining in gallantly. Some of them looked a bit cold, they never seemed to wear enough clothes for the boat trip. I eagerly asked who had the mail and took it off them thumbing through impatiently for expected letters. No, I'd have to wait till we had sorted things out and, keeping it tucked under my arm, I helped load the dumper. One visitor marched off up the hill with his heavy rucksack, oh well, that was up to him! Then someone spotted a puffin, they were lucky, it was the first week in August and most of them had gone. 'Isn't it small? How many are there? Will it stay?' And so on. Fingers fumbled in pockets or bags, cameras came out and a little blob on the sea was registered. The man with his rucksack dropped it and ran down to look. We all admired the solitary puffin for a minute or two case it was the last one we saw.

Ray coaxed the dumper into reverse and backed up the hill, bags and cases jumping around precariously in the front, always a mighty hairy business I thought. That was just the first of two or three loads. 'Did our flour come? Anyone seen the meat? How was the crossing?'. So went the disjointed conversation as we traipsed up the hill to the buildings.

There were many new faces, some of which expressed relief at having arrived safe and dry, whilst others looked positively excited by the novelty of being on a small island packed with seabirds, and perhaps some interesting migrants too. Visitor retraps looked about them knowingly and whispered to us that they would like such and such a room if possible. The questions began immediately, those hundreds of questions every Saturday, where do we get water? Can we walk anywhere? What are the chances of a Grassholm trip? Those who had been before stood by passively, smug in the knowledge that they knew the ropes, and as usual we endeavoured to delay answering in order to gather everyone together for the assignment of rooms. Lunchtime was the time for all those pressing issues to be discussed. It was not always easy trying to ascertain who was with whom, and in what relationship, and was that a man or a woman concealed in that spacious anorak? They soon put us right if we made a mistake and usually made a joke of it!

That was a typical Saturday, as I remember it, at least so long as the boat came. If it didn't, and the weather looked all right to us, then there were hours of uncertainty, waiting around, trying to do constructive things, making decisions about whether to

The Sharon landing visitors

serve lunch or whether people should be allowed to make phone calls etc. If the sea was obviously too rough, it was easy, you just got stuck into another day, although once or twice we were caught out much to the dismay of those who were bad sailors. Saturdays were our weekly markers and if the boat was delayed, the days became muddled.

Living on a beautiful island, with most of the work so enjoyable, was undeniably satisfying, but there were times when slaving over a hot stove cooking breakfasts for fifteen or so visitors seemed exactly what I didn't want to be doing. It was a always a cooked breakfast, something different everyday, with cereal first and toast afterwards. Tuesdays was scrambled egg and everyone looked anxiously at the washing up rota to see who was going to be lumbered with that particular saucepan! There was in unlimited supply of tea or coffee with every meal, and we had a teapot that took a strong arm to lift, but there were plenty of gentlemen in those days! Kettles were constantly on the boil.

In fact it was only breakfast that was such a chore, the other meals could be prepared in a more leisurely way, and in advance, so that we could make the most of the rest of the day (largely to do other work!). My routine of making lunchtime cakes or scones before breakfast, left the rest of the morning fairly free. Cake making was something I never envisaged doing much of in a normal life, it was merely for the titivation of the visitors palate. We had chocolate fudge cake, banana, orange, coffee and walnut, coconut, fruit, scones, flapjacks, all freshly made, no ready-mix for us, and not even self-raising flour. Most had generous layers of icing too. One of my favourites was chocolate ripple because it looked really difficult to make, but in fact it wasn't, you just layered the two mixes in the tin. Lardy cake was a speciality, but I shudder to think of all the lard that went into it in these cholesterol conscious days. Success breeds success and after the lardy cake experiment came hot cross buns and doughnuts. That kind of novel enthusiasm was probably more evident in my early days of cooking. My tiny Be-Ro recipe book was my bible. Mike was so keen on the cakes that he always came in to scrape round the mixing bowl. One day, I made a classic mistake, one which sounds impossible but was nevertheless accomplished, and quite innocently too. I must have been in a hurry for somehow I put salt in the mix instead of sugar. I soon realized it, as my own palate needed titivating from time to time, and I discarded it, but not without leaving rather more in the bowl than usual. In came Mike, thinking either he had struck lucky or cook was being extra generous, and took a whacking great spoonful. It was too much for even his voracious appetite. That taught him to have complete faith in my cooking!

Lunch at one-o-clock could be prepared easily in an hour. We invented a variety of hot snacks which it would be tedious to list, but one which I continue to relish to this day is apple and cheese on toast. You simply toast a piece of bread, slice some apple on to it, cover it with slices of cheese, sprinkle it with pepper and put it under the grill to melt the cheese. It is delicious. In those days I could even make pastry, and bacon and egg pie with beans was a favourite – gulls eggs of course!

We changed the main meal from midday to the early evening. It was much better for us, because again it left more of the day free. Judging by the amount they ate, I imagine it rendered many of our visitors inactive, so perhaps it was better for them too. It was scheduled for 6.30pm and so didn't need preparing until late afternoon. Our routine weekly menu also helped us to organize our time efficiently. We had a different meal each day of the week, and if someone stayed a fortnight we cursed but made an extra effort to see that they didn't have the same meal twice! Unfortunately, being unable to resist picking at food, my stomach was usually well satisfied before I even served the meals! I probably ate more crackling off the pork joint than all the visitors put together. Carving the meat was a job I hated, so there had to be some recompense. Puddings were always available. Ray's fortés were pineapple upside-down pudding and lemon meringue pie, whilst mine were treacle tart and steamed puddings.

Island specialities were served from time to time – rabbit casserole, scrambled gulls' eggs, locally caught fish, blackberry pie (only once), and parasol mushrooms. These last were sometimes as big as the frying pan itself and were absolutely delicious. To anyone unfamiliar with them, they look rather alarming because of their size and their shaggy tops, but they are absolutely delicious. Some visitors refused them on grounds of suspicion; they didn't know what they were missing.

We had little food left over and what Mike wouldn't eat, the chickens did, or was it the other way round! We would cringe at the sight of him attacking a sticky mushy mess that was yesterday's steamed pudding or gooseberry crumble whilst we tackled our weetabix at breakfast time. Left over cake was often served up with coffee in the common room later in the evening, and nothing was ever left for the mice. Once, I found some very old, very stale cornflakes hidden away and put them aside for the chickens (I knew even Mike would reject them). A helper had offered to set out breakfast and into the bowls went those cornflakes, without my knowledge of course. When the kind lady got to our bowls at the top of the table, she ran out of them and opened a new packet. So how were we to know why the table suddenly went quiet and why everyone seemed to be chewing so avidly, our cornflakes were fine and we crunched away merrily. Someone must have politely said something because all of a sudden it dawned on me what had happened!.

There was always so much going on in the summer that the cooking seemed incidental to everything else, especially with it being shared between Ray and myself. Mike and a friend, Bob Gomes, once relieved me of the evening meal while Ray was absent for a week, Bob concocting a fine curry and Mike taking on the dessert. This last was to be a wonderful mousse but it wasn't given a chance to set because they never stopped opening the fridge door to see if it had reached that final stage. Likewise the curry for the dinner was tasted so many times (A little more lemon? A little more sugar?), there was very little left! Such are the delights and stresses of cooking for other people.

Mostly, it was a pleasure catering for our visitors; they were always hungry and so appreciative. I never felt that our efforts were wasted. We ate every bit as well as any-

Parasol mushroom

one on the mainland, if not better, with excellent cuts of meat for roasts, joints of ham, fresh vegetables and salad etc. Mealtimes were sociable affairs and it wasn't always easy to shift people once they had got into a deep debate about some pressing issue. Fortunately they were responsible for washing up, not us, and so we were quickly out the door! Potato peeling was a visitor chore too and we cooks almost forgot how to do it. It wasn't a bad task as it could be accomplished sitting outside in the sun whilst chatting to other members of the team. It was organized on a rota basis with the washing up, and it was surprising how much that rota was discussed and analysed. To save arguing we divided everyone into groups according to where they sat on the Saturday of their arrival. The fact that we were excused meant that we could use as many saucepans as we liked when we prepared the meals! I was accused many times, probably rightfully, of using every conceivable pan and implement available to me.

Mike dutifully took part in these domestic chores, no doubt dreaming of the latest shearwater marriage or a new brood of wheatears, but he never got the hang of our swish potato peeler. One regular visitor went to the length of bringing his own tool for the job; he was familiar with the enormity of the task! It was a bucketful after all!

The spring migration attracted many visitors but, because of the unpredictable weather and the possibility of being stormbound, the autumn was not so popular. Often we had quiet weeks in July and August too. Most people were keen ornithologists, happy with whatever birds they saw and the fact that there were plenty of them, but others were of the twitching fraternity. Three in particular come to mind; their competitive natures compelled them to stay in view of each other throughout the whole day lest one should be seen off! It was for them that we commissioned a visiting artist friend to paint a potato in the guise of a bluethroat and set it in the Wheelhouse sycamore tree. It was good enough for them to be taken in for a while, but eventually it became necessary to view the back of the bird, which was not by any means perfect in that it looked spudlike and lacked a tail. Tail-less bluethroats that remain stationary in trees for ten minutes naturally arouse suspicion, and thus it was revealed a fake, but it was taken in good heart.

The enthusiasm and regularity with which some keen birders ran the Heligoland traps had to be quelled sometimes. The island attracted trainee ringers and also many people who simply liked to see birds in the hand and take part in our seabird ringing activities. So it was that, when the time came for renewal of the lease in 1976 and the cessation of ringing, concern began to mount as to whether we would be able to attract a sufficient number of visitors each year. We never knew much about the financial situation, but thought that we were probably supplemented by the more lucrative business of charging day trippers to land on neighbouring Skomer, which was leased by the Trust from what was then the Nature Conservancy Council (and now The Countryside

Council for Wales). The Trust began to advertise field courses on Skokholm to be run by ourselves and guest lecturers. In 1977 and 1978, we ran courses on birdwatching for beginners, seabirds and general natural history, and succeeded in attracting fairly good numbers of people. There was no shortage of subjects of interest, especially with the general courses. Moth trapping proved to be a fascinating and popular activity, even for those who had never seen it done before. The Trust also agreed to a boatload of day trippers being brought over each Monday, a scheme organized by the National Parks. There were up to thirty people on the boat and we had to lead them round the island. That was fine but we both felt that thirty was too many. It was hard to control those avid photographers who would keep disappearing down the cliffs out of our view. We were perhaps a little too sensitive, but our main concern was the birds.

My voice does not carry and I usually found myself quite hoarse after such a walk. After the first year we were in favour of stopping them, particularly as half the time, they didn't make it because of the weather. In 1994, however, I blessed them as it was the only way that I could get to the island. Arriving unannounced, I spent a perfect day looking over old haunts and renewing my acquaintance with the wildlife.

So in 1977, we had a new role, and we both (by then Mike had left) enjoyed participation in the new ventures and particularly the courses, which meant brushing up on our facts and figures. We had more time without the ringing, but there was still census work and a million other jobs with only two of us to deal with them. Promotion was evident only in that one of us was able to occupy the warden's seat at the top of the table. We were probably paid more too, but I was blissfully ignorant of such matters in those days. They were Ray's concern, and as long as we were able to eat and sleep, that was good enough for me. Many visitors came each year to enjoy birds, but also because they grew very fond of the island itself and the simple, uncomplicated lifestyle. After a year or so we were welcoming back visitors like old friends and looked forward to the arrival of the boat each Saturday, bringing them and our long awaited mail. Kind people often asked what we would like brought over when they returned. For me it was chocolate and, by the sixth year, I kept up a veritable store. Anyone who wonders why I disappeared so quickly after dinner may now know that it was to my hidden chocolate store I went for a private treat. Pretty soon they even got to know which type I preferred – dark with roasted almonds. I thank all those kind people who made life even better than it was already. Mike's weakness lay in peanut butter and jam and, apart from the peanut butter we filched as bait for the mouse traps, he had plenty of it all for himself and ate it with great relish. I believe he acquired the taste in America and we listened with disbelief to his tales of specially prepared jars of layered jam and peanut butter which were available over there. Ray's weakness was whisky, particularly malt whisky.

It came as a surprise to me how quickly you could get to know and become fond of someone in just a week (perhaps the chocolate had something to do with it!). The Trust provided us with a list of visitor names beforehand and so we knew who was coming, apart from very late bookings. Once, on the list, we had a Dickie Bird, and I don't know to this day whether that was his real name. Another was Miss P. Witt (alias Rita Morris), a retrap from a BBC television crew who had a subtle sense of humour and with whom I remain friends. Miss P. Witt had a desire to sleep out in the open air with the other pee-wits and, as I too enjoyed these exploits, we took our sleeping bags to Windmill Gully and found a pleasant spot beside a group of parasol mushrooms which were picked fresh in the morning and fried for a delicious open-air breakfast.

Of film crews we had a few, and our friend Miss P .Witt came originally with the BBC to make a film of some research carried out by ex-warden Mike Harris on the island's gulls. For myself, I remember peering through their enormous telephoto lenses with a mixture of awe and envy, and comparing them with my meagre 400 millimetre lens. Those town folk were a strange presence on the island with their leather coats and boots and fancy cravats, and the same can be said for the Yorkshire Television crew who came in July 1973 accompanied by the man we longed to meet, Ronald Lockley himself. He too must have felt their presence odd because he was as elusive as he could possibly be and the most common phrase heard that week was an impatient 'where's Ronald'. It must have been an emotional visit for him and I imagine he was well out of their sight most of the time enjoying his dream island on a more personal level. He was not a big man and neither did he have an imposing manner, far from it. I had always admired his unsentimental enthusiasm for nature and his passion for adventurous travel. At times I thought perhaps he was a little impassive, but probably he was not at all, maybe it was just an ability to stand back and look on without becoming emotionally involved. Such people are often more effective in handling conservation issues. A pity then that his stay was short. He had travelled to Britain from his new home in New Zealand and was accompanied by his wife Jean.

The arrival on the island of some of the Yorkshire crew deserves comment. The first ones to arrive came by helicopter unannounced and included an Italian cameraman called Mustapha. We had one guest on the island who, at the time of their landing, was at the lighthouse and unaware of their arrival. Imagine then his face as he turned into the yard and spotted this gentleman from the Mediterranean in white suit and dark shades reclining on a sun lounge smoking a fat cigar, a mafia type image for sure! Was it a take over he wondered as he backed off. It was made worse by the fact that no staff were around and the place appeared to be otherwise deserted. Greg Glendell, for that was his name, crept away and hid behind a rock to await events. We note that no investigations were made on our behalf as to our fate

(Kidnap? Incarceration?). The truth was that Clare and myself were whisked away in the helicopter with a shopping list, as we had more people to cater for than we were told about, and Ray and Mike had business elsewhere (Sleep? Cup final?). We girls suffered a culture shock when, within a short time of leaving our island retreat, we found ourselves in a huge supermarket car park, myself gawping at the first dog I saw and Clare trying to resist the purchase of a large, multi-coloured beachball that caught her eye. We were unprepared and made a mess of the shopping too, but the helicopter ride was exciting.

Other celebrities that visited Skokholm were Hugh Miles and Bruce Pearson before they each became famous, Bruce as an artist and Hugh as a film cameraman with many superb natural history films to his credit. The late Sir John Hunt, of Everest fame, came with his wife and took a great deal of interest in the island and its wildlife. We resisted the temptation to ply him with questions about the mountain, after all he was on holiday, and it is to his credit that he never talked about it unless prompted. I remember him as being a strong character and delightfully modest. Peter Archer, Solicitor General at the time, also visited and at the time I didn't have the faintest idea what the title meant. Today, I'm not much wiser.

We were always told of the impending visit of anyone of notoriety so that we were properly prepared to make a good impression, but we were too busy to think about that. Skokholm was a wonderful place for people from all walks of life to mix together and share a common interest, which usually meant a great fascination for wildlife. Labourers mixed with judges, scientists with artists, doctors with shopkeepers etc., and nearly everyone got on. It has to be said that now and again we had individuals who were the proverbial pain in the neck, like Wingeing Walt from Texas and Yellow Trousers, but they added to the variety and spice of life. One man, paranoid about food, went on and on about the nutritional value of everything he was presented with. The cornflake packet, he declared, had more goodness in it than the cornflakes, so what did he get for his breakfast the next day – a torn up cornflakes packet, milk, sugar an' all! One lady evidently thought the place very unhygenic and washed, scrubbed and disinfected everything three times over. Not for her a rough, flagstone floor, wooden tabletops and Tilley lamps. Linoleum, formica and clean electric lights were her scene.

Most visitors went off birdwatching, but one lady sat behind a wall on the Knoll and spent the entire week reading a book. Another, wearing a long skirt and wellingtons floated round the island in a dream, totally absorbed in something, what, we knew not, but it wasn't the birds. She plucked a flower occasionally and stroked the odd hen, but she didn't know a puffin from a rabbit. Others enjoyed the social side as much as the wildlife, and would talk well into the early hours, especially if fortified by a few drinks.

Some even fell in love on the island; who wouldn't in such a romantic setting. We never knew if the romances lasted, but we would liked to have known!

Schools we had plenty of, some of them regularly like Forest Hill, High Arcal and St Edmunds Ware. The children were there to learn as well as to enjoy themselves. I felt sometimes that the school projects weren't imaginative enough for such a special environment. Limpet movement graphs became a standard joke, they didn't vary from year to year – the projects or the graphs! Not having much time myself to look about on the lower shore, I enjoyed wandering into the lab and looking at the trays of marine organisms laid out and labelled. The children (some of them were hardly children at fifteen or sixteen) showed me a wonderful selection of brittle stars, anemones, worms, seaweeds etc. Dozens of plants and animals of weird shapes and colours that *we* hardly ever saw! For example, I remember the first time they brought in a blue rayed limpet (*Patina pellucida*), a small, semi translucent shell set tightly into a shiny brown Laminaria frond and with beautiful rows of electric blue dashes radiating out from the point. They told me that the colour faded with age and that older individuals are to be found on the holdfasts.

Forest Hill week was eagerly looked forward to both for their good company and for the crate of gin and tonic that the staff brought over for their pleasure, and ours. Cook found lunch so much easier to prepare after a tumblerful of spiritual refreshment and plonked the poached egg on the toast with great gusto, often missing it altogether! Forest Hill were led by their headmaster, Dave Stanbury who had been coming to the island since the 1950s. He was a man with a strong presence whom we all liked and respected, as did all of his pupils and staff. His bright alert eyes, deep penetrating voice and inquiring mind are some of the characters I remember him by. In my mind, I see him in a faded blue fisherman's smock and a red kerchief round his neck, walking round the island with a walking stick, which I never thought he needed, but he apparently did. He was a man fully in command and must have been an excellent headmaster. The news of his sudden death early in 1997 came as a great shock.

At some time during their visit Forest Hill would disappear down into South Haven for a session of grovelling amongst the rocks in search of the toothed topshell. We had a colourful population – an infinite variety of reds, blues, greens etc. but they were no cherished subspecies, they were just daubed in enamel paint. The project had been ongoing since 1959 and was set up by Dave Stanbury in collaboration with John Barrett, marine biologist and warden of Dale Fort Field Centre at the time. The mark/release experiment brought to light some interesting facts about the population structure, growth rates, mortality etc. The single surviving painted topshell from 1959 was still there in 1974 and was therefore fifteen years old. Such detailed studies are of value not only in the specific data extracted from the analysis but also for the future

Forest Hill schoolboys 'having a ride' on the dumper truck

monitoring of environmental effects such as pollution or climate change. Will any changes be detected after the *Sea Empress* incident one wonders? The most significant natural disaster affecting the population until then had been the very cold winter of 1962/63 which had depleted numbers considerably.

Other school projects were in progress including the notorious limpet movement study by St Edmund's Ware, but it always seemed a shame to me that they were all projects that could equally well have been carried out on the mainland. Not so the riotous evening drinking sessions of one group which, in my strictly disciplined schooldays, would have been considered as justification for expulsion, but in that case was encouraged by the teachers themselves! Practical jokes abounded and we didn't escape them just because we were staff!

In June 1973, a student with the Berkshire College of Education undertook a study of our one and only species of newt, the palmate newt, which had been recorded in all three ponds, but most frequently North Pond. Our pond life tended to be ignored in favour of the birdlife, so this was a most welcome and refreshing study. Ian Vernon caught an amazing one hundred and ten newts, and was able to divide them into three colour types – dark, light and yellow. One interesting aspect of his work was discovering the amount of detritus brought to the pond by bathing gulls in the way of guano, salt and vegetation. This, he suggested, increased the productivity of the pond.

Palmate newt

Whoever they were, every visitor had a fair chance of being stranded on the island because of bad weather. It was most entertaining for us to witness the effect on them of being stormbound for several days. From carefree, happy individuals, some of them would quickly become anxious and irritable. They loved the island certainly, but an upset in their carefully planned itinerary they could not cope with. Wives were waiting, their companies would fall apart if they were not there at nine o'clock on Monday morning, and anyway they were out of cigarettes! As non-smokers ourselves, we watched with interest as they grew more fractious by the day, some of the more enterprising of them (or the really desperate ones) collected dry heather to smoke. First, cook had to give it a spell in the oven, with the bread of course as we could not waste gas. Some even pretended they enjoyed it! One of our young visitors, Bob Burgess, even began to bring over a supply of cigarettes for purchase in case of such an event. Spurred on by success, he later extended this underhand business to Mars bars and crisps, and soon realized he could up the price daily as the cravings increased with time.

Visitors who were particularly concerned about their stormbound state in respect of work or family commitments were able to make quick phone calls at the lighthouse to report their situation. This posed no problems, except on one occasion when a visitor went a little over the top in dramatizing the event – we had no food, he said, and were being forced to catch and eat rabbits for survival as well having to prise limpets off the rocks for frying etc., both of which were true, except that all that was on top of a normal, ample diet. The coastguard, who happened to be listening in, didn't know that though and alerted HMS *Brawdy* who took immediate action and sent out a rescue helicopter! What a drama, we were even in a national paper under the headline 'Birdwatchers hoodwink RAF'. They landed on Home Meadow in under ten minutes and took our people off in fine humour. I'm sure they all enjoyed the ride. The highlight of the incident for us was when a crew member jumped out and presented us staff, starving as we were, with two loaves of Mother's Pride sliced bread – awful stuff! It wasn't a patch on our 'home-baked' which only stormbound visitors were treated to!

Visitors were never stuck for more than three or four days, unless they wanted to be, as was the case with two runaway boys who absconded to the lighthouse when they heard a rumour that the long-awaited boat was on its way. They were fully acclimatized to their stormbound situation and evidently wanted to extend it. Extend it they did, for ten days, as the boatman refused to accept responsibility for them and it was the end of the season anyway. They eventually left on a Trinity House boat, still reluctantly. That wasn't the only time that our visitors were rescued by the lighthouse service either; several times they opted for a rough passage on the *Winston Churchill* all the way back to Swansea, a long way from the car park at Martinshaven!

We too were shipped off occasionally for medical or dental attention and it was almost embarrassing how we were given preferential treatment so readily. 'From the island? You'll have to get back before it blows up', was how we were greeted, and that without any pleading from us. Fortunately, we never suffered from anything much and the only occasion that could have been serious was when Ray proved the theory that earwigs are called earwigs because they have a propensity for disappearing inside people's ears, a theory that is hotly contested by many entomologists! When he woke in the middle of the night complaining of a thunderstorm in his ear, I did what I thought best and poured in a jug of water. Out came a fully grown earwig!

The RAF rescue craft was not the only helicopter that landed on the lawn. From inside the Wheelhouse one day, I heard a thunderous roar and ran outside to leap up on the bench and see what was going on. I was more annoyed than pleased to see this alien, yellow thing with whirring propellers just twenty feet from me, because I saw my chickens in a state of utmost terror dashing in all directions. 'No eggs' was my first thought. He was a potato merchant, evidently a wealthy one, but he didn't bring us any potatoes for his cheek, instead he flew us round the island to take dozens of aerial photographs, and we were more than happy with that. However, we impressed on him that he shouldn't make a habit of it! Helicopters cause tremendous disturbance by flying low over seabird colonies and we had our Trinity House pilots well trained.

One day I spotted a small boat coming in to South Haven and rushed down to fend it off, as there was positively no landing by private individuals. When I saw a lady approaching me on the track with a pleading expression on her face and Ronald Lockley's book *The Island* clutched in her hand, I softened at once. 'It could have been me,' was what I thought. I would have done exactly that, and would been very upset to be turned away. After all, she could do no harm, especially if I showed her round. So I did, and hopefully she returned for a week's stay in later years as she said she would.

One week, there came a visitor whom I will never forget, and who triggered off what was later on to become a fanatical interest, in fact an obsession. A being of high intelligence and a streamlined body that moved through the water with ultimate grace and boundless energy. This visitor lived life to the full, judging by the spontaneous display of joyful activity we were treated to. He came to the island under his own steam, with the boat but not actually in it. He was of course a bottle-nosed dolphin.

Donald, otherwise known as Beaky, arrived in the Martinshaven area in April 1975. As Terry sculled out to the *Sharon* in his small dinghy, Donald would go to greet him and act out his self-imposed duty as an escort. It was said, although I'm sure it wasn't true, that he had fallen in love with the dinghy! Dolphins are more intelligent than that, he merely loved playing and exercising with it. Rushing exitedly around Martinshaven while outgoing visitors boarded the *Sharon*, he would then accompany her out to the islands. We didn't have the pleasure of watching him leaping alongside or riding the bow wave. Nor did we see him nosing along behind with his beak dangerously close to the propeller or mischieviously making splashes in an attempt to soak people, but we did see him leaping and bounding around the boat as she drew in. We watched and admired his sleek body as it left the water glistening with silver droplets, and he seemed to be looking at us all the while with a bright gentle eye. We saw too, the pronounced beak that gives the species its name. Donald Dolphin stole the show. Newly arrived visitors, the mail bag, Terry and everything else took second place all the time that fascinating creature was in sight. He seemed to be something more than a species of cetacean living out his role in the marine environment. There was something powerful emanating from that animal, something alluring and, I felt, enviable.

Now after much reading and reflection, I acknowledge that dolphins and cetaceans, whilst possessing a large and complex brain comparable to a human, are unburdened with any of the material and moral complications that bring about disharmony amongst human beings. Maybe that is the reason for their apparent lack of aggression and their gentle manners towards their own kind, and indeed towards man as well. I didn't even think about that then, but the arrival of Donald on the scene had sparked off something which I was to take more seriously in years to come. Had it been today, I couldn't have resisted the temptation to jump into the water with him. Will we ever understand very much about dolphins and whales and their complicated communication systems, and more to the point will we condescend to learn anything from them. I certainly hope so!

Donald eventually left the area and turned up in Cornwall. He finally disappeared from there and was never seen again. Those who knew him could not but fear the worst since fishing boats were operating on the area using large purse seine nets. These long nets are deployed to completely encircle shoals of mackerel, and a dolphin could not hope to scan the entire net. Hopefully, Donald did not drown in a net but, if he did, the joy he brought to so many people may help to save others of his own kind.

As we ourselves were a part of the human element on the island, it would be a grand omission not to say a few words of how relations between us developed. As may be expected in such a situation, a certain amount of acrimony arose between ourselves and Mike for various reasons. First and foremost there was the situation itself – three people confined to a small island and living in very close proximity to each other. Tensions were bound to arise but, young and inexperienced as we were, we did not realise then that it was all part of 'normal' island life. We later called it 'islanditis' and recognised it as a temporary loss of perspective. Some of the symptoms were hyper-sensitivity, irritability and failure to see another's point of view. It was sometimes diffi-cult to conceal this underlying tension from visitors as we all ate and sat together reg-ularly. Although most of the tension was between us and Mike, it has to be said that Ray and I also had our bad days and it wasn't always easy to conceal an icy counte-nance towards each other at mealtimes!

The tensions arose mainly because we felt that Mike was too much the research stu-dent and too little the warden and shouldn't have expected so much assistance from us on the research side, primarily because of the general workload we already had. That was a bit of an irony because we both enjoyed that side of the job most of all. Perhaps the best way to describe it is that we felt more used than appreciated. It may be true, as Mike has pointed out since, that, because we shared the work of cooking and assistant wardening, we each felt the burden of two jobs. It certainly was an advantage in one way for us, but perhaps it did give us a false perception. Also, Mike was in a difficult position as he felt that he was trying to serve several masters who were pulling in different directions, i.e. the Edward Grey Institute at Oxford, the West Wales Naturalist Trust and our visitors. Exactly where our responsibilities lay was not laid down in black and white and, because we had seen the island being run differently in 1971, we assumed we knew our roles. We inevitably voiced our complaints to the Trust, they in turn involved the EGI and between them they tried to sort it out. Meanwhile the atmosphere fluctuated from bad to good and back again. Tempers rarely flared, mostly it surfaced as a cold, awkward indifference. However, eventually a compromise was reached, our workload was eased a little and matters were greatly improved.

It couldn't have been easy for Mike, with him being alone and us effectively a unit, but there was another contributing factor that enhanced the difficulties. We were from different walks of life. Mike's background was very different to ours. He had had little experience of dealing with the likes of us and it was a long time before we realised that, let alone tried to understand it as part of the problem. This created a further rift which made it nearly impossible for us to talk the matter over like sensible adults. Indeed, it took a few contemplative sessions on Spy Rock for me to analyse the problem and see it more clearly. Indeed, matters were already considerably improved when Mike and myself talked it through over a pleasant meal in Oxford and cleared it up once and for all.

It all seems very trivial now, but we learnt by it, and most importantly, it didn't affect our work or our enjoyment of the island. It was a part of the overall experience, and pales into insignifice when compared with the more positive elements.

CHAPTER 11

Summertime

Swimming was one of the great, physical joys of summer. It was a powerful revitalizing agent and a sensual pleasure. Initiation was on a warm sunny afternoon in May, when most of the birds were laying eggs or thinking about it. I would grab a towel and head towards South Haven for the first dip of the year. The water, turquoise and crystal clear, would be lapping gently over the white-limed steps and looking so inviting. Not for me a rough sea with waves that explode in your face before pulling you under! Always there were flotillas of puffins cruising beneath Alice, who I liked to think kept a watchful eye on me because I preferred to go it alone on this first swim. It was undoubtedly one of the best swimming pools in the world, tucked beneath those warm cliffs, bright with flowers and buzzing with insects and birds.

It would either be a rash jump or a sliding in gingerly from one step down to the next until well and truly submerged. Either way it was a hell of a shock, one that I still experience here in Cornwall. That first time, short-lived as it was, was by far the worst, and never again during the season did it feel so cold. After that it became more of a pleasure than a rude introduction ceremony. It is often hard to describe the perverse pleasure one gets from swimming in icy cold water, but for those who don't understand, there is always the pleasure of getting out!

Time spent actually languishing on the steps in the sun came later on in July and August when most chicks had done the decent thing and fledged, and then we were not so busy with our ringing pliers. To gaze across the sound to the beautiful and extensive sandy beach below Marloes didn't make me envious. You could see people densely packed around the place where the path descended to the beach and, away from there, humanity was sparse. Very nice, but there was something much more comfortable and secure about being on an island. You knew exactly who and what was around! It was warm (probably warmer than on that beach) on those white steps, often baking hot in fact as the sea breeze blew into the west side of the island. Most of our visitors left the island with an impressive sun-tan.

When easterly winds roughed up the sea in South Haven, it meant going across to North Haven for a swim. This was a lovely cove with varying amounts of sand on the tiny beach, but it was not much in the sun. However, my swim before breakfast was nearly always taken in this cove, and so were the only swimming lessons I ever gave to a friend when I was swept away in the swell, but fortunately deposited on the sand at his feet by the next incoming wave! There ended the lessons. The evening dips in North Haven were by far the most memorable. Sometimes, as darkness fell, I watched shadowy petrels flitting over my head as I lay floating on my back, and sometimes a seal came closer than normal to investigate the strange pale body lounging in the water. There were midnight swims too, often spontaneous affairs organised by visitors or students, where no one bothered about bathing costumes, but the presence of lots of people meant no encounters with wildlife. Seals often came into the haven by day, but they would never allow a close approach. A pup was born on the little beach one October, rendering it out of bounds. Anyone who has seen a newborn pup with its big doleful, eyes and silky white coat will understand how protective we felt about it.

I remember days and days of sunshine, but there must have been bad weather too. The long hot summers of 1975 and 1976 brought drought conditions and scorched the turf brown. That, I didn't like. We longed for rain then to revive and refresh the island, and it didn't come until September. The rabbits were desperate, out feeding by day and chewing anything that was green, thistles, ragwort etc., The dust parched our throats and blew around in clouds on the dry cliff slopes where erosion was particularly bad, exacerbated no doubt by the trampling of the birds. Those years, the shearwater colony was extemely bare and so fragile with little vegetation to bind the soil. Light warm, easterly winds blew incessantly, but at least we were able to cool down in the sea.

Trips to Grassholm with Cambell on the *Dale Queen* were some of the highlights of the summer seasons. First a breathless lighthouse keeper would appear at the wheelhouse door during breakfast with a message that the boat would go if there were enough willing participants, for a small fee of course. There were always enough, for what visitor would have missed the chance of a visit to that spectacular gannetry. The keeper was soon despatched with instructions to send a positive reply. Then it was bedlam with people gulping breakfast down, grabbing cameras and anoraks and myself frantically cutting sandwiches to pack into large biscuit tins. Gallon containers were filled with orange squash and piles of paper cups stuffed in the rucksack of anyone who happened to be standing around. One or two of us staff would go as crew because numbers were restricted by the Board of Trade licence. It actually meant little more than grabbing ropes and helping visitors on and off the boat, although we were allowed to take the wheel sometimes under Cambell's supervision. For staff left on Skokholm, it was like taking a holiday, hardly anyone to get lunch for and the island almost to yourself for a day.

Someone would be posted on lookout for the boat, just as on a Saturday, and as soon as she was sighted there was a rush for the landing. Boarding was generally straightforward, but there was one day when everything went wrong at the start. First, a vis-

Martin Garnett and Clare Lloyd on the boat to Grassholm

itor stepping into the dinghy was overcome with a feeling of insecurity and refused to let go of the steps with his hands as it drew away. He formed the classic human bridge, but was manhandled to safety before he took an involuntary dip. Then we lost a rowlock, and then an oar as we tried to recover it. As if that wasn't enough, when we pulled away from South Haven, some person with a cool head noticed that the dinghy was drifting away in the current. No one had tied it on! Somehow, we got it back and survived the rest of the trip.

Away we went on the seven-mile journey, spirits high and everyone on the lookout for anything unusual in the way of birds or cetaceans. We either went through Broad Sound, looking intently through our binoculars at Skomer's Mewstone for a sighting of the nesting peregrines, or we went round the south coast of Skokholm where the crazi-

Euan Dunn on the boat to Grassholm

ly folded and tilted strata of the sandstone rock captured our attention, before being diverted by waving lighthouse keepers. If we were lucky, we would go through the Wildgoose race without too much tossing, and then on through relatively calm water until we got to the boiling seas around Grassholm where many currents met in a swirling, confused mass. Often on the way we encountered auks feeding. When Clare was with us she took careful note for her study of how many miles out those feeding zones were. She found that, from an area some six to seven miles out, there was a constant stream of auks going to and from the islands (this in itself a useful guide for the birds as to the whereabouts of good fishing grounds). Always we would see shearwaters and just occasionally petrels treading daintily on the surface picking off plankton. These sprite-like birds, seen so fleetingly by twilight, moonlight or torchlight by our visitors, suddenly became real birds of the ocean. They were so dainty, so small and yet so perfectly adapted for life on land and sea. It was a great thrill for those seeing them for the first time.

Quite often we saw the rolling backs and small triangular fins of porpoises. The calmer the sea the easier they were to locate. Sometimes concentrations of diving gannets gave us a clue to their whereabouts. It was always worth checking beneath them (and that applies off the Cornish coast too). We saw no very large groups, as did naturalist T. Warren Davies in 1928 when he reported several hundred, possibly a thousand, just inside Milford Haven estuary. Interestingly, the present wardens on Skokholm, Graham Thompson and Teresa Purcell report regular sightings in the tide race, south-west of the island. Today an alarming number of porpoises and dolphins are caught in mono-filament fishing nets, resulting in a severe reduction in numbers. Hopefully, the new restrictions on drift netting for tuna fish will alleviate the situation.

We also saw dolphins occasionally, but at that time I could not have distinguished between species. They were most likely common, bottle-nosed or more rarely Risso's dolphins. From the boat, we could see clearly the gently sloping outline of Skokholm, its flat surface pimpled with rocky outcrops. It rose gradually towards the south-western end, the highest point being only one hundred and seventy feet above sea level. Nothing dramatic or impressive about it, it was just the island we all loved. Even with Skokholm miles behind us, it seemed to take ages for the humped-shaped lump of basalt that was Grassholm to draw nearer. When eventually it did, the white line extending over the top of it's twenty-two acres became better defined as a mass of closely packed gannets, and there were always hundreds of them soaring over the island and the surrounding sea.

Soon we would be wallowing in the rough water off the gannetry, all of us hanging on to the boat rail and quite overcome by the spectacle before us. Most apparent was the fierce stench of guano and rotting seaweed that assaulted our pampered nostrils, not really unpleasant but certainly a memorable part of the experience! The noise was overpowering, but what else could you expect from a colony of seabirds forty-thousand strong not counting non-breeders! It was a vibrant picture, an everchanging collage of dazzling white, jet black and sea green, all electrified by the fierce sunlight. Their torpedo bodies fell from the sky all around us, piercing the sea in pursuit of mackerel, spouting jets of white water everywhere. We saw gannets cruising leisurly just a few feet above the surface and then suddenly they would tip over, draw in their wings and slice down into the water. Others flew much higher, using their acute vision to locate the fish, stalling first, then flipping over before a fast dive shot them beneath the water. Out of sight for only a few seconds, they bounced back up with fish already swallowed or else lost.

Cambell or George were skillful in manoeuvring the boat into a narrow gut in the rocks on the sheltered south-eastern side. The slightest swell made the landing tricky and, in anything other than relatively calm weather, quite impossible. A small colony of kittiwakes had cemented their nests to the ledges and I'm afraid must have been disturbed by our landings. Fortunately it didn't happen too often. They never bred on Skokholm (although a pair once built a nest there), so the good views we had of those slender gulls with soft ebony eyes and dove grey backs, were an added bonus.

One by one we had to leap off the boat on to the rocks, timing it precisely as she rose and fell with the swell. Then came the scramble ashore and over the thick fescue turf on to the island proper. There were no rabbits out there to keep down the grass and no farmer these days would go to the trouble of ferrying grazing stock out to such a lonely retreat. The ground in places was treacherous, a series of huge tussocks separated by narrow winding channels, all this hidden by the long grass ready to twist an unwary ankle. The irregular surface was said to be the result of collapsed puffin burrows. The books (mostly Lockley's) tell of 250 000 pairs of puffins around 1890. This knowledge was apparently gleaned from the locals; just how they came to that figure (or any figure for that matter) is a mystery, but there certainly must have been a lot out there. They are said to have moved across to Skokholm, where small numbers already existed, leaving the island to about two hundred gannets. There were no records of gannets before 1820. Once, small numbers of the latter were taken as bait for lobster pots until they were protected in 1890 by the owner. Since then there has been an incredible expansion of the colony and the island is now fully protected, with landing either prohibited or severely restricted, a wise move by the RSPB. We were lucky in those days because, apart from the occasional boat from Dale Fort (the *Lord Hurcombe*) run by the warden, David Emmerson, we were the only trippers out there.

After the sea journey of nearly two hours, lunch was taken in a suitable quiet place to soak up the atmosphere and to give us time to advise our visitors on what they should

Kittiwake

Gannets on Grassholm. Adults and chicks

and shouldn't do. People ready with cameras were told the strict rule of not trying to go in amongst the gannets and to keep at such a distance that the non breeding birds on the fringe of the colony remained there. In fact those wary birds nearly always flew off. Then everyone went their own way to look at the colony or to explore the rest of the island. Inevitably some still felt queasy, if they were not actually sick, after the boat trip, but I don't think anyone ever regretted going.

At that time the gannets had not begun to spread over the brow of the island (as they have now) and it was easy to view them and take pictures from the highest elevation without disturbing them. Over the years they had been spreading from the west side towards the east, and the increase is still going on. It was a truly wonderful sight, thousands of portly, white birds regularly spaced out on their nests. These were built on hummocks, years worth of accumulated material, composed of dried grass and seaweed mixed with guano and combined with all kinds of debris. With gold on their heads, dagger-like bills and eyes of the palest silver blue, the gannets sported a noble countenance. If they were sitting on eggs the scene was fairly orderly, but if they had chicks there was a great deal of commotion with much stabbing at neighbours as they came and went. Pairs raised their beaks to the sky in graceful salute, necks almost intertwined and bills clashing. When about to leave the nest, they stiffly raised their bills and turned about (sky-pointing). There was little room for a misunderstanding, so all those elaborate signals were necessary; each pair was only at pecking distance from its neighbours. Well grown chicks looked comical as they sat upright gazing about them, just enormous heaps of white down with stark, black faces. Later on in September/October time each year, they were deserted and, clad in their new dark grey feathers, they were left to run the gauntlet through the colony and down to the sea. Their breeding season was a long one with birds present on the island from mid February until October.

After making several trips to Grassholm, I liked best to creep away from the nucleus of gannets and look at the other wildlife there. It was on Grassholm that I first looked into the pale green eye of a nesting shag and fully appreciated the lovely metallic sheen on their feathers. The very young nestlings were dark and strange, like little reptiles, and they clung together in the bowl of the untidy nest which often incorporated bits of coloured fishing line. As with the incident involving the raven chick told in an earlier chapter, this material often caused problems with gannets and indeed, over the years, many birds have been freed or found dead, held fast to the nest by this lethal stuff. The RSPB now runs a trip out to Grassholm in the late season to deal with the unfortunate chicks. Currently, monofilament nets are responsible for the deaths of thousands of seabirds, mostly auks, each winter.

Seals were always there, basking on the rocks at low tide, and offering us closer and more intimate views than we had on Skokholm. For us regulars, it was easy to relax just like they were, and loaf about contentedly on the rocks just enjoying being there. Many times I would find myself gazing westwards to the Smalls Lighthouse, a tall and lonely tower rising abruptly a further ten miles out to sea. I often expressed a wish to go there but never dreamt I would. Well I did, thanks to Cambell and this is how it happened. In 1973, our first year, we set off one day for Grassholm rather later than usual with our visitors and with Clare on board too (another Smalls enthusiast). Just prior to landing Cambell said to us 'are you getting off here or are you coming to the Smalls?' I doubt if he'd ever had such an enthusiastic crew. It was glassy calm, a perfect day and good enough to land stores, as this was strictly a business trip under contract from Trinity House. Even on such a day, there was a hefty swell washing round the reef as we edged in and greeted the exiled keepers who smiled quizzically at us. Being out there for a month at a time, they probably couldn't understand our obvious

Shag

excitement. We found the atmosphere rather eerie, such isolation and such austere simplicity in the huge concrete tower looming above us, built primarily for strength and purpose. We looked for the tea stains reputed to be blatently evident beneath the windows where the keepers threw their dregs. They were there all right.

Around the tower at low tide is a spread of rock, the keepers' only playground, and one which is decidedly precarious. We didn't land unfortunately as this wasn't a social visit and we couldn't justify the extra time involved. The keepers were relieved by helicopter so there was no question of them being marooned for weeks like in the old days. Maintenance men were still occasionally landed there from one or other boat.

Out there we saw many more storm petrels, and porpoises were ever present. Too soon though, it was time for the ten mile trip back to Grassholm. After picking up our deserted visitors on Grassholm, we had further treats in store that evening in the form of thousands of shearwaters rafting on the sea between Skomer and Skokholm. We arrived back late, but highly exhilarated after a most memorable day.

Ray and myself usually took it in turns to go to Grassholm. The one who didn't go cooked the evening meal and that was a spirited affair after such a day out.

Fine summer's evenings were ideal for barbeques and, looking back, I think it a shame that we didn't have more. Wood for fires wasn't easy to come by and we scarcely had enough for our cottage fires on cold autumn evenings. One way of getting half a bucket of coal was to follow the dumper truck to the lighthouse after a delivery and pick up the fallen pieces. The amount you got depended on the recklessness of the driver. It usually happened that they took pity on our peasant-like ingenuity and rewarded us with a sack now and again. Our only wood source was driftwood and much effort and time was needed to search for it and then recover it from the awkward places where it would get washed in. When dry however, this wood, so impregnated with salt, burned hot and bright. Some visitors made it a personal challenge to collect as much as possible and their help was greatly appreciated. Their enjoyment of the task was insatiable and I'm sure primitive instincts were at work!

Wood for barbeques then was at a premium, and perhaps that's why we didn't have many. One such, that took place in South Haven, immediately springs to mind. It happened because a visitor called Bruce took it on himself to build a huge spit on which to roast rabbits. He did a splendid job and we had to do it justice. We procured some rabbits and down they went to South Haven with mountains of other food and plenty of home brew and wine. Somehow we had loud music, I can't remember how, but it was good and loud enough to get people dancing on the landing until four in the morning! That was interesting, bearing in mind the steps going down to the sea and the effect on one's balance of copious home brew. The only concession cook received was a half hour delay on breakfast next day.

There were special culinary delights on offer for picnics and barbeques which involved a bit of adventuresome scrambling about, but you needed a very low spring tide. You also needed a long wire hook to poke into large crevices. Crab Bay, as its name implies, was the best place to find large edible crabs. Crab Bay Rocks to be precise. We would mount an expedition an hour or so before the lowest tide and set off with an empty sack and plenty of optimism. We usually came back with the empty sack minus the optimism, but there were times when we struck lucky and found one, or even two large crabs, but they didn't go far between us. More important was the spirit in which everyone took part and also the exceptional beauty of the place. It was a different world down there. Long ribbons of gleaming ochre seaweed billowed and swayed in the blue limpid water and swirled round our legs, soothing us with its clammy coolness. We saw starfish, exquisitely patterned topshells, squidgy red anemones and tiny blennys flashing across rock pools. It was a colourful, fascinating environment, never mind if the bag was empty and we had nothing to show for it. We always regretted the tide coming in and hastening us back to the cliff.

Butterflies were plentiful on the island in summer; there were colourful migrants, like painted ladies, red admirals, clouded yellows and peacocks, and also a number of resident species. The sun-bright flowers of golden-rod and ragwort blazed with red-patterned wings angled this way and that, daubed with powder blue and yellow, flashing black velvet or chequered black and orange. With the immigration of painted ladies, came silver Y moths that flew by day as well as by night. Migrant clouded yellows were rare most years. They were unmistakable, butter yellow specks scooting over the dark green bracken. You could often watch migrant butterflies coming across the sea to the island, sometimes perilously close to the waves. I thought it remarkable that many of them came all the way from North Africa. They were such fragile creatures, with only a tenuous hold on life, and yet they were winging their way across a vast ocean expanse, often alone but evidently with a great purpose.

Among the residents, three generations of small coppers defended territories in bracken clearings where their foodplants (*Rumex sps.*) grew. Their close relatives, common blues, sought out the heather belts, where they sipped nectar from the flowers and laid their eggs on birds-foot-trefoil growing in the turf between the tussocks. What a beautiful mix of colour were those pastel blue wings among the heather flowers. I remember my surprise when I learnt that the irridescent colours of these last two species were not pigments at all, but were created physically by light striking tiny corrugations on the wing scales.

In 1976 a few dark green fritillaries were seen in fast erratic flight over Orchid Bog. They were not altogether unexpected since their foodplants, violets, were very common on the island. Once, a small pearl-bordered fritillary turned up, probably blown in from the mainland. Large and small white butterflies were abundant most years, but they included many migrants among their numbers. We had no trouble with them, but only because we planted no cabbages! We also had a population of green-veined whites, and I had no idea what their foodplant was except that it would have been a crucifer. Graylings and wall browns were scarce, both of them having caterpillars that fed on grasses. However, most numerous and dear to my heart was another brown butterfly, the meadow brown *(Maniola jurtina)*.

In 1976, the year of the drought. Dr David Lees from Cardiff University visited the island with a party of students. He had a special interest in the meadow browns on Skokholm, fostered by studies carried out on the Isles of Scilly by E. B. Ford. With the imminent introduction of our non bird ringing status the following year, it seemed a good idea to get involved in alternative studies. So, before I could blink, I was brandishing a net and setting forth into one of three designated study areas, decked in shorts and wellingtons, the most suitable attire for the job. In hot pursuit of the butterflies, Dr. Lees and myself would fly around catching them in a single sweep of the net (jurting we called it), and then dispatch them into cardboard pillboxes for further examination in the laboratory. This entailed counting the number of tiny spots on the hindwing of both males and females, a character which had been shown to vary across England – the frequency of high-spotted individuals increasing towards the western extremities i.e. the Scilly Isles and Cornwall. We decided to undertake detailed population studies and that entailed marking them individually, first with cellulose paint and then, more successfully, with marker pens. Nearly every day during the flying season, which extended from 28 June to 23 August in 1976, the year of most intensive study, saw me out and about after as many as I could catch. Dozens were processed on most days and even on dull days it was possible to flush them out of the bracken. For some idea of their numbers, it was estimated that roughly one hundred a day were emerging. The work continued in only one area, that of East Bog, in 1977 and 1978. The butterflies were found in distinct colonies separated by certain physical factors which inhibited their dispersal, such as the broad expanse of short turf comprising Home Meadow. However, our studies showed that there was some movement between colonies. We also sampled butterflies from the small island of Gateholm on the mainland opposite.

'Jurting'

I have to admit that at first I was not too sure of the questions we were trying to answer, but simply enjoyed the exercise and the sport of catching them. Certain facts and features that came to light struck me as interesting in themselves, like the age of the oldest known male and female, both at twenty-four days, and that the average life span was four to six days. It was one thing to be told that the eye spots on the wings were to attract the attention of predators away from the vulnerable head region, but quite another to find the clearly defined outline of a bird's beak on the wing, a bit like a pencil mark. It was good to know that the butterflies really can escape that way. Also of note, was the ease with which the slow-flying males were caught in the net compared to the larger, faster flying females, implying that the latter were better equipped for eluding their predators. As mentioned above, marking demonstrated that some individuals moved round the island, but whether by intention or as a result of strong winds we never knew. The whereabouts of all those butterflies at night and in dull weather was food for thought, especially as the colony around North Haven totalled three thousand by our estimate. They were, of course, hidden deep in the vegetation.

As expected our studies demonstrated that our butterflies were certainly high spotted. Not a significant character in itself, but it was suspected that the gene responsible was also connected with an adaptability to maritime climate, isolated populations and dispersal ability. Our work went a little way to verifying that theory, as well as providing data on population dynamics. The work was written up and published in the *Biological Journal of the Linnean Society* and is listed in the references at the back of the book. In 1981, a colleage of E. B. Ford, W. H. Dowedsell, who studied the variability of spotting throughout Europe, published a monograph called 'The Life of the Meadow Brown'.

With all those butterflies around, one might have expected to find the odd caterpillar feeding on grass of one or other species. The trouble was they fed at night and hid by day. A few nightly expeditions in spring or autumn (they overwinter as larvae) did reveal a few, but I was glad it was the adults that were the subject of my study, there was enough nightwork already!

In 1977, I began the butterfly monitoring programme initiated by Ernest Pollard of Monk's Wood in 1976. This extremely pleasant task involved doing a standard walk of about half a mile or so, incorporating a variety of micro habitats, and recording any butterfly that flew within an imaginary ten foot box around you. Conditions had to be relatively still and sunny and it was undertaken once a week (there were weeks when the weather didn't permit, so our summers couldn't always have been good!). It was a simple procedure, the only difficulty being not to get distracted by the other wildlife. The results were useful for detecting fluctuations in the populations from year to year, and could also be used to detect any change in the habitat. Since the size of the rabbit population influenced the vegetation, any major changes in that respect would have been reflected in the numbers and species of butterflies.

Dr Lees also brought to the island a Robinson mercury vapour trap to begin a moth trapping programme. Since it revived a childhood interest, I was more than happy with this and ran the trap regularly in 1976 and 1977. It was not just the scientific value of recording which species were there and in what kind of numbers that made it so enjoyable, it was the fact that the moths were so beautiful, even the plainest and less colour-ful ones were worthy of close study. Their need to be cryptic has led to all manner of design in shape, wing pattern and colour, and I know at least one nationally respected artist whose work has been inspired by the patterns and colours displayed by moths.

The trap and the accompanying generator were rigged up by the well. That was con-venient for us and, with its sloping south-easterly aspect, it was expected to attract moths from all around. It is possible that moths from the mainland may even have been attracted to it sometimes. The theory goes that moths are guided by the moon at night and fly in a line at right angles to it, hence they fly across the earth's surface rather than away from it. They therefore spin in ever decreasing circles around any light that they are attracted to. Once they were attracted to and circling the bulb in the trap, they were deflected downwards into it by a ring of plastic, passing down through a funnel into the main container. Inside this were layers of egg boxes to which they could cling and settle on for the night without damaging each other. It is a mar-vellous theory but it still puzzles me why they don't all end up on the moon!

For my part, I had to quickly learn identification skills, and also how to set a specimen of each for the island collection. This latter I didn't enjoy, but I did it nevertheless. It was unpleasant having to kill them and it was a fiddly task setting them. Their bodies soon stiffened and one had to be quick. Identification was slow at first but, once the common species became familiar to me, naming them became easier and each time a new species turned up it was with great anticipation that I turned to the book to find it. In those days we used *Moths of the British Isles* in two volumes by South. Several migrant species came to the trap as would be expected, including dark sword grass, the gem and the vestal. Certain moths were very striking, among them I recall ruby tiger, angle shades, frosted orange and ghost swift. Perhaps there's something in the name as well! The angle shades is a classic example of camouflage, with its crinkled wings and broken pattern of pink, buff and green markings to mimic perfectly the ground vegetation. Not surprisingly, because of the lack of foodplants, the only hawk moth recorded was the migrant humming-bird hawk, a nectar loving moth of whirring wings and extensile tongue.

Many other moths had wonderful camouflage and one could imagine them blend-ing in perfectly with lichens on rocks and trees. Their wings were often covered in lit-tle pearls of merging colour, grey, green, dull brown or white, and encased in thin curv-ing lines of black just like the thallus of a lichen. I am thinking particularly of moths like the marbled green and the marbled beauty, but the commonest was the marbled coro-net. The pale brown wings of netted pugs were broken by a network of very thin, dark lines, like many of the encrusting lichens. I spent some time searching cliff faces and rocky outcrops in the day to find out where they hid, and I found some too. To my surprise however, they were resting on plain rock and were quite conspicuous, but of course that is why I found them! Unlike a foraging bird though, I wasn't interested in eating them! The diurnal yellow shell was exceedingly common, but their yellow ochre wings with hundreds of concentric rings like a seashell were no camouflage on the red rock either. There were many more moths that came to my trap which are deserving of comment but there is too little space here.

One evening I spread a sheet over a plastic dustbin containing a Tilley lamp out on Northern Plain with the idea of attracting moths and examining them at my leisure. Apart from a few moths, I also caught the attentions of a passing helicopter from HMS *Brawdy* which came low and circled several times to investigate the phenomenon. It must have looked just like a grounded UFO! Some moths flew only at dusk and were seldom attracted to the trap, and so 'dusking' with a butterfly net became another popular pastime. A very pleasant way of 'mothing' was to take a Tilley out to the ragwort in the Bog and search over the flowers. Silver Y moths and several noctuids were drawn to them, and anyway it was a lovely atmosphere out there on a calm summer's night with the bright yellow flowers and fluttering insects.

After intensive trapping in 1976 and 1977, I brought up to date the moth list for the island. Other recorders had operated on Skokholm and, by the end of 1977, a total of 165 species of Lepidoptera had been recorded, including butterflies. The list was published in *Nature in Wales*, volume sixteen, number three. Trapping programmes over the years had also brought to light (no pun intended) several other interesting facts about the moths. One was that the resident populations of several species seemed to fluctuate considerably over the years, and this could have been connected to food availability (ref. the cyclic nature and unpredictability of many plant species), weather or immigration. Cinnebar moth, heart and dart and smoky wainscot were examples of these. Other species appeared to be subject to periodic extinctions and recolonizations, probably due to severe localization of the food plant. The small wainscot and the frosted orange may have been thus affected. Some appeared to be recent colonizers like the rosy rustic and the Barrett's coronet. Easterly winds characteristically brought over certain moths from the mainland, like the muslin moth, a lovely velvety brown creature with a softly hairy thorax, and most of these were unlikely to be resident because of the absence of their foodplants. Although migrants were frequently recorded, the origin of an American moth, the beautiful *utetheisa*, which was caught in 1961, remains obscure.

Since anything that flew was of interest, the damselflies did not escape my attention. I knew none when I came to the island and I only knew two when I left. Those were our resident species, *Ishnura elegans* and *Coenagrion puella*. They were thin, wispy-bodied insects that darted here and there in the bogs, allowing no more than a fleeting glimpse before they penetrated the rush clumps and seemingly evaporated. I knew nothing about them at first, but finally I caught one each of them by drawing them into glass tubes as they rested on their stems, so that I could study the details of their anatomy. Eventually they were given names and a real existence. There were momentary sightings of larger dragonflies scooting at tremendous speed over the bracken in search of something or somewhere (prey perhaps or a breeding pond?). Any hopes of pinning names on those were quickly abandoned.

Even bumble bees were given a go, and we proudly named three large species of Bombus, each with different colours on the tip of the abdomen. *Bombus lucorum*, *Bombus lapidarius* and *Bombus terrestris* were dutifully recorded and that was the end of the foray into the more difficult insect groups. If you had the time, it was never ending, but time was always a limiting factor. Pity, for our sakes, that the glow-worms released many years ago in South Haven didn't survive. To see those tiny green lights glowing on our banks or walls would have been magic indeed.

Lastly, even though the ants were small and normally didn't attract any attention, they could not be ignored on certain days in July, when the first hot, calm and humid weather triggered off their nuptial flight. Home Meadow and the skies above were a humming, fidgety mass of tiny insects, with a tendency to drift away in the slightest breeze. Their summer was short, vital and highly productive. Gulls, chickens and several other birds had a field day, rushing about gorging themselves on the spontaneous and unexpected feast.

A fine evening in July finds a group of people sitting quietly on the north slopes of Twinlet Bay. The light is fading rapidly and we stare intently at the cliff face opposite with binoculars. They are focused on a tiny, black and white object teetering on the edge of a ledge, a razorbill chick on the point of fledging. It has no down left on its body and is a minature of its parent, even showing the beginning of a white eye stripe. It flaps and jumps about on the edge, falters, turns and makes as if to return to hide beneath its parent's wing again. We sigh! It is preparing for the biggest moment in it's life, a timely jump that will take it down to the swirling sea below, which is all it will know until, if it survives, it returns to the cliffs in two or three years time as an adolescent. But now it is on the edge again, the activity becomes frenzied, we watch with bated breath, unable to bear the suspense any longer. It has already kept us there for two evenings running, behaving just like this and convincing us that we were about to witness the great event. Each time we have been disappointed. Tonight is sure to be the night, we think. Will it, won't it?

At last, and very suddenly as if we ourselves had willed it, it is off, taking the plunge; we raise a cheer of triumph, but its not safe yet. It descends swiftly, flapping furiously on wings that have scarcely begun to develop any primary feathers. We are aware of the adult bird following close behind it and we assume it is the male, as Clare's studies indicate. In a second or two, the chick is beneath the water. Our anxious faces peer down on to the calm, dark water in the gully, looking for it to reappear. At last it does and immediately gives out a series of loud, penetrating whistles 'wee-oo wee-oo'. With relief, we see the adult making towards it growling continually; this is the contact call. They unite, the fully grown parent with newly fledged chick, the latter less than half its size and only nineteen days old, two days over average fledging age. They swim away from the cliffs heading for the open sea. A predatory gull cries above and then lands a little way from them. We become tense and struggle to see the pair in the dim light; they dive immediately and expertly, although this is the chick's first encounter with the sea. Thankfully, the gull loses interest and takes off. They emerge some ten feet away; we can just see them swimming away and eventually they lose themselves in the impending darkness. We wish them a safe journey and hope the chick will be among those that return to the island. Many will come back here, in fact two-thirds of nestlings return to their natal colony. A very few may end up on Skomer, or even further afield in colonies on St Margaret's Island.

We knew that if this chick had lingered any longer on the ledge the adults would have left it alone for increasingly longer periods and it would have become vulnerable to predators. The parent bird had done all it could to encourage it this evening, standing alongside it, preening, nudging, flapping and stooping over the edge in readiness. It needed to get to sea to begin the moult process and was already suffering from the effects of post-breeding stress. The chick had persistently returned to the back of the ledge, and most reluctantly the attending adult had commenced brooding it. Now, at last they were gone safely.

We stare at the deserted cliff face, that fledgling had been the last to go from Twinlet and Guillemot Point. The guillemots' chicks, with an average fledging age of eighteen days, have all gone too. We will see them no more because they will swim well off-shore to feeding grounds where the chick will learn to feed itself, unless of course we encounter some of them on our trips to Grassholm. Tomorrow morning, there may be one or two adults standing around, perhaps with fish in their bills, mates of birds who have recently gone off with their chicks, but soon even they would go, leaving the cliffs bare. All around the island the auks have been slowly disappearing, the razorbills and guillemots taking the plunge from their ledges, as we have just seen, or scrambling and tumbling over boulder scree in places where they couldn't jump. For these two species, it is evidently more energy efficient for the young to leave prematurely and be taken to the food, rather than have the food brought to them. The fully grown, adult-sized puffin chicks, however, have made their own way seawards during the short summer nights, after a much longer fledging period of thirty-five days, a different strategy alto-

Grassholm island

gether, but evidently a successful one. Now all the auk chicks face the task of learning to feed for themselves, with or without the assistance of their parents. The puffins will live off accumulated fat, but the razorbills and guillemots will be with their parents for many weeks before becoming independent. They will face storms, predation and various hazards connected with humanity. Mortality of auk chicks is very high at this time, particularly if there are storms. Many chicks will never return. We discuss the odds as we trudge home, wondering especially what will be the fate of that last chick to leave the Twinlet ledges. We may even know in the future because it was one of the few that were ringed.

That razorbill chick was one of twenty-one that I had witnessed fledging between mid-July and mid-August 1974, when I undertook a special study of fledging behaviour. Twinlet was one of many colonies where fledging was observed. I became very involved in the fate of those chicks and fortunately saw no incidents of predation, although there were several prior to fledging. Indeed, all the ones I watched fledged successfully. Predation by gulls did not seem to be a serious threat on Skokholm although, in the past, chick remains had been found in the pellets of great black-backed gulls whose numbers were then much higher. A few chicks had died due to flooding of the nest site, others were just found mysteriously dead or they simply disappeared in the early stages. Even so, departure at dusk was evidently the safest time to leave the cliffs, with less risk of drawing attention from the gulls, while at the same time taking advantage of the remaining daylight to make contact easier between adult and chick.

This latter, I deemed very important, since some chicks from boulder sites landed many metres from the sea and took up to half and hour of jumping, scrambling, flapping and falling to reach it. Often it was a real strain to see them as the darkness fell, but for the white breast feathers it often would have been impossible. There was constant whistling and growling whilst adult and chick were separated, but when together they stayed silent. The chick often went ahead when the journey was easy, but if obstacles appeared, like large pointed rocks, clefts etc. the adult took the initiative. I was on tenterhooks if a chick fell into a deep crevice that looked as if it had no escape route, but they always surfaced in the end with much coaxing from the anxious parent. Actual physical aid was never witnessed. Although I never saw it happen, there must have been occasions when this kind of predicament led to failure, and if I had been sure of such failure, I would have gone to the rescue, rightly or wrongly! Parental behaviour and mostly the maintenance of parent/chick contact seemed to be the key factors in successful fledging. Only once did two adults accompany a chick and, another time, an 'auntie' from another ledge tried to join up with the pair but was rebuffed. Incidentally, the chicks showed that they had some control over their flight, as I saw on several occasions when they pulled out from near vertical drops to reach the water's edge.

Just occasionally, in late July or August off the coast of Cornwall, I hear that whistle and it tugs at my heart strings. I always expect to see a chick lost and struggling along on its own. Nearly always though, an adult bird pops up beside it. The whistling was just to keep the pair in touch during diving lessons!

CHAPTER 12

The Lighthouse

One entered the lighthouse via a heavy wooden door, painted bright green, which took you into a small lobby, exited by another door leading into the main part of the building. There were a couple of steps up to each door and the arrangement, so they proudly told me, rendered it mouseproof. On the strength of this, I had always felt comfortable about releasing the many mice we caught in Longworth traps into the island quarry, which happened to be adjacent to the lighthouse. The idea was that it was a long way for them to return to us, and they might think better of trying once they discovered the multiple tunnelling system and the various nooks and crannies that the latter had to offer. As it happened though, the mice had other ideas, and lighthouse keepers are as good as anyone else at leaving scraps of food around. So it wasn't too long before the keepers were visiting us, especially to borrow tins, boxes, etc., for what purpose they didn't disclose at first and then it dawned on me what was happening. I sheepishly asked if they were having a spot of trouble with a mouse or two dozen. After that our Observatory mice were taken elsewhere to start their new life.

In spite of its dubious mouseproof qualities, the lighthouse was immensely strong and well built, as they all are, and need to be in their extremely exposed positions. Building began on Skokholm in 1914 and was completed just before the war, the station remaining manned until 1983. It is now monitored and controlled from the Trinity House Operations Control Centre at Harwich in Essex.

Inside, I remember a comfortable living room with the radio/telephone (RT set), a television, lots of comfortable chairs, and a coal-fired stove. This room was occupied by the watchkeeper, and the other keepers when they were off duty and not sleeping. Some keepers bagged their own chairs and were very jealous of anyone else sitting in them. High on the wall opposite the east-facing window, was the lighthouse clock with 'Skokham' written across it. This odd spelling, we were told, was a clerical error on the part of Trinity House. Downstairs, there was also a well fitted kitchen, a bathroom and a noisy generator room. All fixtures were electric of course. We had an open invitation to use the shower, which Ray and Mike made good use of, but I preferred our primitive bath! Upstairs, they each had a bedroom and were better off, they told us, than on certain lighthouse towers built on small isolated rocks, where the bunks had to curve with the wall. I never really knew if that was true, but it possibly was. There was a small stairway with brass rails leading from the second floor which gave access to the tower housing the lantern.

There was continual noise from the generators, but a certain amount of soundpoofing was incorporated into the building. The foghorn didn't bother the keepers much, nor us, although in a south-westerly wind we could hear it very well. One June, however, when the mainland was basking in sunshine, we had the brute going for eight days solid and this did try our nerves. The keepers came down often during that week to get away from it a bit. I always said, as they did, that I could fall asleep easily while it was going but woke when it stopped! I've since tried to fathom how we worked that one out. How did we know it had just stopped when we woke up?

It was another matter if you were walking beneath it when it started. It sent vicious, sonic vibrations through your body, and you felt you were lucky not to have been blasted over the cliff! Visibility had to be down to about a mile-and-a-half before it sounded. The other danger you were exposed to when walking behind the lighthouse was that you were in line of fire of the keepers' rubbish as it came hurtling over the cliff from behind the white walls that surrounded the building. I certainly had to dodge a few bean cans and I suspect that, in one or two cases, it wasn't just chance. Most keepers were friendly, but we had our share of oddballs!

There were three keepers on for a month at a time and then they were relieved by another crew of three, each with a Principal Keeper (PK) in charge. Their period of duty had been decreased from two months to one. They told me that originally the lighthouses only had crews of two, but that an incident occurred on a rock station when one of the pair died, leaving the other with all the work, as well as being frightened of accusations of murder! The story goes that the remaining keeper suspended the body on a rope outside a window until relief came! After that they recruited crews of three.

The majority of men were well settled into their monthly routine, even the married ones; one in particular claiming that he had a honeymoon each time he went home! Most were stationed on the island for several years but, before they became established, they had spent six months training as supernumaries, during which time they could have been sent anywhere in England, the Channel Islands or Wales, but not Scotland as it had its own service not run by Trinity House. There was even a post on the Rock of Gibralter!

We came to know many of these supernumaries, as well as the regular keepers. Five years was supposed to be the maximum stay on any one station, but a few outstayed that period, whilst others were moved unexpectedly or because they asked for a move. Often it accorded with where their home on the mainland was located. Even on their months off, they could be called out somewhere, but that was a very rare occurrence.

Sometimes I felt jealous of all the remote and beautiful places that some of them had been to – Lundy, Bardsey, Alderney, not to mention the mainland lighthouses. I often felt that I wouldn't have minded being a lighthouse keeper myself and I still would if they weren't already an extinct species!

The keepers were a mixed bunch with a wide range of personalities, hobbies, likes and dislikes. For some, it was undoubtedly just a job; they could earn rather good money and not work terribly hard, have a paid month off and be relatively secure. One obvious disadvantage was the irregular hours they had to get used to for sleeping and eating. Each twenty-four hour day was divided into four and eight hour shifts, arranged so that each keeper had a twenty-four hour period off every third day. They all seemed to cope with it pretty well. The other disadvantage was the enforced isolation, although some of them positively enjoyed it, knowing it was for a limited time only. Skokholm though, like Lundy and Bardsey, was different in that it was peopled and there were opportunities for socialising, unlike being on the Smalls or the South Bishop, both of which were visible to us in good weather. Out there, they only had each other for company and we frequently heard of personality clashes, which were no doubt exacerbated by their restricted environment. Those conditions brought out the best and the worst in their characters. There were very few times when we sensed an acrimonious atmosphere on Skokholm, but it wasn't unknown. They were full of stories that were probably grossly exaggerated but nevertheless very entertaining.

A few keepers were prone to consuming large amounts of alcohol when ashore and used their month on duty as a drying out period. The bottle of medicinal rum in their first aid kit was often referred to jokingly, but as far as I know it was never consumed. Alcohol was forbidden in the lighthouse itself. The crew always arrived on the island looking very smart in their uniforms, ready and willing to take up their responsibilities even if they were well hung over! One day our Saturday lunch with the newly arrived visitors was interrupted by two very inebriated keepers just off the helicopter, who burst into the Wheelhouse clutching beer cans as well as each other, off duty of course! Most were very conscientious and that was a one-off event, which our visitors were fortunately much amused by. They were, after all, just two more examples of our infinitely variable wildlife!

The helicopter relief was a big event for them and, in a way, for us too. We would be welcoming back old friends and taking advantage of an extra chance to send mail, especially when we had no weekly boat at the beginning and end of each season. Lighthouse keeper Jack (see below) was not to be trusted with letters, his excuse – he didn't always get to the bottom of his suitcase before returning! Once, he actually produced, quite voluntarily, a cluster of crumpled, well-travelled letters from months before.

On relief day, we could hear the Trinity House helicopter coming and going as it systematically relieved all the lighthouses in the district. It was a small craft with only room for three keepers and the crew. One keeper was badly overweight and was always

Lighthouse relief

forced by the others to sit in the middle to retain stability and to allow escape in the event of ditching! The Trinity House pilots were the Bond twins, who were very good and had the reputation of being dare-devils. Apparently, one of them had been the first helicopter pilot to perform the loop-de-loop! Some of the crew were nervous of their flying antics and perhaps that explains the drinking! By arrangement, the pilot kept well clear of our seabird colonies.

We kept well out of the way during relief, but would sometimes watch at a distance so that we could tease them about their uniforms which they discarded straight after the event. The only other time we saw them worn was during the annual visit of the much revered Elder Brethren, the men at the top, visiting in their ship, the *Patricia* (known to us as the floating gin palace!). The EB's came to inspect the lighthouse to make sure all was up to scratch. Prior to the event, there was much frantic activity, cleaning, polishing, painting etc. The actual landing was another entertainment that we enjoyed watching, preferably from somewhere concealed. It was strange to see the *Patricia* at night moored off South Haven and lit up like a Christmas tree. The other Trinity House boats, that called to drop off coal and oil, didn't elicit any such ceremony. There were two of them called the *Stella* and the *Argus*.

Apart from their full uniform, the keepers had work clothes issued – navy blue pullovers and trousers, white shirts etc., all good quality. They could do as they liked in their leisure time, but we only managed to turn one of them into a birdwatcher and that was our friend Jack, a Mancunian with a fine accent. Jack's way of a first introduction was a handshake followed by a 'likkle bokkle' of navy rum! He soon equipped himself with binoculars and became expert enough to be able to supply us with a list of birds he had seen in our absence overwinter. He was nicknamed 'Jack the Light', and it has stuck, even though he is redundant now and hasn't 'got a light' anymore. He remains upset about his Marmora's warbler which Mike politely rejected. Jack was, and still is, a bachelor and was thoroughly enjoying two lives, one on the island and one on the mainland. Every third night he would turn up at the Observatory for a game of darts or crib and some home-brewed beer. Darts matches took place in the Wheelhouse with the board fixed up on the shelves to the right of the wheel. Below was a bucket in which Mike soaked his socks for a week or two before he dried them. To have to delve into it to retrieve a wayward dart was penalty enough for missing the board! Occasionally, we would invite a visitor to join us in a match by slyly winking at them in the doorway of the common room. Now redundant from the lighthouse, Jack is a night porter in a hotel and tells me how hard it is, after more than twenty years in the service, to remember to turn lights off at night instead of on!

Other keepers were keen fishermen, the more adventurous ones trying their luck in such out of the way places as South Gallery Rocks. One of them caught a razorbill which bit him on the nose while he extracted it from his gear. 'Serves you right' we said as bird-lovers. Some were very creative, one making window frames whilst he was on the island to sell on the mainland (or to us when we needed them), others painting or trying their hand at gardening. They watched television a lot, certain keepers being forever glued to the screen and I grew to dislike it more and more as it distracted from the conversation. We were invited to watch whatever we liked, but I never took up the offer except when we featured very briefly on a film about Skokholm. For relaxation (or escape!) I prefer books. There were so many other things to do and life was too short. Just prior to our leaving computer games came out and, when one was brought on to the island, many keepers spent hours trying to stop a jet crashing into hazards like chimney stacks and blocks of flats! I tried my hand and decided I was better at catching razorbills.

There were many 'characters' within the lighthouse personnel. One was a PK called Bob Rattey. He was very strict and rules had to be obeyed, but he was much liked and respected. The lighthouse, under his supervision, looked splendid, with the brass polished almost daily and everything spick and span. Taking visitors or ourselves up into the tower to view the lantern, he would request that nobody touch the shining brass handrails for fear of greasy fingermarks. Broken legs and unsteady nerves were OK but not soiled handrails! He took great pride in his job and that was obviously why he was made a PK. His tall form, brandishing a home-made walking stick to fend off attacking gulls, was regularly to be seen striding round the island on his constitutional walk. He had the look of a sea captain, with handsome features, greying hair and intelligent grey eyes. On my desk I have a dimpled whisky bottle, inside which is a replica of a fully rigged schooner sailing on a fabricated blue sea. It is five-inches long and three-inches high, beautifully constructed in wood, card and clay with the most intricate detail, even down to the ship's lifeboats on the deck and a tiny flag hoisted on the stern. The neck of the bottle is less than an inch wide and, by some clever mechanism using thread, the sails were raised when the boat was inside the bottle. This is one of many made by Bob and given to me by a friend, a fitting memento of our association with the lighthouse.

Bob well overstayed his allotted time on Skokholm (but not his welcome) seeing out ten years of service there, and he loved it. Unfortunately for us, he left in our first year to take a position at St Ann's on the mainland opposite and it was strange to see this man trying to hold back the tears during a leaving party we gave for him. Myself, Clare and Ray had made a cake in the shape of a lighthouse, complete with red dumper truck in the yard (the breadboard!) which was spinkled with 'chocolate' gravel. We even made some model goats and rabbits, all edible of course. A glass was inverted on the top to emulate the lantern. It was an emotional moment when the cake was carried into the wheelhouse with a little candle glowing inside the tower.

There were several other PKs whose company we enjoyed, including Bill O'Brian, Mike O'Sullivan, Simon Reynolds and Ken Chapman: the first two were keen fishermen whilst Simon was an avid reader. It was obviously a great asset for them to have such hobbies. There were a few assistant keepers who appeared to have no interests at all and they sometimes got up to mischief, such as joy riding on the dumper, disregarding the shearwater burrows of course. One man we definitely disliked and I believe he was responsible for some strange goings-on at the lighthouse involving some shearwater research being carried out by a DPhil. student from Nottingham called Dave Whitehouse. That keeper was in the habit of visiting us too often and one day I decided to hide when I heard the sound of the dumper approaching. Out of the Wheelhouse I flew and into the dormitory, where I concealed myself very uncomfortably in a small wardrobe. As he was in the habit of searching around for someone, this seemed a good hiding place, especially as I left the door open for him to see that the room was empty. It never occurred to me that the absence of myself and the others would encourage him to sit around and wait for us to return. He wanted his cup of tea and that was that, so he sat on the bench outside and started his chain-smoking routine. I hadn't bargained for that and prepared myself mentally for a long and painful stay, cursing myself for my stupidity. After twenty minutes, I tried to think of an excuse I could use when the cramp became unbearable and forced me into premature emergence. Painting the inside of a wardrobe hardly sounded likely and neither did falling asleep in there. Apart from that, it was boring and I had work to do. In the end I was saved embarrassment by the arrival of another keeper on foot who needed to return the dumper and there was no way that man would walk back. I was never so pleased to hear that engine start but I could hardly walk afterwards.

Another character was Jim Doran, an assistant keeper and a northerner with whom I had many long, heated debates about social issues. He accused me many times of being an escapist and knowing nothing about the hardships that existed in the inner cities. In some ways of course he was right, islands are a means of escape for people who find life becoming too cluttered and complicated, but is it really that selfish to go for an alternative existence which is more personally fulfilling, while still being able to contribute by helping to enrich the lives of others? I talk here of looking after our visitors, who came from all walks of life, and with whom we did our best to share our knowledge and joy of the island and its wildlife. I would love to meet Jim Doran again and see how we each have changed. In spite of our differences, Jim was a good friend and a talented individual in many ways. He was responsible for painting a face with gorgeous eyes on the front of the dumper and he also made a mermaid for the wind vane at the lighthouse. Another one of his legacies was the small pond above Dip Gully which he dug out – Jim's Pond. It didn't attract many birds generally, but he was

Bob Rattey, Clare Lloyd and the lighthouse cake

mighty proud when a heron began to visit it. It was under Jim's supervision that I was allowed to turn the light on one night and off again in the morning, something I had always wanted to do. It was a simple procedure, mainly involving pushing the right buttons! But it also included taking the protective curtain down from around the lantern. This was accidentally left up one night and nobody noticed for several hours, but fortunately no ships were wrecked that night!

Jim was an excellent cook and taught me how to make a delicious rabbit pizza. One little incident deserves a mention. He had said many times over that he had a great desire to have a custard pie thrown at him, a real one. I don't think he really expected anyone to take it up, but in my younger days that kind of challenge was irresistible and I could make a mean custard pie. So I did and carried it up to the lighthouse, knowing exactly when his duties were and certain of where he would be sitting at the time I arrived, which was very conveniently just behind the living room door. He was there all right and he got it right on target. I never saw anyone laugh so loudly and so hysterically for so long and I was scared for a while that he had flipped his lid. However, he hadn't and he didn't mind either. Perhaps he was grateful to me for ridding him of his perverse desire!

Something else that Jim taught me was how to take the meat off a rabbit in less than five minutes without gutting it. The main reason for doing it this way was that the rabbits on Skokholm were small and not well endowed with flesh, making it pointless to bother about the meat on the ribs. One simply slit the skin up the back, peeled out the front and back legs, cut them out and then slit along the backbone each side, easing away with the knife the two long strips of back meat. That was it and there you were with the meat and hardly any mess. For two or three of us with no fresh meat at either end of the season, a rabbit casserole was a frequent and delicious meal. I still do a rabbit that way if I'm lucky enough to be given one.

Twiggy was a keeper that I remember more for his cat than for himself, although he was a likeable fellow and often very helpful. I believe his real name was Brian Twig. Without asking permission from anyone, he took a small white kitten out to the island one winter. In spite of it ridding the Observatory of many mice by the time we arrived in the spring, we were horrified, and I fear somewhat angry as I think any bird lover would be at such an intrusion on a island important for seabirds. Cats and birds don't mix well in any situation, never mind on Skokholm. In these days, when birds are already under threat from sundry other factors like habitat loss, pesticides etc., predation by cats must be harmful to their populations. Still, many bird lovers keep cats and often not one, but many. 'Why?' I ask myself. Many decreases, and even actual extinctions, have occurred on islands because of the introduction of cats, particularly with some species of petrel. The world's only population of flightless wrens on Stephen Island was hunted to extinction by feral cats. Hundreds more examples could be cited.

That sweet, snowy white kitten soon turned dirty yellow and ran semi-wild in the island quarry where our storm petrels bred. Steps had to be taken; we were already discovering petrel corpses strewn about the rocks. It was difficult, but the culprit was finally caught and deported in a basket. I was later surprised to read that even Ronald Lockley brought a cat to the island to rid the buildings of mice.

The lighthouse had a roving band of mechanics and electricians who were never allowed to tread on each other's toes as far as work was concerned and neither were the keepers allowed to tackle even the simplest jobs themselves. The unions were responsible of course and great expense was incurred when the maintenance boys had to be flown or shipped over for small, straightforward tasks. Sometimes though, their skills were very necessary and their stay prolonged. One year, a Portacabin was erected to house the extra workers and it was quite an operation for the helicopter to bring over all the sections piece by piece. It had to be well roped down, as in no way could it have stood on its own against the elements in its exposed situation. It was rigged up without too many hitches and well used, although it wasn't too many years before the lighthouse went automatic.

The mechanics and electricians were a lively bunch and on several occasions joined up with us to form a Skokholm football team for a match on Home Meadow against the visitors. One electrician, called George, dressed as if he was heading for a London nightclub in the 1960s, with white trousers, pink shirt, winkle-picker shoes and a teddy boy haircut. What a treat for us when George performed his Elvis Presley imitation, strumming his guitar and singing 'Wooden Heart' while he gyrated on a flat rock at the bottom of Crab Bay. This while we feasted on a crab barbecue and waited for him to lose his balance! How anyone made it back up the cliff that night was a miracle. His workmate, Pete, was a man with a broad grin, a mop of Beatle-cut hair and a large stomach. It was Pete who gave me a driving lesson on the dumper, but forgot that the brakes weren't working as we trundled down the steep hill to South Haven! There was no option but to drive up on to the rocks on the seaward side of the track. It was the best thing I could have done for neither we nor the dumper came to any harm! Many years later, as I strolled along the cliff path above Tater-Du lighthouse in Cornwall, in the company of Jack the Light, I saw, protruding from an open door, a stomach which I seemed to recognize. It was none other than our friend Pete from Skokholm.

Another keeper, Mike, only stayed a short while before he was moved to the Eddystone Light, forty miles off Plymouth Sound. He wrote me strange and fascinating letters describing his experiences and sightings. It was interesting to hear of the happenings on his lonely outpost.

There were many other keepers and maintenance men who deserve a mention for their personalities or eccentricities, but there is little space in this book to describe them

Left to right: *Bill O'Brian, Jim Doran and Peter McGilloway*

all except to say that I remember most of them with affection. I especially loved to linger on the balcony around the lantern, with the protective curtain drawn back so that I could admire the huge, light-reflecting prisms arranged around the four sides of the bulb. They glittered brightly and split the daylight into rainbows of colour.

The view from the balcony was impressive too, with much of the island's surface visible. From high up, Skokholm looked more like the gently sloping plateau that it was, broken only by small ridges and knolls.

A significant, but not so good alteration to the lighthouse in recent years, was the change from a red light to a white one. It gave a flash every ten seconds. White lights, as I described in Chapter 6, are hazardous to birds when rain or fog brings them low down. However in 1999, after a little pressure, Trinity house fitted a red filter to the lamp so that only the seaward sector is white. This will at least reduce the fatalities. Other islands with white lights, like Bardsay, sometimes witness heavy mortality. St Ann's lighthouse is not a problem apparently because it doesn't flash. No really bad incidents have occured to date on Skokholm but, in 1996, before the filter was fitted, between forty and fifty birds were picked up at the lighthouse, presumed to have been attracted to the light. Slightly less than half of them were dead. We loved Skokholm's red light; it was friendly, individual and, above all, safe for the birds. Various other devices have been tried over the years to minimize the danger, for example the erection of spotlights on the ground below to light the building.

CHAPTER 13

End of Season

Autumn, with its mellow tints and colourful sunsets, was a most welcome arrival. The russet, purple and faded green tones of the vegetation were ever a source of inspiration to me, as was the ocean panorama beneath the fickle September skies. Nights became colder and, on fine mornings, heavy dews sparkled on the bracken and grass, while faint mists lingered in the hollows.

Gale days were vastly different, bringing spectacular seas that urged us out of doors to witness the indomitable waves surging over the landing steps and washing halfway up the track. The winch would completely disappear under a towering plume of white water and, when it reappeared, it would be dwarfed by the next wave, threatening obliteration. South Haven became a mass of swirling white foam and the wind spun up balls of froth and carried them over the cliffs to nooks where they lay and fizzled into oblivion. We rushed to take photographs, and some of us would fight our way to the west coast, bent almost double to oppose the most violent gusts. Cowering behind a rock, we then witnessed Mad Bay in the peak of its madness, grappling with an advancing army of white-streaked waves, marching on to the dark purple frontier, another gripping episode in the ceaseless battle between land and sea. Trickles of water, seeking an outlet to the sea, defied gravity and spurted back over the land in miniature fountains; in really bad gales it was nearly impossible to stand up, making it foolhardy to go anywhere near the cliff edge, but to see some of the birds, particularly the fulmars, toying with mini-tornados whipping around the cliff tops was humbling indeed. It was natural to lean into a gust of wind, but when it suddenly dropped you all but landed flat on your face! Thus, keeping away from the precipitous cliff's edge was a necessary precaution. If you felt like making the effort in the evening of a rare summer gale, Head Bay Rock was an excellent vantage point to enjoy the company of thousands of shearwaters careering by in a never-ending stream. Their free and easy flight seemed to soothe the troubled waters. In such weather, especially at high tide, turnstones and purple sandpipers were driven up the cliffs, to stand around misplaced on the salty, yellow turf waiting for the sea to drop and leave exposed their rocky refuge. It was strange seeing them standing there so conspicuously, after being accustomed to having to search so thoroughly for them down on the rocks. We would see curlew too, crouching tightly in the grass in an attempt to shelter from the storm. The wind showed no mercy.

One autumn day, the eye of a storm passed over us. The wind had been a south-easterly force ten for many hours when, suddenly, within seconds, total calm ensued. Anticipating all kinds of birds being blown in, we hastened to North Pond to find it teeming with ducks – teal, shoveler, mallard and wigeon. Five minutes grace was all we had, for no sooner had we identified the ducks and enjoyed the spectacle than a north-westerly force ten was blowing hard!

I enjoyed every kind of weather on Skokholm for one reason or another; the settled spells of sunshine and blessed calm when you could hear every sound, the eeriness and shrouding beauty of the sea fog that distorted and magnified everything, the fantastic rainbows whose intense, multicoloured arcs stretched from horizon to horizon and the drama and invincibility of sudden storms. There was even a good side to heavy rain because, apart from filling our water tanks, it sent our ducks into a frenzy of joyful activity, affording us much amusement. Likewise, while hailstones stung our faces, the chickens rushed about snapping up the unexpected bonanza of heaven-sent food with a greed that surpassed hungry schoolboys on chip day! Even after the discomfort they must have suffered, they didn't learn anything because, after that, they added snow to their dietary experience! The snow came one April and sent us rushing for our cameras as everything became sprinkled in a white, ethereal dust. The island was a blanket of pastel colour, soft green, brown and pink, depending on what lay beneath, and it brought with it the impalpable silence of a snowy landscape.

One day, I managed to get lost out in the Bog in thick fog with visibility down to a few yards. It was an eerie experience walking in the direction where I imagined the buildings lay and then finding myself on the cliff edge. Eventually, I found North Pond and it was straightforward from there. Once, in fog, a disorientated arctic skua pitched on the roof of the old Cook's Cottage and, until then, I had never seen one of those pirate birds close to. It was a superb, light phase skua with a neat black cap and a chocolate brown back. We seldom saw skuas but, during a south-westerly gale in October 1977, I watched several bonxies (great skuas) filing west past the Stack. Their formidable looks and slow calculated flight impressed me, but not so much as the numbers of kittiwakes did. There were so many that it reminded me of a snowstorm, so pure white and so light of wing were they, as they passed in flurries of hundreds against the leaden grey sea.

By late August many of our breeding birds had departed. The deserted cliffs looked austere and lifeless without the bustling auk colonies and the central plain, like a deserted city, assumed an eerie quietness after the hoards of screaming gulls had moved away. A somewhat diminished flock remained with us and shed their moulted feathers liberally over the ground, particularly on the Neck where they chose to roost, or on the ponds where they bathed. The moult had begun in June and lasted through to

The landing during a storm

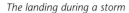

September.   Shearwater and storm petrel chicks lingered in their burrows, a few remaining into October, although by then our attentions were drawn away from the breeding birds to the migration and dispersal.

From the end of July onwards, we had witnessed the beginning of the return passage with the arrival of early willow warblers and several species of wading birds. The piping whistle of a whimbrel flying in to roost with the curlew flock, the sharp tick of a robin or a sandpiper picking about on the rocks were stirring reminders of the approach of autumn. It was a time to watch the ponds for migrant waders, remembering to be cautious when approaching them so that the birds didn't exit in alarm, or else they were gone for good. If they did fly away, there was at least a chance of them calling. Thus I learnt the triple whistle of a greenshank, the sweet, disyllabic call of a ringed plover, the magical, flute-like note of the golden plover and several more besides. Apart from the personal pleasure this tuning-in to calls brought me, it was also useful in that many waders passed straight over, often calling as they did so. There were never many (except for the curlew flock), usually only singles or small groups. Our three main ponds were not extensive, but were evidently attractive enough for some of them to use as temporary feeding and resting places whilst on route to more productive grounds. North Pond was by far the best. When rainfall had been high, a series of small depressions to the north of the main pond filled with water and they often attracted some of the smaller species, such as dunlin. These pools were known as North Lows. The birds usually circled a few times before landing and once down would stay, sometimes minutes, sometimes hours and sometimes days, as long as there was some mud exposed to allow them to feed.

July arrivals included greenshank, ringed plover and dunlin. August brought a greater variety, with knot, redshank, spotted redshank, ruff, green and wood sandpipers, or more rarely curlew sandpipers. I remember also, two very tame knot which allowed us to approach them within a few feet. They looked so small and were so pretty, with faintly streaked heads and fine scaling etched on their backs and wings as if executed by a thin paintbrush; it was actually the composite effect of pale edging on each of the feathers. As the breeding range of the knot was well to the north of us in Greenland, arctic Canada or Russia, they were honoured visitors to our pond. We were used to seeing most of the waders more or less in winter plumage, which was usually rather plain, and so it was a real treat to see one in breeding attire, or at least partially so for most had begun moulting. There were godwits with breasts daubed rufous, spotted redshanks in charcoal flecked with white, and golden plover with gold spangled backs and coal black breasts.

We made good use of the hide at that time of year. On windy and wet nights, Mike would creep out to go dazzling for waders and, on returning, would appear in the doorway of the common room, dripping wet and grinning like an apparition, but with a stunningly beautiful wader held in his hand. How elegant were those birds and how bright and alert their eyes when they were seen in the hand. We would admire his catch and, after ringing, the bird would be placed in a box to be released in the morning.

Met. Heath was the best place to find a dotterel. When recording the weather in September, if was my habit to look among the heather clumps for a head moving hurredly away. They rarely flew off, they just scuttled away, and if you didn't look hard you would miss them. The broad, curved supercillium and breast band were diagnostic and so, usually, was the fact that they were creeping about on Met. Heath, which must have been the nearest thing to their summer home on dry rolling moorland in the north. They were scarce visitors but were remarkably consistent in their arrival dates between 13 and 17 September. We recorded several over the years.

August saw the first snipe dropping into the long grass and rushes of the interior, and from then on we were increasingly likely to flush them from any damp area. They gave harsh, indignant squawks as they rose up from underfoot and weaved from side to side, only to fall steeply again and go to ground a little further on. It was the snipe that rose silently that excited us and particularly if its flight path was more or less straight, for

chances were that it was a Jack snipe, but we needed to see the shorter bill to confirm this. Whilst strolling at dusk on October evenings, we sometimes startled woodcock from the bracken. An aura of mystery surrounded those birds, at least to my mind, because I never saw anything more than a silhouette with a long bill. It wasn't until after I left the island that I was able to admire in daylight the exquisite marbling and the warm, autumnal tints of their plumage. These make for a perfect camouflage when the bird squats amongst crinkled, dry vegetation.

Rarely, our silent footsteps disturbed a short-eared owl hiding in the long grass. They often waited until the last minute before rising, adding an element of surprise to good fortune. Light and bouyant was their flight, tipping this way and that as if some hidden substance kept them afloat. The late afternoon sun would highlight the golden wing patches, which were a striking feature of those owls. Flying with utmost grace, an owl would hold me spellbound until settling again or disappearing back to Skomer or the mainland from whence it most likely originated. We once kept an injured short-eared owl in a cage constructed inside the garden trap and were kept busy with our mouse traps until it was successfully released. The only other owl that came to us, apart from the little owl, was a superb long-eared owl which we had the thrill of catching in 1975.

Late summer and autumn was a good time to see some very special visitors from Skomer or the mainland. Like the owls, the choughs were not migrants but part of a local dispersal movement. They alerted us with twanging cries that echoed all round the island. We could hear them from the buildings, wherever they were, and would rush out to watch them playing in the air currents; swooping, tumbling and falling with marvellous elasticity of flight, fingered primaries curling as the air flowed over their broad, square-edged wings. They frequently alighted on the short turf above Crab Bay to search for ants or suchlike. From Spy Rock we could watch them probing the ground with curved bills of scarlet to match their legs, royal trimmings on black feathers touched with a purple gloss. The groups were small, the largest consisting of about a dozen individuals. They had bred on Skokholm in 1928, and have done so recently. The important link between grazing and chough feeding habits has been established now with, it appears, dung beetle larvae featuring largely in the diet during the lean months. With all the rabbit dung, why should they not breed on Skokholm successfully? As to the general decline of choughs in Britain, once again agricultural intensification is the culprit, but it must also be said that they are on the northern edge of their breeding range and are badly hit by severe winters, making the population doubly vulnerable.

August brought southbound flycatchers, wagtails, whinchats, wheatears, redstarts, willow warblers and chiffchaffs, many of which were caught and ringed. Passage con-

tinued throughout September. Each year, one or two water rail were caught in the Heligoland. They are well known for their skulking habit and we generally only saw them when they were trapped. Returning to the island some years later, I found a freshly dead one lying on the side of Spy Rock and it was in good condition except that it was emaciated. That bird now looks down at me from a top shelf in my study, head down and in typical retiring pose. It has lost the strong red colour on its bill, but it still retains a smoky blue flush on its breast and fine, black and white striping on the flanks. The long toes, ideal for walking over soft mud, are still intact but are little more than bone. Years ago, they had bred on the island. In August 1973, Mike flushed an elusive spotted crake, but I had to wait for years before I saw my first one in Cornwall.

Once again we were busy looking for new arrivals, and especially more unusual ones. Our autumn rarities included red-breasted flycatcher, tawny and Richard's pipits, woodchat shrike, scarlet rosefinch, wryneck, melodious and icterine warblers, yellow-browed warbler and a greenish warbler. It was incredible how the yellow-browed warblers turned up on nearly the same date each year, which was between the 22 and the 26 of October. Also, quite remarkably, three of the four greenish warblers ever to have been recorded on Skokholm, our 1976 bird being one of them, were seen on the 31 August!

My rufous bushchat in 1977 was among the autumn rarities and, although rejected by the ten wise men, it was the first for Wales. Initially, it was seen through the kitchen window, foraging on the edge of the bracken while we were washing up. There was never a dull moment!

Most intriguing was the arrival of birds which seemed to be altogether in the wrong place, for example a kingfisher. Whilst walking along the west coast one day my eye was caught by a streak of irridescent turquoise flashing over the rocks below. I could hardly believe what I was seeing, but I have since seen them around the Cornish coast in August so perhaps it wasn't that unusual. It was evidently part of a post-breeding dispersal movement. A treecreeper fussing around on the rocks produced a similar reaction, in fact even more so! Tits always seemed misplaced, but we had autumn records of blue tits, long-tailed tits and coal tits. There must be few places where a house sparrow can be the cause of great excitement, but one caused a sensation when it appreared chirruping on the top of a water butt.

Swifts began to arrive just prior to the return hirundine migration in August, which continued until the end of October, with some very late swallows in November. There were no wires for them to gather on, but they often sat in rows on the rooftops, chattering incessantly. However, it was the visible migration of hundreds of finches and thrushes that came later in October and November which I really enjoyed. Much, of this took place on calm, clear nights and, before going to bed, I would often spend a

few minutes standing outside listening for the high pitched calls of redwing flying high overhead; invisible travellers driven by a vital force, ancient and primeval. There was no light pollution on our island (unless you count the lighthouse!) and no intrusive noise to disract from contemplation of the night sky, so that I was often tempted outside to listen for birds just for the pleasure of being there! From the island, we could see many lighthouses - Skokholm of course, St Ann's, South Bishop, the Smalls, St Gowan's lightship and, one night from Spy Rock, we believed we saw Lundy Island. Clear Skokholm nights were seductive and alluring.

Swift

After a few years on the island, the different calls made by thrushes flying overhead became imprinted on me; song thrushes at last were distinct from redwing, while wheezing blackbirds and clacking fieldfare were easily recognizable. The call of the less common ring ouzel sounded sufficiently different from a blackbird to be able to distinguish it easily. The dull brown female or juvenile ouzels had faint grey panelling on their wings and an indistinct breastband, but they still resembled blackbirds at a distance. Many of the thrushes came from Scandinavia, eastern Europe or Russia. Cold weather to the north and east of us would drive hundreds of them down through Britain in search of mild temperatures and soft earth containing their invertebrate food. They never stayed long, usually continuing flying south or west. It was a treat to see the handsome fieldfares, never numerous but so striking in their cold grey, brown and black plumage, most suitably attired for announcing the imminent arrival of winter. Some days we had up to one hundred and fifty blackbirds on the island, something which particularly thrilled me because of my special affection for those garden-loving birds.

In the early morning hours of a typical October day, even before the dawn broke, waves of smaller migrants passed overhead. With no wind to mask their calls, it was easy to pick out individual species. Most common were chaffinches, greenfinches, linnets, siskins, bramblings, skylarks and pipits, with one or other species dominating on different days. Learning all their calls became quite a challenge and eventually I was able to pick out more unusual species like snow bunting, lapland bunting and redpoll. One morning, late in October 1977, I awoke to a series of unfamiliar notes coming from the Wheelhouse yard, which was just behind our room. It struck me as similar to the musical twitter of a linnet and I guessed before I left the room that it (or they) were twites. They were my first and, as it happened, a birthday treat!

There were October mornings when every bit of cover, seemed to conceal a goldcrest. Although the high pitched call was easily recognizable, it was often difficult pinpointing exactly where it was coming from, but then maybe that was the idea because would-be predators might have the same trouble! On such days they would be discovered (or at least heard) just about everywhere on the island. They were difficult to count when

they were spread around in the bracken and we could only make rough estimates. Easiest to see were the ones foraging on the cliff faces, or of course the ones we caught. We marvelled at their tiny bodies dwarfed by our clumsy human hands. Much dexterity and care was required in handling a goldcrest, you needed to be gentle but firm. The gold and black head stripes were their crowning glory, with most of the rest of the plumage being plain olive, but it was the much rarer firecrest which came to us on a few dates around mid October that was the real gem. It seemed to me to be a symbol of late autumn, reflecting the season's colours in its fiery orange crown stripe and lustrous, golden bronze shoulder patches. In the watery sunlight of October, the stripes on the head look crisp and clear and the body feathers positively glowed.

With many small and often exhausted birds around as well as a proliferation of rabbits and mice, it wasn't surprising that we had many visiting predators towards the latter end of the season (apart from the short-eared owls that is). Some days up to five kestrels hovered over the rough pasture, their posture a brilliant co-ordination between airflow and wing beat. One minute they were still, and the next flapping madly, with tails fanned to stabilize their bodies, and eyes ever alert to any flicker of movement in the grass that might betray the whereabouts of an unwary mouse, a venturesome frog or a late butterfly. On the other hand sparrowhawks seemed to appear from nowhere, dashing into the corners of buildings with a terrible rush of wings that signalled instant death to some small bird. The agility of the hawk amazed me; they would streak towards the walls with frightening speed and then extricate themselves faster than the eye could follow. A scatter of feathers floating in the air, a limp bundle held in a dangling claw and the hawk would fly away unscathed with its victim. From the feathers we could sometimes identify the prey which, more often than not, were meadow pipits. During a chase, the hawks sometimes entered the traps and were caught. Then gloves were needed to take them from the box as protection from the needle sharp claws and tearing beak. Sometimes they startled me as I prepared a meal, dashing themselves against the Wheelhouse window in pursuit of something that had dived for the cover in the nettles around the sump.

Buzzards were omnipresent, often three or four individuals at a time, cruising, soaring, mewing, taking advantage of the lesser numbers of gulls. They were masters of leisure.

Proud and imperious was the peregrine falcon, whose infrequent visits instilled drama into our relatively peaceful existence. A young falcon came once and perched on the wall behind the Wheelhouse, its terribleness as a predator accentuated by the black hood and the glaring, yellow-ringed eye. The upper bill or cere was yellow too, but the sharply hooked beak for tearing prey was shiny enamel blue. I watched the eye when a small bird flew over and saw it register the movement with a calculated flick, but it didn't give chase.

END OF SEASON

Late October or November often brought a migrating hen harrier which stayed for a day or too, systematically quartering the banks and walls in search of prey. They were always brown ring-tails (female or immature), never the silver grey males.

The autumn song of the robin is sweet and a little melancholy. Late August brought us an influx of these out-of-season songsters and some struck up winter territory. I didn't know then that both males and females sing to defend that territory, which is an interesting and unusual strategy among British birds. Neither was I aware that the song of the female is shorter and more subdued. They are mainly insectivorous birds and apparently benefit from driving away competitors during the winter months, in the same way that they do during the summer. In all, between thirty-five and forty robins came and most of the bays around the island were occupied. Females and juveniles normally move away from their breeding territories in mainland Britain, so it was most likely to be these robins that came to us, while the males stayed behind. We had no ringing returns to indicate where they had bred, but ringing had shown that some birds returned on consecutive years. With the imminent arrival of winter gales, cold temperatures and a bleak prospect generally, it was heart-warming to listen to them, so earnest and cheerful were they. I only wished we could have seen the winter through with them! They helped to fill the gap left by the absent seabirds.

Peregrine Falcon

Along with the robins came a variable number of wrens, up to two hundred one year, many of them staying until the early spring. Sometimes it was hard to tell if the tiny, brown creature you glimpsed darting into a burrow was a wren or a mouse! They were especially mouse-like in the quarry as they crept between the stones. All we heard from them was a harsh scolding if we ventured too close.

Finally, in September we would begin to see a few different birds on the sea. Black-headed gulls would fly with the kittiwake flocks. They looked remarkably small and slender beside our three gulls. Strings of common scoter would file through Broad Sound, strange dark duck whose appearance was a mystery to me then. Since hundreds of them winter in Cardigan Bay, they were not uncommon, and hopefully they are not now, in spite of heavy mortalities caused by the *Sea Empress* disaster. Terns appeared sporadically, usually in groups of two or three, in the first stages of their long journey south to Africa. We saw more in the autumn than in the spring due to their numbers being boosted by juveniles. They were usually sandwich, common or arctic terns, but little terns were also recorded.

The departing boat all but disappears round the corner. We try hopelessly to sustain the forlorn and lost expressions on our faces, but to no avail. A broad grin creeps over the faces of each of us and it is all we can do to refrain from jumping up and down with glee. The last remaining visitors are gone. Now we are free with the whole island to

ourselves save for the keepers at the far end. After weeks of solid routine, regular meals and millions of questions, we can relax and enjoy ourselves with absolutely no pressures. We love the job and the company, but seven days a week with no break for fifteen or more weeks is exhausting. This moment has been eagerly awaited.

It was true though that the island felt a little empty with both the visitors and most of the breeding birds gone. Even the atmosphere around the buildings, normally resounding with laughter and lively chatter, fell rather flat. When there was only two of us left in 1977, with Mike moving on to higher things, we felt it even more keenly, but the autumn was a beautiful time and the return migration continued to excite us. We soon adapted and began to enjoy the island in a different way.

Then was the time that I let the island take me over, and for several weeks I revelled in the remoteness, the blissful solitude and above all the natural beauty about me, which was so hard to tune into when diverted by work and people. It was the other side of island life, a side that I enjoyed immensely and one of my main reasons for being there. Only the weather, the tides and our whims governed what we did. The time of day scarcely mattered, and without our Saturday boat it was easy to lose track of the days. Brilliant dawns and sunsets, wild storms and cold sharp winds only heightened my senses and made me ever more reluctant to think of leaving. In the evenings bright driftwood fires put a glow on our wind-tanned faces, and on stormy nights, with rain beating hard on the windows, the Cottage felt snug and safe. The island had me under its spell and those are the memories I cherish most of all.

It was usually during the first part of September that the visitor season ended, so we had the rest of that month, the whole of October and much of November to indulge in our solitude. The ringing of late migrants continued until autumn 1976, but with the traps dismantled in 1977 we had to rely on looking harder each year. We always hoped for an Indian summer, but even without one life continued to be stimulating and most enjoyable. When I went to bed on Skokholm, it was with impatience for the start of another day. I remember saying that to a visitor who looked at me as if it was an unheard of state of mind! Life on the mainland, I decided, would be a big anticlimax. Happily our final departure date each year was always vague.

As we had no boat, we depended on our chickens and the rabbits for fresh meat. I would disappear into the workshop, rummage about and set off across the island with a bundle of stop snares under my arm in search of rabbit runs. Eventually I became adept at catching them. I found that the most successful snares were those placed at the bracken/turf interface on Green Heath and Home Meadow. Checking them every hour, I would call on Ray to dispatch the animals quickly. The snares didn't hurt the rabbits, they held them round the body without tightening too much, so that I could

let them go if I had caught too many. Rabbit catching had a great appeal for me, it was as near subsistence living as I was likely to get. For the sake of eating good, fresh protein rather than tinned meat it seemed quite acceptable, especially as there was no shortage of them. Many were destined to die in the winter anyway, with the population sometimes dropping to a few hundred, and using them for meat was undeniably an island tradition. After two years there, I became partly vegetarian and ceased to eat meat except for rabbit and free range chicken. My criteria was, and still is, based on whether the animal has a reasonable quality of life in the first place.

There was nothing more delicious to my mind than a rabbit stew or casserole cooked with our home-grown vegetables and flavoured with fresh mint from the island. The stews, made with a few rabbits, would last for two or three days and tasted better as they matured! I have never enjoyed meals so much since, but perhaps the primitive and beautifully lit atmosphere in the Wheelhouse contributed to that. So too did the regular tot of whisky that we looked forward to afterwards! Rabbit curry, rabbit pizzas, rabbit pies, we made them all and never got fed up with them. A plump, young cockerel provided an almost equally delicious alternative. We kept these surplus birds separate from the hens and ate them at ten to twelve weeks old when they were tender and succulent. It was imperative that we didn't get too fond of them! The dormitory was used as a skinning and plucking room.

Alas, my main involvement with the rabbits was in eating them and so I have written very little about them so far. It is a serious omission since, as well as being a major component of the ecology, they have played a vital role in the island economy since they were first introduced by the Normans in the fourteenth century. The Pembrokeshire islands were once regarded primarily as huge rabbit warrens from which they couldn't escape. From the 1300s onwards, they were exploited for fur and meat and often payed the rent too. The meat could be salted down and preserved when the weather was too rough to cross to the mainland.

Later on, during the farming era, walls were built, some of which, according to Lockley, may have been rabbit proof. He claimed that one of the jobs of the farm labourers in the days when crops were grown was to stop up the holes in the walls made by rabbits trying to gain entrance to the fields. The rabbits were said to be barricaded out by placing cuttings of heather and gorse on the tops of the walls. The fields were evidently cleared beforehand. Nevertheless, after our first gardening attempts, I find it hard to believe that any large fields on the island could have been really rabbit proof. Other literature states that sometimes rabbit catchers made holes in the walls to give them dry breeding and sleeping places.

Lockley tried many ways to rid the island of rabbits to make easier his early attempts at farming, but soon put a stop to the gin traps laid by his rabbit catcher

when a buzzard was caught. In the end gassing was the most effective measure, but even then a remnant population remained around the cliffs to breed and spread. He himself drew revenue from the rabbits and had plans for a chinchilla breeding farm which, unfortunately for him, fell apart when market prices dropped (see *Dream Island Days*).

Our rabbits were slightly smaller than mainland ones, which is why we needed two or three for a good sized casserole! There were various introductions of domestic rabbits which bred with the wild ones and we saw several genetic throw-backs. There were individuals with white blazes or white saddles, and some with both, and there were also long haired individuals originating from the angora type. Black rabbits regularly cropped up and where there was one there were usually several. They were true melanics and generated lots of interest among visitors who hadn't seen them in a wild population before. They were very conspicuous and we had a never-ending argument as to whether they were more susceptible to predators because they were black or whether predators avoided them. In fact the former is true, according to a report by Sam Berry in 1977, who also claims that they are less timid and feed more in the day, which is why they continue to survive. None of those attractive varieties were ever caught in my snares.

I once hand-caught a rabbit on the Knoll and thought I had achieved the impossible, only to discover by its ancient ear tag that it was most probably dying of old age!

The story of the introduction of myxamatosis on the island has been told in Lockley's books. We saw very little positive sign of it, but we did occasionally see weak ones with swollen eyes that must have been suffering from it. We were led to believe that the Skokholm rabbits had no fleas to communicate the disease, and it is interesting that there was an outbreak recently which caused a considerable decline in the population. Fleas or no fleas? As would be expected though, considerable changes to the vegetation were noted.

Diana Bell, one of Britain's authorities on the wild rabbit, once came to stay and told us many interesting things about them. We then realized that they were more than fluffy bundles of meat that disappeared down holes, they actually had an interesting social structure. Of more interest to us was the fact that they must have many encounters with burrowing birds, most of which possesed beaks sharp enough to make even ferreting for rabbits unsuccessful. Overall they seemed to have a pretty hard time of it. However, my resolve to spend some time watching them didn't last long. I was too distracted by the birds! Rabbits didn't seem to do enough, and they weren't nearly so attractive!

Domestic arrangements at the end of the season became lax, and we relaxed! Dinner was inevitably late when the two of us were left on our own. All hours of light were to

be taken advantage of as far as I was concerned and the last hour or so of my day was usually spent in the hide at North Pond. Not only was I held there by the infinitely variable sunsets and dramatic afterglow effects, all splendidly reflected in what was by then a large expanse of water, but I wanted to witness the incoming flight of duck that used the pond as a nocturnal roost. By the time they came all that remained of the day-

North Pond

light was a supernatural green glow and they were no more than black silhouettes. I enjoyed their arrival as if it was a secret between them and myself. Even though I saw little detail on the ducks, the profiles of different species became familiar to me: the long-billed, sleek headed mallard, the smaller, neater teal and the round-headed, plump-bodied wigeon that flashed white on their wings. Even though they are common, I was mightily pleased when my first shoveler came winging in and I picked out the huge, spatulate bill and flattened forehead. Other species of duck were rarely recorded, but there were occasional visits from shelduck and pintail. No true diving ducks ever came, the pond was too shallow. Often I stayed in the hide until the light was completely gone, or so it would have seemed to anyone stepping out of a well lit room, but to my accustomed eyes there was light enough to see by even without a moon. The first time I stayed well into the darkness I caused unnecessary anxiety to Ray, and after that I made a point of voicing my intentions.

Just an hour or two earlier than the duck arrived, we received more overnight visitors. Flocks of curlew came winging in from the mainland, their cries echoing across the increasingly pallid sky. Skokholm was a safe and relatively undisturbed roosting place for them and their numbers built up as the days got shorter, sometimes reaching several hundred. Because I was not tied to work and therefore less tired, it became tempting to sleep out under the stars. Some of my best memories of Skokholm are of sleeping out on the Knoll on nights that were still and crystal clear. The light of a bright moon would glisten on the white roofs below like a phosphorescence and, beyond, the sea shimmered beneath blackened cliffs. Lighthouses winked and a thousand stars twinkled in an indigo sky. Eventually I would sleep, but the best was yet to come. When exactly the curlew came on to the Knoll, I never knew, although I heard many anonymous scufflings as I lay dozing, but one has no worries there and so they remained anonymous. As dawn broke, several curlew stood around on the hill so that when I stirred, stiff and wet with dew, they left one by one with a fluted 'coo-lee'. So close were they that I could hear the sound resonating in their throats. What a beautiful alarm clock! Not that I needed one, sleep came only fitfully, otherwise I may as well have stayed in bed!

In the evenings, I desired no entertainment other than books and we had a good selection in the library. Many set my feet itching to travel and see other islands. There were books on St Kilda, Lundy and Fair Isle. Frank Fraser Darling's books on North Rona and the Summer Isles, Williamson's book on St Kilda, Roscoe Howell's on Skomer and many more, as well as dozens of books on birds (it was indeed the yearning for new places and more experiences that culminated in our eventually leaving the island). We put our trust in visitors to borrow and return the books, not dreaming that anyone would make off with any and it was heartening that none of them went missing. Unfortunately though, books were stolen after we left.

Ray sometimes went to the lighthouse in the evenings leaving me with the Cottage to myself. That made me acutely aware that I would have enjoyed a period of absolute solitude on the island just for the sake of the experience, but that was impossible so I just had to stop thinking about it. It was so comfortable and pleasant with the wood fire in the common room that we moved a mattress in there and slept in front of the dying embers, perhaps in the manner of the old rabbit trappers! Nights were quiet with few shearwaters calling; the only other sounds, the wind and the mice scratching.

We knew very little of the outside world once the visitors were gone and there were few of them who wanted to discuss political issues or tabloid sensations. For most people the idea was to get away from all that. Ignorance of world affairs was pure choice on my part because there was a television at the lighthouse and I also had a radio cassette player. No news was good news as far as I was concerned, even at the quiet end of the season. It surprised and even shocked me if a visitor brought on a radio and listened to lengthy news items in the common room. Few did, and when they did others usually complained. I even shuddered at the Archers which now has me rushing to switch on! During my very first visit in 1971, silence was demanded at the meal table while the warden had his daily dose of the Ambridge clan (or was it to shut everyone up!). Shipping forecasts were my limit and they were the only broadcasts that affected us. Once, whilst tuning in at ten to six, I caught the end of a broadcast of Winston Churchill's message to the nation when World War Two broke out and for a minute my heart stopped, I thought the dreaded World War Three had arrived! Not as silly as it sounds as it was in the thick of the Middle East crisis, but I was out of touch, and out of touch I stayed. Ray was better informed because of the television. My small collection of cassettes was not inspiring, a few Bob Dylan and the mournful, monotone voice of Leonard Cohen singing 'Bird on a Wire' which provoked Chris Perrins to ask how I could listen to such abject misery, and the truth was that I couldn't for long!

There were few social events save for our evenings with Jack and cups of tea at the lighthouse. I always celebrated my birthday on the island in October and, apart from the inevitable cake, there were sometimes practical jokes. One of these deserves a mention. The afternoon prior to the event, I happened to be standing on the bench beneath the drinking water tank peering over the wall, whilst I waited for a vessel to fill up. The sight that met my eyes was intriguing and most certainly new to me. It was a cold, windy day and Mike, who had never, even on the hottest summer's day, worn anything but long trousers, was walking up the wall adjacent to Alice's Knoll in his underpants. To say it was out of character would be an understatement. Had he flipped? Should I confront him with a pair of trousers? Or should I run away? I didn't do anything save keep my head down, but my curiosity was naturally aroused. At dinner, I regarded him critically, looking out for signs of abnormal behaviour. There were none. There happened to be four of us at the Observatory because Martin Garnett, helper and shearwater slave, was staying and that was comforting because it meant that there were three of us to cope with Mike's behavioural problem.

My birthday dawned, as usual I felt nothing, but mid- morning Mike rushed in to say there was a king eider duck in South Haven. That was what I called a birthday present, but where were the others. Mystified, I set off towards South Haven, but not without sensing that something was amiss. What I was afraid of was the statutory dunking instead of an exciting new bird. As South Haven came into view, I saw that indeed there was a bird on the water, a boldly marked duck, but that wasn't all. Who was that creeping round the rocks? Then the bird dived; well, it sort of dived and then it sort of rolled and appeared to be dragged beneath the water. They hadn't quite got it right! The model wooden duck was perfectly made and painted, but the rig set up to make it dive was a trifle primitive and perhaps a little ambitious. So what did that have to do with Mike and his devious behaviour? I asked myself. A lot it seemed. It transpired that, the day before, the bird was undergoing trials – swimming and diving on the end of an assemblage of wire and string operated by Martin. Although it was only a model, it proved a bit lively for them and broke loose. Then came the rescue attempt with Mike setting out on an oil drum in a bid to retrieve it. He did, but not without a few mishaps which resulted in his one and only swim on the island. Hence the apparition of the day before. I certainly appreciated their insight into what would have made a very special birthday present for me if only it had been real. The eider, modelled excellently by Martin, was officially handed over and I kept it for years.

In mid November, we were on standby for departure and lived in a state of half readiness. The books were taken over to the lab, save the few we were reading, along with blankets, chair covers etc., as the lab was reckoned to be the driest room. Curtains were taken down to be shipped off and laundered during the winter, clothes (the few we had) and some of our belongings were stuffed in rucksacks and surplus food was packed away. We didn't always get a message from the lighthouse that the boat was on its way and, if we did, it gave us precious little time so there was often a panic in the final few hours. The main problem was the livestock. Our twenty or so free range chickens, scattered around the buildings and the yard, were not easily persuaded to climb into a box and board the boat no matter what I promised them at the other end. The departure was traumatic enough for us never mind our peace-loving hens, and the cockerel was always there to attack us when we tried to catch them.

'If we had known you were coming, we would never have let them out,' we would proclaim to Terry or Cambell as we mustered forces to gather them up. Chickens are ten times more difficult to catch than shearwaters because they can run fast! Cornering was the best tactic, even if it meant charging through the thick nettles at the back of the Wheelhouse with the evil smelling sump nearby. Rugby tackles were moderately successful but a bundle of feathers isn't very grippable, although legs are. Moth net, razorbill hook, bribing with titbits, we tried them all. Perseverance won in the end and only once did we nearly leave one behind. She was determined, but not as much as I!

We had long shed any ideas that dress was something to worry about and usually left the island looking a little dishevelled. Ray was often considerably more hairy than the billy goat he was escorting. I was what my mother would have described as 'the Wreck of Hesperus', but it was Mike that topped the bill in his ragged Barbour and long, black, sun streaked hair. To finish off the 'wild islander' image one year, he wore one thigh wader and one baseball boot that had seen better days. That year, as I struggled across the mud in Sandy Haven clutching my box of chickens, an alarm clock stuffed in my pocket gave out its shrill reveille, causing the chickens to pop their heads out through the breathing holes cut in the lid. They wanted to know what was going on!

Terry was always relieved to get us off the island because that meant his responsibility for us was ended and he could take his boat out of the water. In 1973 and 1974 we went back to his farm for a day or so before returning to winter in Hampshire. At first our chickens spent the winter there with us, but after that we rented cottages in Wales and found them lodgings. Always we looked forward to enjoying the things that were lacking on the island – electricity, cars, hot water on tap, flush loos etc., but the novelty never lasted longer than a day or two. By the time February came round again we were desperate to return.

We didn't know that when we left on the boat in 1978 it was our last season. We were a little earlier that year because of a planned trip to Cape Clear in southern Ireland. It was the year of the *Christos Bitos* oiling incident. The news reached us in Ireland, but of course there was nothing we could do except pray that not too many Skokholm birds would be affected. We also heard the news of Ray's successful application for another job. So that was it, we were moving on. I remember experiencing the most peculiar mixture of emotions – sadness, guilt, dreaded uncertainty, but also a cautious excitement at the thought of new places, new birds and a new life. Could I leave Skokholm really? I doubted that anywhere else would have quite the same appeal, but that niggling restlessness would always be there. So we made the decision to go and, looking back on that day in October 1978, I am glad I didn't know then we were leaving for good, because it would have been agonizing.

Ray's new contract was to begin in January. We were still in Pembrokeshire in December of that year, awaiting the chance of a last visit out to the island to collect our gear. It was a beautiful Sunday and Rita (alias Miss P. Witt) was visiting us with Jack the Light. The message came early that David Emmerson of Dale Fort would take us that very morning. The day sticks in my memory, the experience was so magical. So much so in fact that it found a place in Rita's book of special days, which tells of a calm blue sea, gorgeous weather, North Pond brimming with duck, finishing the home brew, and finally a wonderful boat trip round the island.

So it was goodbye to the island. There were no regrets, but we needed to adjust to what did turn out to be a more mundane existence. There were still the memories and that is what this book is all about. It is for me as well as for you!

References

Betts, M. *Birds of Skokholm* (Updated bird list). Bioline, University of Wales College of Cardiff, 1992.

Brooke, M. Lees, D. and Lawman J. 'Spot Distribution in the Meadow Brown Butterfly'. *Biological Journal of the Linnean Society*, 24; 337-348, 1985.

Brooke, M. *The Manx Shearwater.* T. & A. D. Poyser, London, 1990.

Chambers, B. *The Birds of Skokholm.* (Complete bird list for sale on Skokholm only)

Fisher, J and Lockley, R. M. *Sea-Birds.* Collins, London, 1954

Gillham, M. E. 'Ecology of the Pembrokeshire Islands.' *Journal of Ecology*, Vol.43, No.1, 1955.

Gillham, M.E. 'Ecology of the Pembrokeshire Islands.' *Journal of Ecology*, Vol.44, 1956.

Goodman, G. T. and Gillham, M. E. 'Ecology of the Pembrokeshire Islands.' *Journal of Ecology*, Vol.42, No.2, 1954.

Gynn, E. G. and Bos, F. *Flora of Skokholm* (Complete plant list printed for purchase on Skokholm only).

Lawman, J. 'Jackdaws on Skokholm.' *Skokholm and Skomer Report*, 1974.

Lawman, J. 'Observations on the Fledging of Razorbill Chicks.' *Nature in Wales*, Vol.14, No.4, 1975.

Lawman, J. 'Skokholm Lepidoptera.' *Nature in Wales*, Vol.16, No.3, 1979.

Lewis, J. *The Islanders.* Quotes, Northants, 1997.

Lloyd, C. S. 'The Breeding Biology of the Razorbill.' D Phil thesis. University of Oxford, England.

Lockley, R. M. *Dear Islandman* (Letters compiled by R.Lockley and edited by Ann Mark), 1996.

Lockley, R. M. *Dream Island Days.* H. F. and G. Witherby, London, 1943.

Lockley, R. M. *Flight of the Storm Petrel.* David & Charles, Devon, 1983.

Lockley, R. M. *Letters from Skokholm.* J. M. Dent & Sons, London, 1947.

Lockley, R. M. *The Island.* Andre Deutsch, London, 1969.

Lockley, R. M. *The Private Life of the Rabbit.* Andre Deutsch, London, 1964.

Skokholm and Skokholm Reports. Compiled by the island wardens (1962 onwards). The Wildlife Trust, West Wales.

The Island Naturalist. Journal of the friends of Skokholm and Skomer. The Wildlife Trust, West Wales, 1997.